The Data Hero Playbook

The Quiet Hero Playbook

The Data Hero Playbook

Developing Your Data Leadership Superpowers

Malcolm Hawker

WILEY

Copyright © 2025 by John Wiley & Sons, Inc. All rights, including for text and data mining, AI training, and similar technologies, are reserved.

Published by John Wiley & Sons, Inc., Hoboken, New Jersey.
Published simultaneously in Canada and the United Kingdom.

ISBNs: 9781394310647 (Hardback), 9781394310661 (ePDF), 9781394310654 (ePub)

No part of this publication may be reproduced, stored in a retrieval system, or transmitted in any form or by any means, electronic, mechanical, photocopying, recording, scanning, or otherwise, except as permitted under Section 107 or 108 of the 1976 United States Copyright Act, without either the prior written permission of the Publisher, or authorization through payment of the appropriate per-copy fee to the Copyright Clearance Center, Inc., 222 Rosewood Drive, Danvers, MA 01923, (978) 750-8400, fax (978) 750-4470, or on the web at www.copyright.com. Requests to the Publisher for permission should be addressed to the Permissions Department, John Wiley & Sons, Inc., 111 River Street, Hoboken, NJ 07030, (201) 748-6011, fax (201) 748-6008, or online at www.wiley.com/go/permission.

The manufacturer's authorized representative according to the EU General Product Safety Regulation is Wiley-VCH GmbH, Boschstr. 12, 69469 Weinheim, Germany, e-mail: Product_Safety@wiley.com.

Trademarks: WILEY and the Wiley logo are trademarks or registered trademarks of John Wiley & Sons, Inc. and/or its affiliates, in the United States and other countries, and may not be used without written permission. All other trademarks are the property of their respective owners. John Wiley & Sons, Inc. is not associated with any product or vendor mentioned in this book.

Limit of Liability/Disclaimer of Warranty: While the publisher and author have used their best efforts in preparing this book, they make no representations or warranties with respect to the accuracy or completeness of the contents of this book and specifically disclaim any implied warranties of merchantability or fitness for a particular purpose. No warranty may be created or extended by sales representatives or written sales materials. The advice and strategies contained herein may not be suitable for your situation. You should consult with a professional where appropriate. Further, readers should be aware that websites listed in this work may have changed or disappeared between when this work was written and when it is read. Neither the publisher nor author shall be liable for any loss of profit or any other commercial damages, including but not limited to special, incidental, consequential, or other damages.

For general information on our other products and services or for technical support, please contact our Customer Care Department within the United States at (800) 762-2974, outside the United States at (317) 572-3993 or fax (317) 572-400. For product technical support, you can find answers to frequently asked questions or reach us via live chat at https://support.wiley.com.

If you believe you've found a mistake in this book, please bring it to our attention by emailing our reader support team at wileysupport@wiley.com with the subject line "Possible Book Errata Submission."

Wiley also publishes its books in a variety of electronic formats. Some content that appears in print may not be available in electronic formats. For more information about Wiley products, visit our web site at www.wiley.com.

Library of Congress Control Number: 2024953068

Cover image: © liu_miu/stock.adobe.com
Cover design: Jon Boylan

About the Author

Malcolm Hawker is the CDO of Profisee and is a thought leader in the fields of data strategy, master data management (MDM), and data governance. As a former analyst, Malcolm has authored industry-defining research and has consulted some of the largest businesses in the world on their enterprise data and analytics strategies. Malcolm has held senior roles in both product management and IT leadership and has more than 25 years' experience at the forefront of data-enabled business transformations. Malcolm is a frequent conference speaker on data and analytics best practices, and he cherishes the opportunity to share practical and actionable insights on how companies can achieve their strategic imperatives by improving their approach to data management. When not sharing his passion for data or recording episodes of the *CDO Matters* podcast, Malcolm is an avid hobbyist landscape photographer and lives with his wife and two dogs in a small beach town in Florida.

Acknowledgments

This book would not have been possible without the love and support of many people throughout my life and my professional career. I am eternally grateful to my wife and soul's friend, who inspires, challenges, and supports me through all my endeavors. She is my home and my heart, and I am a better person and a better professional because she chooses to walk beside me. I am beyond blessed to be her partner and her husband. Over the years I've spent hundreds of nights away from home in hotels across the globe because of work travel, and even though something in our home breaks down practically every time I leave, she's never complained. Through it all she continues to support me, trip after trip, with her steadfast devotion making each departure that much harder than the last.

I am also grateful to my amazing parents for teaching me the most important lessons in life. My mother taught me the importance of agency and self-sufficiency, and my father taught me integrity and hard work. Together, they worked tirelessly to ensure that I was best positioned to flourish in every aspect of life once leaving their tutelage, and I would not be the man I am without their love and support. The same is true of my beloved sister, who is a wonderful human with a heart of gold who patiently mentored her annoying little brother with a gentle guiding hand that influences me to this day.

There have been many incredible people I've had the honor to work with, and learn from, over my 30+ years – far too many to list individually. Some of my work and team experiences have left an indelible mark on my life and my career. Those include my amazing work tribes at AOL, Neustar, and Hoover's. If you were in my tribe at any of those places, then you know who you are, and you know the types of special experiences we shared. What we built and what we experienced goes beyond the résumé, and I will forever be grateful of the friendships we created.

I must also thank the amazing team and leadership at Profisee, particularly Reed Gusmus, who has supported me in this undertaking. I am beyond blessed to work for a company that deeply embraces a growth mindset, and it's even better that I get to work with an amazing group of extremely talented people day in, day out.

Lastly, I need to thank all the incredible and like-minded people who are a part of my ever-growing network of data professionals. Many of you I know only through our online exchanges on LinkedIn, where you are providing the constant stream of constructive and candid feedback needed for me to become a better advocate for our profession. Others I've had the amazing opportunity to collaborate with on books, articles, or other research efforts. Your camaraderie and your professionalism are inspiring, and I am constantly amazed by how much I learn from you. If you're in the small group of data people I regularly connect with at data events, or those who I choose to associate with outside of work, I treasure your friendship. My many thanks to all of you for your support and your dedication to our industry. You are all my data heroes.

Contents at a Glance

Introduction		xv
Chapter 1:	The Data Hero Origin Story	1
Chapter 2:	The Data Hero Superpower: A Positive Mindset	17
Chapter 3:	The Anti-hero: Limiting Mindsets	41
Chapter 4:	The Wrath of the Anti-hero in Data and Analytics	63
Chapter 5:	Reinforcement Mechanisms in Data and Analytics	103
Chapter 6:	Putting Your Customer at the Center of Everything You Do	147
Chapter 7:	Integrating Product Management as a Discipline Within Data and Analytics Teams	163
Chapter 8:	Embrace Agility and a Relentless Focus on Value Delivery	195

Chapter 9:	Look Inward Before Looking Outward	215
Chapter 10:	Looking Forward	235
Index		259

Contents

Introduction		xv
Chapter 1: The Data Hero Origin Story		1
Chapter 2: The Data Hero Superpower: A Positive Mindset		17
What's a Mindset?		17
Mindset and Corporate Culture		21
Traits of a Positive Mindset and Acts of Data Heroism		24
Adaptability and Willingness to Change		25
Resiliency		27
Innovation and Risk-Taking, Reduced Fear of Failure		30
Open to Feedback and Criticism		34
Seeks Opportunities to Collaborate		36
Chapter 3: The Anti-hero: Limiting Mindsets		41
All-or-Nothing Thinking		42
Lack of Accountability		45
Blaming Others		49
Avoid Challenges, Reluctance to Take Risks		52
Embrace the Status Quo, Resist Change		56
Failure to See Positive Intent		59

CONTENTS

Chapter 4: The Wrath of the Anti-hero in Data and Analytics ... 63
The Unwillingness to Quantify the Value of Data ... 64
Data Literacy and Blaming Customers for Product Failures ... 69
Extreme Forms of "Data First" or "Data Driven" ... 76
Data Culture Is a Dependency to Deliver Value and Is
    Somebody Else's Problem ... 80
Garbage In, Garbage Out ... 83
Seeing Negative Intentions in Others ... 88
Deterministic, "All-or-Nothing" Thinking in a Probabilistic World ... 96

Chapter 5: Reinforcement Mechanisms in Data and Analytics ... 103
Market Realities ... 105
Information Technology Ecosystem Feedback Loop ... 105
Analyst Influences ... 112
Consultant Influences ... 120
Vendor Influences ... 128
Social Media Influences ... 133
Technology Influences ... 140

Chapter 6: Putting Your Customer at the Center
    of Everything You Do ... 147
Become Customer Driven, Not Data Driven ... 149
Focus on Customers and Their Business Processes, Not Technology ... 152
Assume Positive Intentions, Have Empathy ... 153
Better Aligned Incentives and Success Metrics ... 155
Proactive Engagement and Feedback Loops ... 157
Revisit Organizational Structures, Roles, and Responsibilities ... 158

Chapter 7: Integrating Product Management as a
    Discipline Within Data and Analytics Teams ... 163
The P&L North Star ... 165
Hire a Product Manager ... 167
Embrace User- and Customer-Centric Design Methodologies ... 169
Hire a Value Engineer and Measure the Cost and
    Benefit of Everything ... 172
Implement a "Go to Market" Function; Repackage
    Governance and Literacy ... 178
        Changing Your Data Governance Function to a
            Customer Enablement Function ... 179

| Contents | xiii |

Changing a Data Literacy Focus to a Customer Training Function	183
Separate Data Management from Data Product Management (and GTM)	185
Evolve Your Organization Toward Customer and Product Centricity	187
Data Supply Chain Management	189
Data Product Manufacturing (or Development)	189
Data Product Management and PMO	190
Finance, Planning, and Analysis	192

Chapter 8: Embrace Agility and a Relentless Focus on Value Delivery — 195

The Data Strategy MVP	196
Success Metrics/Business Cases	199
Scope, Approach, and Roadmap	201
The Data Governance Model	203
The Data and Analytics Organizational Model	205
D&A Product Management	206
Technology and Infrastructure	208
Wash, Rinse, and Repeat	210

Chapter 9: Look Inward Before Looking Outward — 215

Be Humble	216
Embrace Critical Thinking	219
Lead by Example	221
Make Room for Failure	228
Be Practical	232

Chapter 10: Looking Forward — 235

Natively Digital	235
Data and AI Haves and Have-Nots	240
DataOps and the Convergence of Data and Product Functions	241
Data Monetization and Widespread Data Sharing	243
Data Consortiums and Governance Networks	246
Data Sustainability	249
Data as an Asset	254
In Closing	256

| Index | 259 |

Introduction

Despite billions of dollars invested in data teams and technologies, many organizations struggle to extract meaningful value from their data. Chief data officers (CDOs) and other data leaders face persistent challenges, including short tenures, dissatisfaction with data programs, and unrealized returns on investment. Why? Thanks to the explosion of AI, there is a growing and seemingly unsatiable desire for data and the insights it provides, yet the chasm between the unrealized potential value of data and it's actual value is greater than it has ever been. And it's getting bigger every day.

This is creating a "do or die" moment for CDOs and other leaders of data and analytics functions. The time for heroic action is now, lest data leaders be slowly replaced by others more able to overcome the many barriers that have beguiled the data industry for the last two decades. The key challenge facing CDOs isn't a lack of technology or best practices – it's a limiting mindset that prioritizes the status quo over innovation and customer impact.

During my tenure as an industry analyst, I engaged with thousands of senior data leaders across many industries. The patterns were clear: they struggled because of a failure to embrace a growth-oriented mindset. These CDO struggles play out within an industry rife with forces that help to reinforce old and outdated approaches to managing data that have been proven, time and again, to simply not work. However, there is a better way. This book introduces the **Data Hero Mindset**, an approach that empowers data leaders to focus on business value, adaptability, and customer needs – which are necessary ingredients for data leaders devoted to breaking free from the crippling grip of the status quo.

This book explores how ingrained mindsets hinder data success, the cultural shifts needed to overcome them, and practical steps data leaders can take to become true data heroes. It's not just about governance or frameworks – it's a call to action for completely rethinking the role of data leadership in the AI era. If you're ready to challenge the status quo and become the data hero your organization needs, let's begin this journey together.

Chapter 1
The Data Hero Origin Story

About two years ago on a sunny summer day in my home in Florida, I had a realization. For several years prior I had been ruminating on the issue of why so many data leaders fail to deliver meaningful value to their companies. Despite a recurring string of major technical innovations and no shortage of best practices, frameworks, and expensive consulting engagements – and massive ongoing investments in data functions dating back over a decade – the statistics on chief data officer (CDO) performance have been consistently bleak.

By 2021 the question of why so many data leaders are failing had become something of an obsession for me. Then out of the blue, I figured it out.

I had long known the core issue was a "people problem," because if it was process or technology related, the problem would have been solved a long time ago. But simply saying it's a "people problem" isn't itself meaningful – such is the case with all platitudes.

What I came to realize is there's an epidemic within the world of data and analytics. It's affecting everyone in one way or another, and worse yet, it's so insidious, most are completely unaware of its reach or its impact. It influences every major data initiative, every technology deployment, and every analyst and consulting engagement. It hinders every attempt to fix the problem, and it's running completely amuck.

The epidemic is an ongoing and widespread embrace of a highly limiting *mindset that favors the status quo over growth*. This mindset is manifested in how we express our beliefs related to our customers, our roles, and our data. And because it informs how we view our world, it touches everything.

This book explores these limiting mindsets and what data leaders must do to overcome their negative impacts. So, if you're a data leader or CDO tasked with promoting a culture of data-enabled decision-making within your company, then you've come to the right place. This book is dedicated to sharing insights on the behaviors, and more importantly the mindset, that data leaders must adopt to succeed in an era of constant change and artificial intelligence (AI)-fueled disruption.

What exactly do I mean by a mindset? Before we deep dive into the world of data and analytics, here's a story to help explain what I mean.

Let's imagine you're a baker with 10+ years of experience, backed by a degree from a well-regarded culinary school. Your passion is baking bread, and you've just relocated to a small town where you're the only person in town who still makes their bread the old-fashioned way, by hand and with great attention to quality and detail.

You open a new storefront, and every morning you line your shelves with your freshly baked bread. For a small store there is an amazing assortment of breads, and your bakery is located on a main thoroughfare with steady foot and vehicle traffic in the middle of the town. Better yet, you're the only bakery in town.

Unfortunately, several months after launch it becomes abundantly clear that you're struggling to grow your business. You are paying your rent, but you've had to let go of the one employee you originally hired to help with your launch. You're working 60–70 hours a week and just barely making ends meet. Your business is floundering, and you're uncertain how much longer you'll be able to operate. It quickly becomes clear that if drastic action is not taken, it's likely you'll be unable to continue.

What state of mind will best serve you in your attempts to rescue your business?

At a high level, you have two choices: embrace a mindset that will help you grow from the situation or embrace one that will reinforce the status quo but most certainly means the demise of your business and your physical and mental health.

Taking a more positive, growth-centric mindset requires you to acknowledge that something isn't right with the product and that improvements need to be made to what's being offered to better meet (and understand) customer needs. An individual with a positive mindset would acknowledge the challenge, be grateful for candid feedback from their customers, and seek opportunities to improve. You may think that you have the key to making the best, most-beloved bread in the country, but your customer feedback tells you differently.

In contrast, a baker who embraces a mindset that reinforces the status quo is one who chastises the customers for a failure to appreciate the hard work invested in the breads and for being ignorant to the nutritional superiority artisanal breads have over their heavily bleached and bland big-box competitors. Rather than acknowledge a failure and learn from it, the baker with a more limiting mindset seeks to point fingers, avoid ownership, and embrace a victim mentality.

As counterproductive and toxic as these limiting mindsets are, in the world of data and analytics, we embrace them often. And we do it so often, most of the time we don't even know we're doing it.

My desire to identify the root cause of why so many CDOs are struggling came to a head during my time as a data and analytics analyst at the notable research firm of Gartner. In that Gartner role, which I held from 2019 to 2022, most of my time was spent talking with chief information officers (CIOs), CDOs, and others in senior leadership roles supporting data functions at companies around the globe. It was my job to impart the knowledge and data management best practices I had gained after more than 25 years in similar technology-centric leadership roles and while also working as an IT and product leader, a consultant, and a software and data vendor.

What I learned while an analyst, among many things, is that the problems caused by these limiting mindsets are utterly pervasive. The challenges caused by these mindsets were starkly juxtaposed to the growing belief that data is critical to business success in the digital age.

Regardless of its status as the new oil, or the new gold, or the new whatever, by late 2021 the latent potential for data to fuel competitive differentiation had become front-of-mind for many chief executive officers (CEOs) and corporate boards. Study after study showed the unrealized value of data within organizations, and by the height of the global pandemic (and partially because of the pandemic), companies were anxious to make that potential a reality.

This data gold rush had its beginnings more than a decade previous but had lost significant traction due to the failure of "big data" to drive meaningful benefits for most companies implementing it. The pandemic reinvigorated a C-level focus on data, as disruptions to global supply chains and drastically changing customer behaviors exacerbated the need to have immediate access to accurate and trustworthy insights as not only a competitive differentiator – but for many – their corporate survival. In the span of just a few weeks, fueled by the disruptive force of the pandemic, the need for good data went from a "nice to have" to a "must have" – an evolution I discussed often while a Gartner analyst.

Companies that had a solid foundation of data, supported by exceptional leaders with growth-oriented approaches to data management and data governance, weathered the pandemic storm – and in many cases – prospered from it. Those companies that lacked the leadership needed to successfully leverage the data required to take decisive actions to mitigate the impacts of the pandemic floundered.

This need for data – and the invaluable insights they can provide – further buttressed by the meteoric growth of Generative AI (GenAI) continues to fuel what could rightfully be called a golden age of data and analytics. Characterized by drastic increases in the number of CDOs, increasing investments in data and analytics technologies, and widespread awareness of the transformative power of data, this golden age is only just beginning.

For CDOs and other executives in senior data leadership roles, the AI-driven data gold rush puts those leaders in a highly enviable position of, metaphorically speaking, operating the only gas station in a city with a rapidly expanding population and an insatiable thirst for travel. There's never been a better time to be in the business of data than over the last five years, and – thanks to AI – this is likely to remain true for at least the next five years. Nobody can express with any certainty what an AI-enabled future looks like, but when it comes to AI, three things are for certain:

(1) As a technology and productivity tool, AI is in its early infancy. However, there is a broad and increasing consensus that the potential value of AI is unlike anything we've ever experienced in modern times, including the birth of the Internet. As of late 2024 there are rightful concerns being expressed about the high initial costs (and comparatively low initial returns) associated with this explosion, but the fact hundreds of millions of people around the globe are using GenAI to enhance their individual productivity strongly suggests this technology is here to stay.
(2) It's being widely and aggressively deployed at companies across the globe, which could all be best described as extremely early adopters.
(3) Data is the fuel to the AI gas tank, and the success of any company building or using AI-based systems will depend on the quality of data used as inputs to AI-based processes.

This is why it's a great time to have a data-centric career, and it's a great time to be a CDO. Gartner couldn't have said it any better than in its annual survey of CDOs in 2024, which stated, "The CDAO has the opportunity to be the hero of the information age, with D&A maturity accelerating financial performance by as much as 30%."[1]

---

[1] Gartner (2024). CDAO Agenda 2024: reinvent yourself or risk failure. 12 March 2024. https://www.gartner.com/en/documents/5272363 (Accessed: 7 January 2025).

Given the impeccable nature of the timing, one could assume that any organizations investing in data and analytics functions, including CDOs and other data professionals, would currently be experiencing a bounty of data-enabled riches. Being in the right place at the right time certainly has its advantages, so congratulations to anyone with "data" in their work title. It's a great time to be in data.

This confluence of factors would naturally lead many to conclude that the modern-day data gold rush is providing a bounty of riches for those companies and those CDOs choosing to invest in data and analytics programs. While this is true for a small number of companies and executives, overall the data appears to tell a very different story.

What I experienced while an industry analyst, and continue to witness today, is a prolonged inability of CDOs to bridge the gap between the potential value of data and the actual value data teams are providing to their organizations. In my daily conversation with CDOs while an analyst, I would repeatedly hear the frustrations of those data leaders' inability to drive meaningful outcomes for their companies. The experiences and perspectives I gleaned through qualitative research conducted during my client inquiries were routinely validated through multiple quantitative research surveys, all of which came to similar conclusions: the *potential* to leverage data for competitive advantage is very real, but only a select few are capitalizing on that potential, putting many CDOs in a highly precarious position.

For example, a recent survey of CDOs from Gartner found that only 44% of data and analytics leaders report that their team is effective in providing value to the organization.[2] This number is truly remarkable – especially when you consider that it is a CDO

---

[2]Gartner (2023). Gartner survey reveals less than half of data and analytics teams effectively provide value to the organization [Press release]. 21 March 2023. https://www.gartner.com/en/newsroom/press-releases/03-21-2023-gartner-survey-reveals-less-than-half-of-data-and-analytics-teams-effectively-provide-value-to-the-organization (Accessed: 7 January 2025).

self-assessment and that bias can heavily skew our perspectives of our own capabilities.

Similar studies have shown that only 24% of companies characterize themselves as being "data driven"[3] and that only 30% of CDOs say they are meeting objectives on the return on investment (ROI) from data and analytics.[4] An inability to extract the latent value of data within organizations is reflected in the short tenures of CDO, which are half those of their CIO counterparts – even as the CDO role is now present in more than 80% of all companies.[5] In a 2023 survey of 3,000 CDOs, IBM found that only 8% of them deliver performance that is highly differentiated from their peers, an extremely small group IBM calls "value creators."[6]

What the data for the last 5 years consistently shows is that companies see the potential transformative power and value of data and, as a result, are aggressively expanding their investments in the people, processes, and technologies needed to best support it. Unfortunately, these investments are not yielding the returns that most – including those in data leadership roles themselves expect.

> "Every year you look at the [CDO] survey, and the scores... would start to decline. Do we have a data culture? Do we think the [CDO] role is successful? The [survey] scores were not improving, so clearly something is amiss."
> Allison Sagraves, former CDO of M&T Bank;
> CDO Matters, *Episode #31*

---

[3] Wavestone (2023). Newvantage CDO study, 2023. https://www.wavestone.us/wp-content/uploads/2022/12/Design-2023-Data-Analytics-Survey-Report.pdf (Accessed: 7 January 2025).
[4] Gartner (2021). CDO Agenda 2021: influence and impact of successful CDOs in the Sixth Annual CDO Survey. 31 March 2021. https://www.gartner.com/doc/4000087 (Accessed: 7 January 2025).
[5] HBR.org (2023). Why do Chief Data Officers have such short tenures? https://hbr.org/2021/08/why-do-chief-data-officers-have-such-short-tenures (Accessed: 7 January 2025).
[6] IBM (2023). 2023 Chief Data Officer Study: turning data into value. 20 March 2023. https://www.ibm.com/thought-leadership/institute-business-value/en-us/report/cdo-2023 (Accessed: 7 January 2025).

This divide between the potential value of data and the actual value data are providing was expressed in stark terms in late 2023 when Gartner noted:

> Many data and analytics governance and MDM programs continue to fail despite decades of effort. Working harder at cataloging data issues and building large committees does not work. Successful best practices exist but are not being used. To succeed, D&A leaders should jettison outmoded **practices**.[7]

A year later, Gartner suggested that 2024 was a "make or break" year for CDOs, suggesting that a prolonged inability of data leaders to deliver business value could possibly lead to an assimilation of the data and analytics function into the IT department or individual business functions.[8]

Sadly, the career and business risks associated with a prolonged inability of data leaders to drive meaningful value for organizations is not new. Gartner – and plenty of other analyst firms and consultants – have been ringing this alarm for several years.

These poor performance numbers and short CDO tenures, at a time when the potential to extract value from data has never been greater, necessarily begs the question of *why*.

If companies have been significantly investing in the teams and people needed to better manage and govern data for more than a decade and the latent potential of data to transform a business is universally acknowledged, *why are so few companies succeeding at it?* Why is the tenure of CDOs so low, and why are so many data professionals frustrated?

Why, at a time when there are more opportunities (and desire) for companies to leverage data for competitive advantage than ever before, are so few data leaders and professionals able to deliver meaningful value?

---

[7] Gartner (2023). *Predicts 2024: data and analytics governance requires a reset.* December 2023.
[8] Gartner (2024). CDAO Survey: CDAO Agenda 2024: reinvent yourself or risk failure. March 2024.

By the start of 2022, answering this question became a top priority and a big reason why I decided to leave Gartner. I had reached the pinnacle of any career focused on advising C-level technical executives, and I had a great position at a great company. I was disproportionately influential in a multibillion-dollar software industry, and I could travel the globe speaking to thousands of executives at swanky industry conferences. I absolutely loved being a Gartner analyst, but two years into the job, I could feel something wasn't quite right.

Yet, as great a job as being a Gartner analyst was, by early 2022 I had reluctantly concluded that Gartner was one of the many reasons why CDOs were failing to deliver meaningful value, and by association, so was I. Coming to this realization was a painful yet liberating experience that required several months of introspection. I will explain my reasoning in far more detail in Chapter 5, but the short version of the story is that many of the recommendations I was giving CDOs and CIOs every day were having little impact or were simply ignored. Worse yet, some of my recommendations were reinforcing highly antiquated approaches that have been proven ineffective time after time after time – yet were foundational aspects of my analyst playbook.

Once I realized that as a Gartner analyst I was potentially doing more harm than good for some of the professionals I was dedicated to helping it became time to leave. More important, I realized that I had fallen into the very same trap that most of my clients had also fallen into – which is a dogmatic embrace of a mindset purpose-built to reinforce the status quo.

Not only was I doing the same thing over and over and expecting a different result, but I was telling my C-level clients to keep doing the same thing over and over with the expectation of a different result. Coming to this realization that I was helping to reinforce a status quo that does not well serve data leaders was difficult, but necessary. It's also one of the reasons why I wrote this book.

> "The harsh reality is that data governance, as performed today, is not working. So, if we want to lead, we have to recognize that and we have to do something different. Maybe that involves dissecting

things – figuring out what portions really do work, building on them, dropping the rest. Or maybe it means something altogether different. My own view is that we are trying too hard to make things work in the current organizational context, which is just not 'fit for data.' And we have shied away from the big, hard, important problems, such as 'What does fit for data look like?,' 'What organizational structures work well with data?,' 'How do we get everyone involved?,' and 'What does it really mean to be data-driven?'"

Tom Redman, author of People and Data;
CDO Matters, Episode #29

Once unshackled from the many constraints imposed on Gartner analysts (many for good reasons) and having the freedom to explore alternative perspectives on the status quo, I set out to fill in some of the gaps in my industry knowledge that had formed while living in the Gartner thought bubble. To answer my gnawing question of why so many data leaders were failing to deliver value to their companies, I needed a wider perspective from a wider set of people, so with the backing of my new employer Profisee, I hit the road.

Mid-2022 through 2023 I visited more than 20 cities across the United States, Canada, and Europe visiting data practitioners and leaders from across every industry and vertical. I went to multiple conferences – often in speaking roles – and I was able to hold meaningful and frank conversations in ways I couldn't have done at Gartner, and I slowly began to inch closer to answering the one question dominating my thoughts for the previous three years.

At these conferences I was able to meet with other notable academics and thought leaders in the data and analytics space – many of whom I had admired over the years – and some of whom have even become my friends. The community of people who regularly speak at data-related conferences is a relatively small and tight-knit group of experts, all of whom have a lifetime of experiences to share.

However, unlike me, many of them have only limited experience as data practitioners or leaders. The same is true with industry analysts. This doesn't necessarily mean they don't have valuable insights to offer, but it does mean they've never had to implement the things they're recommending.

What I saw at conferences is a tendency for the thought leaders and experts to have some of the exact same frustrations as data leaders, born from years of making recommendations that aren't significantly advancing our profession. As data leaders seem stuck in a respective pattern and unable to drive meaningful value, the same is true of the thought leaders who are supposed to be providing the insights needed to drive meaningful value. Rather than offer advice that works, many of the brightest minds in our industry are consistently reinforcing old patterns that have been proven to not work – many of whom seem blissfully unaware they're doing it.

On top of my travel to conferences, I started building a community of data leaders and practitioners on LinkedIn – which provides insights on the needs and thought processes of data leaders in ways I could never have experienced at Gartner. LinkedIn is not immune to bias and the vagaries of the "algorithm" in terms of what you see and who you interact with, but it's still a fantastic venue to connect with other data professionals who are willing to share invaluable knowledge about the state of the data nation. With 16,000+ followers (and growing!), my LinkedIn presence has been an important part of my daily routine where I am able to share what I know in exchange for learning from others. And learning, I most certainly am.

In June 2022 I also launched a podcast called *CDO Matters*, and more than 60 episodes later, I've had some amazing conversations with some truly brilliant CDOs about their biggest challenges. I've included many transcribed quotations, taken from published episodes of my podcast, from these experienced professionals through the text of this book. Previously in my career I would never have guessed that at an age that qualifies me for AARP, I would have a podcast and be an online content creator and an industry "thought leader." I'm living proof that old dogs can indeed learn new tricks, the least of which now also includes how to write a book. Go figure.

The combination of my incredible appetite for research, my love of complex problem solving, my very fulfilling years of experience at Gartner, my 25+ year career in software and data, my LinkedIn community, my podcast, and the love and support of my wife is what finally led to what you're now reading.

Once I was able to determine that an overly limiting mindset focused on the status quo is the root cause of an inability of data teams to deliver transformative value, many of the associated issues I had been studying for years that previously seemed intractable suddenly made complete sense.

A widespread embrace of a highly limiting mindset provides fertile ground for the creation of a dysfunctional relationship between the producers and consumers of data, and it disempowers data leaders from innovating and influencing any meaningful changes to their organizational cultures. It reinforces an inward focus that puts more value on the management of data than customer satisfaction, and in doing so it inverts the entire data value proposition.

CDOs and those working for them may be implementing the right technologies and following data and analytics "best practices" as diligently as possible, but a mindset that focuses on limitations and problems is having a disproportionally negative impact on CDO results. Ideas or practices that may be good in theory, or even when proven through scientific research, are failing to deliver when implemented in an environment managed by people focused on problems and not on growth.

Albert Einstein once famously said, "You cannot solve a problem with the same mind that created it." This is the sad reality for many data professionals today – where the status quo is so rigidly engrained in the mindsets they apply to their data, their customers, and their companies – that it's hindering their ability to see and appreciate different ways of solving these old problems.

Data leaders and practitioners are not the only people in the data industry who suffer from limiting mindsets. Industry analysts, consultants, conference speakers, and software vendors all play a role in reinforcing these perspectives, and all help to reinforce and repeat approaches that consistently fail to deliver meaningful results. Just as data leaders are stuck in the status quo, so are the various players you would hope are somewhat "immune" to the forces that hinder growth and innovation in the data world. But sadly, they aren't.

This is because a negative feedback loop powers an ecosystem of consultants, analysts, and software vendors that act in unison to reinforce many of these highly dysfunctional mindsets. The inability of consultants, analysts, and other thought leaders to promote meaningful change in the world of data and analytics, or deliver meaningful value to their clients, creates fertile ground for the same frustration, finger pointing, and disempowerment that similarly plagues data leaders. I cover this negative feedback loop in much greater detail in Chapter 5.

These limiting mindsets have taken deep root in our companies and within our people, and worse yet, examples of this limiting mindset are widely embraced as dogma and are almost never questioned by anyone in the industry. Case in point: garbage in, garbage out. A continued reliance on mindsets that disempower data leaders while blaming others for their problem is producing a lack of innovation, rigid thinking, and a recursive negative feedback loop. The more we continue to invest in these highly limiting mindsets (and fail to challenge them), the harder it becomes to embrace the behaviors that are proven to deliver meaningful business value.

> "The thing that kept coming back for me was that data governance was the Achilles heel of most programs and our ability to deliver results. And the simplest thing I did was, I Googled 'data governance,' as I wanted to know how people were defining it. And it came back with a page-long definition. I'm not kidding. It was two paragraphs, and it was a full page. And I remember distinctly, I shut my browser, and I stepped away from my laptop, and I determined that I've got to write a book. There's got to be a better way. How do you succeed with anything that's a page long in terms of how you describe the work? Why are we still doing the same things with data governance in the data space? It's illogical to me."
>
> Laura Madsen, *author of* Disrupting Data Governance;
> CDO Matters, *Episode #9*

Most ironically, an unconscious devotion to these limiting mindsets is helping create situations where data leaders are modeling the *exact opposite* behaviors that they expect others to embrace. This phenomenon is covered in more detail in Chapter 4 on data culture.

Empowering data leaders to do away with these old ways of thinking in favor of new, more productive perspectives is a core theme of the book. I call this new way of thinking the Data Hero Mindset, an approach that jettisons the limiting perspectives that no longer serve data professionals and wildly embraces those that take a more positive view of their role, their customers, and their data. In doing so, the Data Hero Mindset enables hard-working and well-intentioned leaders and practitioners to become the harbingers of growth their organizations so desperately need, and it will finally allow organizations to realize the full potential of their data.

Our journey starts with a deep dive into an explanation of a mindset and examples of limiting mindsets in action in companies today. We'll than transition into a discussion around more positive mindsets in action, which will culminate in specific recommendations data leaders can take to promote the culture needed within their teams to shift toward more positive, growth-centric mindsets. I conclude the book by sharing some of my perspectives on how our industry will change when more of its leaders more widely embrace acts of data heroism.

For many, realizing they may have subconsciously played a role in contributing to the ongoing failure of their companies to realize value from data may be uncomfortable. Breaking the behavioral patterns that have disempowered data professionals for decades will not be easy – and I suspect many will choose not to and vilify me in the process.

This book and the perspectives in it will surely be seen by as provocative, if not heretical. It provides a completely different perspective on the root causes of the issue of why companies are struggling to get value from data than anything being shared at industry conferences, on LinkedIn, or in any books on the topic. This book challenges many preconceived notions shared within the data community about why there is friction between producers and consumers of data. It will challenge the status quo and, in the process, I hope make data leaders *think differently* about their roles and the value they add to their companies. In keeping with one of the main traits of a growth mindset, I truly hope that anyone reading this book will receive my feedback in the spirit in which it's given – which is a sincere desire to see the data profession grow and data professionals to thrive. This is especially the case for my fellow thought leaders, partner consultants, and former analyst peers – all of whom I firmly believe have nothing but positive intentions – but who may also be reinforcing a status quo that's crippling our industry.

Before diving in, I should note that what you're reading is an entirely qualitative analysis. I've spoken to *thousands* of leaders in the data space, but the insights are entirely mine and are not backed (yet) with significant quantitative or academic rigor. In the spirit of being more "data driven," I invite any readers who may be more academically inclined to consider research to either prove or disprove all the assertions in this book. After all, if we committed to being data driven, we should be building data to explain why we struggle at providing value from it.

It's also important to note that the perspectives and recommendations I'm making in this book are most relevant to what could best be described as more "centralized" expressions of data teams in most organizations. These groups tend to have a mandate to support both corporate and functional levels of the organization, and they tend to operate from within an information technology function as a shared service – but not exclusively. This is not to say that data teams that exist within functionally aligned departments (like finance or marketing analytics teams) won't also benefit from this book – they certainly will. However, the insights and recommendations are generally provided in the context of a data function that supports every aspect of a business, and not just a subset of it.

Finally, I will say that as excited as I am to have come up with an answer the question that's beguiled me – and an entire industry – for years, the excitement is tempered with the knowledge that I've helped to reinforce many of the limiting behaviors described in this book. However, having all of us take agency over the many previous decisions that have helped create the mess we're in is a key step in moving through it.

So, in many ways, writing this book is a form of therapy that I hope will put others on the same road to a recovery of more positive ways of thinking about how we approach data management – and it's a journey that I hope you'll join me on. Overcoming the mindsets that hold us back will enable all of us to transform into the exceptional leaders our organizations desperately need and will finally allow the full promise of data to be fulfilled in your company.

Let's become the data heroes our companies so desperately need us to be.

Are you with me?

Chapter 2
The Data Hero Superpower: A Positive Mindset

In the opening chapter I stressed the importance of a more positive, growth-oriented mindset. What exactly does that mean? What impact do positive mindsets have on individual and corporate productivity? What behaviors and perspectives typify people with more limiting mindsets, and how could they impact job performance? Could an unproductive, limiting mindset be sufficient to hold back an entire industry from providing prolonged and meaningful value?

In this chapter, we will explore these questions in more detail.

What's a Mindset?

A *mindset* is an established set of attitudes that influences a person's perceptions, beliefs, and behaviors. In the context of a corporation, a mindset can also describe a group's attitude, which in turn affects how individuals in the group approach their work, solve problems, and interact with each other. Mindsets are extremely influential in how we all view the world and, in turn, how we choose to engage with it.

A person with a more limiting mindset will tend to see problems and not opportunities, and they tend to be highly resistant to change. Mindsets that hinder growth are characterized by doubt, pessimism, and complaining – and those who embrace them are prone to blaming external forces and people for a failure to overcome obstacles. These people are also more likely to see another's intentions as negative and not supportive. People with more limiting mindsets tend toward black-and-white thinking and will often see choices in business as an "all or nothing" propositions.

Your mindset influences everything you think and everything you do. The worst (or best) part about a mindset is that they have highly reinforcing properties: if you think positively, you are likely to create more positive situations and outcomes, and if you think negatively, you're likely to create more negative situations or outcomes. And the more outcomes you drive (one way or the other), the more the mindset is reinforced.

I was first exposed to the concept of a mindset when I read *Mindset: The New Psychology of Success*, by Stanford Psychologist and Professor Carol Dweck, published in 2015. I first read this book in early 2022 after joining Profisee because our CEO, Len Finkle, is passionate about the importance of all employees having a growth mindset – so much so he made reading the book part of the company onboarding process.

What Dweck shares in her book is that there are essentially two mindsets that we (and by association, our organizations) can embrace: either a growth mindset or a fixed mindset. Dweck argues that those with a growth mindset, who believe abilities and intelligence can be developed through hard work and dedication, are more likely to achieve success. She asserts that a growth mindset fosters resilience and persistence, which are crucial traits for business leaders and organizations aiming for long-term success.

Conversely, Dweck sees fixed mindsets as those that tend to be more intractable, as embodied within people who choose to avoid challenges, ignore feedback, and give up easily. People with a fixed mindset, according to Dweck, are more interested in being told they are right than in learning, and they are more likely to see their level of intelligence as static. When given the choice between validation and growth, people with a fixed mindset will typically choose the former.

The words Dweck uses to describe either ends of the mindset spectrum are a rooted in quantitative academic research and may often do not completely align to the mindsets that I've encountered over my lengthy professional career – particularly those that stand in opposition to growth. As such, in this book I will use the terms "positive" and "limiting" to describe the opposite mindsets that I see as being mission critical to either promote or change. The perspectives I describe on either end of this spectrum are firmly rooted in, *but not limited to*, the mindset definitions posited by Dweck and other researchers in this space. This is why I've used different words than Dweck to describe these polar opposites, since what I've observed goes beyond the boundaries of Dweck's research.

This is particularly the case in my use of the word "limiting" to describe the mindsets that are the opposite of those needed to promote growth. Being unable or unwilling to grow is one thing, but forwarding perspectives and embracing behaviors that actively subvert the stated goals of your company and your department is another thing entirely. If you embrace behaviors that harm your customer relationships, then the impacts of your choices go well beyond simply embracing the status quo or being "fixed." They hinder your company, they hinder your career, and they are limiting in every definition of the word.

There are many possible psychological explanations for many of the examples of what I'm calling either positive or limiting mindsets in this book. Often, they align to what Dweck would call a growth or fixed mindset. Other times, they may align to other phenomena, and when they do, I'll share those details and cite my sources or experiences.

Ultimately, as you'll read in more detail later, this book is about empowering data leaders. I'm not writing this to judge; I'm writing this to help improve the careers and results of data professionals. If you come to realize that the behaviors and perspectives I'm labeling in this book as more "limiting" describe you, then you have a choice to make. Either you can reject my thesis and double down on the status quo or you can take the opportunity to explore different ways of thinking about old problems. I hope you choose the latter.

That's because the former reinforces the status quo, where available data suggests the odds that you'll deliver meaningful value for your company are significantly worse than a coin flip. Rejecting the status quo will open the door to entirely different perspectives on how to leverage the power of a positive, growth-centric mindset in your job as a data professional. In doing so, you'll learn that growth mindsets are quantifiably proven to increase job satisfaction, retention, and productivity. Embracing more of a growth mindset seems like a winning proposition to me (even if you think I'm completely wrong), but as you'll read in the following chapters, I didn't always have this perspective. I only recently broke free of the mindset that was limiting my personal development and career growth, and thankfully so.

If you are struck by how often your current perspectives may align to a highly limiting mindset, take comfort in knowing things don't have to stay that way. Mindsets can thankfully shift, and I'm living proof. For decades, I embodied the behaviors of a person with a problematic mindset toward the data I managed, my role as a data professional, and my customers. For more than a decade I managed my career in full alignment with more of a very limiting mindset. Yet somehow, I've lived to tell the story of what it takes for a data professional to break free from a mindset that hinders their growth, and you're reading it now.

So, if my use of the words "suboptimal" or "'limiting'" to describe any of the perspectives or behaviors that you embrace causes you discomfort, or perhaps even makes you a bit irritated (or even slightly angry), then good. Let that discomfort be the motivation you need to take a step back and critically evaluate your desired results versus your actual results. Are you where you want to be in your career, or your company? Are you committed to helping your company leverage the transformative power of data? Do you want that big promotion? Do you want to change?

The Data Hero Superpower: A Positive Mindset

If you've read this far, then clearly you answered "yes" to one or more of these questions, and you're interested in finding ways to break from the status quo. That's a great thing, and it's a necessary step in your individual transformation. You're one step closer to becoming your company's data hero.

Mindset and Corporate Culture

The importance of organizational culture cannot be understated – and is the topic of hundreds of books and research papers. The old saying "culture eats strategy for breakfast" reflects the reality that a dysfunctional culture will ultimately thwart all efforts to execute on a business strategy.[1] You can throw all the money in the world at processes and tools, but if the individual people of the organization cannot work together or trust each other, then all collective actions are likely doomed to fail.

An organizational culture is defined by the norms that characterize an organization. Norms are the collective values, beliefs, and practices of the organization. Norms significantly influence how individuals behave in an organization, and like a mindset, they can have both positive and negative impacts. Productive and economically successful organizations are often characterized by the norms of collaboration, innovation, and integrity.[2] Conversely, norms such as a resistance to change, a lack of accountability, and a loyalty to the past can hinder corporate performance.

Certain values can drive behaviors that lead to positive results, and certain values can lead to negative results. This is true at an individual level, and it's especially true at a group or norm level – where the impacts are magnified and recursive. This is how an organization's overall "culture" is intrinsically interconnected with how people think about their jobs.

---

[1] Many people believe that Peter Drucker was the first to say "Culture eats strategy for breakfast," but there is no proof this is the case.
[2] Denison, D. and Mishra, A. (1992). *Toward a Theory of Organizational Culture and Effectiveness.* Organization Science, Mar–Apr.

The difference between a mindset and a value is nuanced. Mindsets shape how individuals perceive and react to situations, while values are the core principles that guide behavior and decision-making. Values influence ethical and moral judgments, while mindsets influence attitudes toward learning, growth, and challenges.

The work of Carol Dweck, and others, has shown that collective mindsets can shape and influence the values of its members. An organization that embraces a growth mindset focused on learning and development will promote values of innovation and collaboration. Just as values can be collectively expressed as norms, mindsets can also be collectively expressed – influencing both individual and group perspectives and, ultimately, corporate productivity.

There is a deep interconnection between mindsets, values, and behaviors within work settings. Mindsets shape values, and values drive behaviors. And in group environments, the behavior of one can have a significant impact on the behavior of others, resulting in situations where one person synchronizes to the behaviors and emotional state of another. The idea my perspectives can influence your perspectives is known as "emotional contagion," where data suggests that emotions can indeed be contagious. Emotional contagion can be triggered by facial expressions, by indirect interactions (like sending an emotionally charged email), or simply by observing the behavior of others.[3] It can even be triggered through indirect exchanges, like through social media.[4]

Emotional contagion can influence all range of possible behaviors, both positive and negative. Positive emotional contagion is linked to better interpersonal functioning and prosocial behaviors.[5] An example of positive emotional contagion is seeing somebody smile and then feeling more positive as a result. Another example

---

[3] Herrando, C. and Constantindies, E. (2021). Emotional contagion: a brief overview and future directions. *Frontiers in Psychology* 12: 712606. https://doi.org/10.3389/fpsyg.2021.712606.
[4] Wakefield, L.T. and Wakefield, R.L. (2018). Anxiety and ephemeral social media use in negative eWOM creation. *Journal of Interactive Marketing* 41: 44-59. https://doi.org/10.1016/j.intmar.2017.09.005.
[5] Marx, A.K.G., Frenzel, A.C., Fiedler, D., and Reck, C. (2024). Susceptibility to positive versus negative emotional contagion: first evidence on their distinction using a balanced self-report measure. *PLoS ONE* 19 (5): e0302890. https://doi.org/10.1371/journal.pone.0302890.

is where you observe somebody expressing empathy or sympathy, where you respond by expressing the same.

Negative emotional contagion works the same way, but in reverse. If you see somebody who is visibility frustrated or deflated, you are more likely to feel the same way. However, unlike positive emotional contagion, data suggests that negative emotional states tend to have a stronger affective impact than positive emotional states.[6] That means if you're repeatedly verbalizing a frustration related to how difficult you believe you job is because you think the data you're working with sucks, then your actions will negatively influence everyone around you – since your negative emotions will have far more impact on others than any positive ones.

The combination of the behaviors we witness in others, and the mindsets we embrace, can significantly influence our work behaviors and, therefore, our corporate culture. Not only can culture be influenced by our own views of the world, but it can also be influenced by the behaviors of the company itself.

In their 1992 book titled *Corporate Culture and Performance*, John P. Kotter and James L. Heskett studied a wide array of companies to conclude that business success can have a positive impact on corporate culture.[7] When managerial actions drive changes in group behaviors, shared values change to reflect the actions required to deliver the desired outcomes. Put another way, *a corporate culture can be meaningfully influenced by business success, and this success tends to act as a feedback loop.*

This idea of a corporate culture being strongly influenced by business success is particularly relevant to data leaders today. While a Gartner analyst, I would often have conversations with data leaders who had convinced themselves that building a "data culture" – which could loosely be defined as a company that values the use of data to make decisions – was a critical *dependency* for CDO success. For many CDOs, this perceived lack of a data culture is believed to

---

[6] Pinilla, A., Tamayo, R.M., and Neira, J. (2020). How do induced affective states bias emotional contagion to faces? A three-dimensional model. *Frontiers in Psychology* 11: 97. https://doi.org/10.3389/fpsyg.2020.00097.
[7] Kotter, J.P. and Heskett, J.L. (1992). *Corporate Culture and Performance*. New York: Free Press.

be *the* primary roadblock to CDO success, a data point reflected in multiple CDO surveys year after year.

There are many CDOs who blame a lack of a data culture for their inability to deliver value – but the finders of Kotter and Heskett suggest the exact opposite is true. *Culture is an outcome of success and not a dependency for it.* This dichotomy is ironic and profound. The misguided belief that a lack of a "data culture" is a dependency for CDO success is also a fantastic example of a mindset that's hindering the ability of data leaders to succeed. Corporate values and culture can indeed change (for the good or the bad), but these shifts take years to develop. As you'll read in the following sections, a culture shift at Microsoft is in its 10th year, so the idea that a newly hired CDO could change a culture as a dependency to deliver short-term business benefits is entirely unrealistic.

With CDO tenures hovering around 18–24 months, it's clear that businesses don't have the patience to wait 3+ years before seeing any benefits from an investment in a data function, or a CDO. The impacts of culture on a company are most certainly profound, but focusing on "culture" at the expense of finding ways to deliver short-term value is a recipe for CDO turnover. It's also completely disempowering.

The mindsets of CDOs, and those who work for them, have a profound impact on the performance of any data and analytic function. Our mindsets can promote growth, or they can promote the status quo or – worse – negative reinforcing loops that erode our organizational health and our business success. The good news here is that mindsets can most certainly be changed. The way we perceive the world around us is not set in stone, and if we're serious about advancing our careers and our ability to affect change, then assessing our perceptions of the world is a critical undertaking.

Traits of a Positive Mindset and Acts of Data Heroism

When looking more broadly at the concept of a mindset, there are no shortage of examples of how a positive mindset may be manifested in the words or actions of people, and companies, at organizations across the globe. Keep in mind that the aggregate expression of individual mindsets will ultimately reflect the mindset of the entire group (and the corporate culture), so any group within a company can also have a "mindset." The following are five key characters or behaviors of people who embrace more positive, or growth-centric, mindsets.

Adaptability and Willingness to Change

People with a more positive mindset will tend to be far more adaptable and are more willing to embrace change. This is because the need to learn and grow, both professionally and individually, is a defining characteristic of anyone with a more positive mindset. This means the need to change, in response to any force (planned or otherwise), would be seen more as an opportunity than a burden.

In the world of data and analytics, the need to adapt in response to changing market or customer dynamics has never been greater. There can be no better recent example of this than during the global pandemic from 2020 to 2022, where companies were required to quickly and drastically alter their operations in response to rapidly changing business needs. While most data leaders I spoke were caught entirely flat-footed by the pandemic (many taking several months to even formulate a response), data leaders who could produce trustworthy and actionable insights into their customers, their supply chains, and their products were able to leverage those insights at the earliest stages of the pandemic for competitive advantage.

There's arguably no better example of this than Nike, which by 2020 was three years into its pivot away from a market focus on retailers to more of a focus on ecommerce and Nike-branded stores. Known as the Consumer Direct Offense, the program was designed specifically to generate more direct-to-consumer (DTC) sales and, as a result, higher profit margins. Starting from approximately 15% DTC sales in 2017, by 2021 that number had increased to 21.5% of Nike's business – at the same time when consumers were locked down and shifting nearly entirely to online purchasing. In response to changing customer needs, Nike tripled its digital fulfillment capacity and continued significant investments in infrastructure and data – all critical components in the massive change to ownership of the customer relationship (and all customer data) from retailers to Nike itself.

Having accurate and trustworthy data on the nature of Nike's relationships with its suppliers and customers was paramount to successfully executing this strategy. This included the acquisition of DataLounge, a machine learning (ML)-fueled data preparation and integration platform, as well as significant investments in AI and advanced analytics platforms – which together allowed Nike to better understand and model customer behaviors for hyper-personalized buying experiences – often for customers who had purchased Nike shoes or apparel in the past only indirectly from retailers.

Having the data and analytics needed to deeply understand their customers and their supply chains, Nike was able to streamline their operations and increase their profit margins, all while also significantly increasing product sales from $34B in 2017 to more than $50B in 2023. This major shift to having more than 43% of its revenue from DTC sales in 2023, up from 15% only six years prior, was especially noteworthy given much of Nike's transformation was happening at a time when many companies were struggling to simply stay alive.

Nike's timing for its focus on a business transformation to DTC was fortuitous (given it started two years before the pandemic lockdowns), but the bigger story here is that Nike's transformation succeeded *despite* the pandemic, not because of it. The company, including its team of data professionals, could have been easily overwhelmed by all the changes required to successfully execute their digital transformation at a time of massive disruption – but they were not. This is why the Nike example is a great testament to the transformational impacts that a willingness to embrace change can promote.

The need to adapt quickly to changing market dynamics is the greatest requirement for any company in an era of constant disruptions – like global pandemics, wars, and major technological advancements such as AI. Any company unable or unwilling to change, through a persistent endorsement of the status quo, will most certainly suffer dire consequences in the long run. The proof of this is highlighted by the fact that only 12% of the companies on the Fortune 500 list today were on that list 50 years ago. Companies come and go, and those that stay tend to be more adaptable to change.

One particularly good example of a company unable to grow or change that stands in stark contrast to Nike is Eastman Kodak. Up to the 1990s Kodak completely dominated the photography industry but was unable to adapt to the changes forced by the digital camera – which ironically – was invented by a Kodak engineer. Fearing digital photography would cannibalize its core film business, Kodak executives shunned the new technology and instead made several investments outside their core business. Over the span of a decade Kodak went from a household name to an afterthought, and by the time they finally decided to change to focus on digital photography in the early 2000s, it was too late to save their business. Kodak declared bankruptcy in 2012.

The Nike and Kodak stories are spectacular examples of the critical importance of a need for both companies and people to be willing to embrace change – and there are plenty more. Blockbuster, BlackBerry, Sears, Toys "R" Us, and Radio Shack are some more examples of large, iconic consumer brands that were unable to adapt to changing customer and market dynamics and therefore suffered the ultimate consequence. The ability to change is key to business success, and people with a positive mindset are more likely to embrace change.

Resiliency

People with a more positive mindset also tend to be far more resilient. This is because failures or setbacks are perceived as a necessary and valuable part of the learning process – and are not seen as an indictment on the value of the person suffering the failure. This doesn't mean people with a positive mindset see the world through rose-colored glasses, but rather, they see challenges as opportunities to develop and grow.

The cross-functional nature of data within large companies means that data professionals will encounter many forms of resistance in the execution of their jobs that others in more siloed business functions simply just don't encounter. There's no better example of this than the requirements for cross-functional data management and governance – where successful execution of these programs will require data professionals to drive consensus on issues that can often be contentious. Even what appear to be the simplest of data governance tasks – like reaching agreement on a common set of business definitions (for things like customers, or products, or employees) – can cause significant disagreement due to the autonomy each of these functions is afforded, usually by design.

I can share far too many stories of situations where I've been given the task of leading a cross-functional group to consensus on a shared definition of our "customers," only to walk away from that experience with little to show for my efforts other than a bruised ego. Sadly, given competing business interests, political fiefdoms, and misaligned incentives, these massive hurdles far too commonly describe many data governance committee meetings in our companies today.

The resilience needed to face these roadblocks and do whatever is necessary to find ways around them is a defining characteristic for many who have enjoyed success in the field of data and analytics. A great example of this is Sol Rashidi, a highly successful five-time CDO with an established career spanning notable companies including Merck, Sony Music, and Royal Caribbean. I first met Sol in January 2024 at the annual Data Day Texas event, where she was attending to give the opening keynote presentation for the conference. I had known of Sol, and her stellar reputation, for several years and was delighted to learn in advance that we would both be speakers at a well-loved data conference in my old hometown of Austin, Texas. Austin is a truly amazing city, and I relish any opportunity to return, especially if the occasion is a data conference.

The Data Hero Superpower: A Positive Mindset

Sol's pedigree speaks volumes on its own, but she also happens to be a confident and compelling storyteller that had me enraptured from the opening sentence of her keynote – where she shared details on the key traits she believes have been most critical to her professional success. A common theme across everything Sol shared in that keynote, and subsequently in far greater detail in the first chapter of her recently published book titled *Your AI Survival Guide*, is her tenacious resiliency. Her resiliency, when coupled with her stubbornness and relentless work effort, forms a formidable combination that has clearly helped Sol to distinguish herself and her career.

Sol's story is one of repeatedly overcoming roadblock after roadblock – in academia, in sports, and in her professional career – each time reaching levels that most of us could only dream about. Sol is by no means physically imposing yet somehow played water polo for a Division 1 school (the University of California) and rugby for the US women's National team. She has no formal technical training yet has led many large data and AI initiatives – and even served as a master data management (MDM) program lead at a $100M project early in her career.

Not many people can say they've succeeded in a large-scale MDM initiative – but knowing what I've come to learn about Sol's character and her resiliency – it's no surprise to me that she counts MDM as one of her many professional accomplishments. The fact she called me out by name as a fellow "MDM person" in her Data Day Texas keynote caught me completely off-guard but was frankly one of the most powerful professional acknowledgments that I've ever received. To this day my face gets red just thinking about it. Sol is as charming as she is resilient.

That January day in Austin following Sol's keynote was capped with some extremely mediocre Texas BBQ, but with an amazing conversation with Sol and a handful of other data luminaries and leaders, including Joe Reis, Chris Tabb, Hala Nelson, and Veronika Durgin (just to name a few) – all of whom I've come to know and appreciate over the last two years. There is a strong community of incredibly like-minded people in the world of data and analytics, and I'm extremely grateful for the opportunity to be a small part of it through my participation in industry events like Data Day Texas.

There's an even smaller group of us, like myself and Sol, who have built their data careers on a foundation of MDM, which for many involves trying and often failing but trying again, and learning so much in the process. The tenacity required to overcome roadblocks, like those common in large-scale MDM and data governance initiatives, in a way where those challenges are seen as opportunities to grow and develop is a function of a positive mindset. Sol is living proof of how the right mindset can be leveraged to develop a prosperous and truly remarkable career in the field of data and analytics.

Innovation and Risk-Taking, Reduced Fear of Failure

People with a more positive mindset tend to be more willing to take risks and are more likely to seek opportunities to innovate. They also look for opportunities to improve, which makes them more likely to break from the status quo and embrace the unknown. Given they view failure as an opportunity to improve (and not a threat to their competence), they are significantly less likely to fear it, and less likely to get stuck in repetitive patterns that tend not to provide growth or learning opportunities.

Research published in 2016 suggests that the perception of failure as either a learning opportunity or a debilitating factor can be passed from parents to children – also suggesting the same may be true of corporate environments.[8] If an organization (or its leadership) sees failure as an opportunity for growth and creates norms that support some degree of measured risk-taking, then it's entirely possible even the most conservative and risk-averse companies could become more innovative over time. So just as a person's individual mindset can hinder or promote innovation, the same is true with the broader mindset of an entire company.

---

[8]Haimovitz, K. and Dweck, C.S. (2016). Parents' views of failure predict children's fixed and growth intelligence mind-sets. *Psychological Science* 27 (6): 859–869. https://doi.org/10.1177/0956797616639727.

The Data Hero Superpower: A Positive Mindset

In the world of data and analytics, I suspect there are few who would strongly assert most data teams are innovative and open to taking risks. Rather, I suspect most, including myself, would broadly generalize the data function as one being inherently conservative and not one widely known as a hotbed of innovation.

Many of you reading this may be saying to yourself but what about all the hype around new technologies? What about things like data products? Or the data mesh? Or the data fabric? Or data observability? Or GenAI? Aren't these all examples of innovation in the data space?

My short answer here is "no," especially in the situation where the innovation is coming from an external software vendor and where the core of the innovation is only technology without supporting innovations in our core operating models – which is so often the case. And when there are significant innovations that marry (or require) people, process, and technology changes, our inability to operationalize those innovations, caused by low levels of maturity across all aspects of our operating models, is a sufficiently large roadblock as to make the innovation largely irrelevant – which is exactly the fate I believe the data mesh is suffering. Sadly, this is also the same fate that many companies are currently experiencing with GenAI, with most still sitting on the sidelines, unable to fully appreciate or understand how to make the AI dream a reality.

Beyond the data mesh or GenAI, plenty of examples of advancements in data and analytics technology exceed the ability of most organizations to operationalize it. The technology to support multiple "versions of the truth" have existed for a long time, yet most companies lack the data governance maturity and investment needed to successfully manage governance policy definition and enforcement for multiple customer master records. Most companies struggle with just creating a single customer master, and even when they create it, it primarily serves only a limited number of business domains.[9]

---

[9] The Gartner 2021 MDM Magic Quadrant quotes data that shows 50% of MDM is deployed in an individual business domain.

So, I stand by my assertion that we suffer from low levels of innovation and risk taking. The reasons here are many – and I'll touch on them in greater detail in subsequent chapters – but I would assert that if we are ever to fulfill the unmet potential of data in most organizations, data teams must find ways to take more risks and to innovate. This is especially the case with how leaders manage a data function, particularly when it comes to the mindset they embrace (and by proxy, they promote).

The status quo is the enemy of innovation, which is a hard requirement in a world of constant change. Keep in mind that innovation isn't just about building the next blockbuster consumer gadget. Innovation can be something as simple as a minor modification to an existing process or methodology or technology platform. Not all innovations need to be market defining, but they most certainly need to happen in an environment where everyone in the management chain promotes an environment conducive to risk-taking and where failures are seen as learning opportunities.

In the world of data and analytics, a company that I've worked closely with that is putting innovation at the core of its data operating model is the Purina division of Nestlé. Brian Zenk, the VP of Data Science for Nestlé Purina, has been leading a team on a multiyear journey to transform and innovate the way data is delivered to internal customers at Purina. This includes major changes to the organizational structure of the data and analytics function, the roles of people on the team, and their supporting technologies.

In 2023 I twice had the honor of introducing members from the Purina team to share their story with audiences at the Gartner Data and Analytics Summits, in both Orlando and London. A core to the new way of delivering data services is a concept Purina calls The Hive, which is essentially a data center of excellence – but it's not positioned that way. It's positioned as a business function and sits entirely outside the IT organization, aligned under Purina's chief *growth* officer.

Zenk describes The Hive as "the place where business, technology, and data and analytics expertise, all come together on one team, with one shared mission"[10] – where that mission is to become a trusted partner to enable AI at scale within Purina. Half of The Hive is focused on enabling capabilities, a focus you would normally see in all data teams. One thing that's fundamentally different with Purina's approach is that the other half of The Hive is focused on "data enablement," which involves working closely with the business to ensure data and insights can be fully operationalized and integrated into business processes and workflows.

At Purina, the goal isn't just the creation of data products; it's also about providing the expertise and support needed to ensure those products are deeply integrated into the business – and are providing meaningful value. To support this, business stakeholders are directly embedded into The Hive in a dotted line relationship (roles funded by the business function), working closely within The Hive to provide requirements, insights on business processes, and feedback on product releases. One way to think of these people is as "ambassadors" of the business within the data function but also ambassadors of the data function back to the business.

The Hive also supports the creation of analytics user communities, which meet twice a month, consisting of more than 500 practitioners and key stakeholders across the business. Resources within The Hive are aligned to "practice guilds" (such as data engineering, AI/ML, and product management), which interface with "swarms" that ensure the output of the guilds can be enabled/operationalized at scale within every business function.

Like many data teams, Purina is embracing the concept of data products. Unlike others, they are doing it in a highly innovative way that is not only focused on managing data at scale but – more importantly – doing it in a way that ensures those products are fully aligned to business needs. This approach is the exact opposite of legacy approaches to products in the world of data, which have primarily involved pushing out dashboards or providing logins to "democratized" analytics platforms. It's a service and

---

[10] https://www.youtube.com/watch?v=82bB3-F7eMk

outcome-oriented approach at Purina focused on making sure customers can use, and get value from, data and analytics.

When looking only at the MDM aspects of Purina's innovation efforts, it's estimated that improvements in customer cross sales and up sales, optimized supply chain logistics, and more accurate predictive analytics built on AI will together drive $25M in incremental corporate revenues over the next five years.

Innovation like this is possible only in environments where data teams feel they can take some risks and where new ways of thinking about old problems are actively promoted at every level of the organization. Embracing positive mindsets that see risk through the lens of an opportunity to learn and develop, and not an opportunity to fail, is an important dependency for any data professional seeking to enrich their career and find ways to deliver meaningful value to their companies – and the people at Purina are a great example of this in action.

Open to Feedback and Criticism

People with more positive mindsets are open to criticism and view feedback as an important input in the development process. Rather than see criticism as an attack or a challenge to their authority, people with a positive mindset will tend to welcome criticism – constructive or otherwise.

The ability to provide feedback is a critical management skill, but quite clearly, the ability to receive it is equally important. I was first exposed to the importance of giving and receiving feedback early in my professional career, having been required to read *Feedback Is a Gift* by Stephen C. Lundin and Marshall Goldsmith in one of my first management jobs in the early 2000s.[11]

The main premise of the book is that managers must work to ensure the receiver of the feedback views it in a positive light – increasing the chances they will use the information to help them

---

[11] Lundin, S.C. and Goldsmith, M. (1999). *Feedback is a Gift*. United States: ChartHouse International Learning Corporation.

grow and develop. As somebody who has always leaned more toward a positive mindset in my professional career (especially prior to focusing exclusively on data), as a young manager I struggled with the idea that anyone willing to extend energy to provide me guidance would be see an anything other than helpful. Yet, I would quickly come to learn that many people under my leadership would see feedback in the exact opposite way regardless of how I tried to delicately manipulate them into seeing it otherwise – which means that for me employee annual review "season" was one of my least favorite times of the business year.

Still, across two decades of people leadership, I consistently worked to hone the skills I needed to deliver feedback in the most constructive way possible, but I'll admit it's still a work in progress. Thankfully, giving feedback is a skill I get to perfect daily at my current company, Profisee, since giving feedback is one of five core corporate values. But instead of "feedback," Profisee refers to it as "constructive candor" and sees it as a critical component of a healthy and productive work environment and overall organizational health.

Our leaders and managers all openly promote the idea of giving constructive candor, regardless of where you sit in the organization and who you're giving the feedback to. We are encouraged to seek feedback from a diversity of people and positions, in whatever method the provider is most comfortable giving it. Training on our company values, including constructive candor, is a critical aspect of all employee onboarding and is something all leaders in the company consistently revisit and reinforce through team meetings, individual reviews, and company-wide gatherings.

A great example of this commitment to constructive candor happened recently, when our CEO reached out to get my input on a presentation he was putting together for our sales organization. He wanted to make sure the tone and content were on point, and given I've been on both sides of the negotiation table (as both a vendor and a buyer), he wanted my input. I learned on that call that I was the third person he had solicited that day, with the other two being outside leadership ranks.

Given this focus on giving and receiving feedback, it should be no surprise that another core value at Profisee is a growth mindset. Management invests in programs to promote learning and development, employees are encouraged to always be seeking opportunities to stretch their comfort zones, and failures are expected as a necessary and essential part of learning.

Profisee is a great example of a data and analytics-centric company with a commitment to develop more positive, growth-minded employees. For Profisee, the benefits of this focus are substantial – both for the company and for employees. In Q3 of Fiscal Year 2024, Profisee announced it had doubled year-over-year sales, a truly exceptional result for an industry that is typified by growth rates in the 5–8% range. It's been voted a "top place to work" in 2021, 2022, and 2023; was certified as a "Great Place to Work" in 2024; and was voted the #1 Technology Company in Atlanta by the *Atlanta Journal-Constitution* in 2023.

The first thing I was asked to do as a new Profisee employee was to read *Mindset* by Carol Dweck, which was my first step in developing a deep understanding of the power of mindsets. Ultimately, reading that book helped to catalyze many of the thoughts shared in this book, and it provided a framework from which to understand why so many data leaders struggle – even when they're working hard and doing what they think are all the right things. The widespread embrace of a growth mindset is a major driver of the success of Profisee, and the company invests heavily to ensure all employees are supported in their efforts to develop the skills needed to both receive and give feedback to anyone at any level, any time.

Seeks Opportunities to Collaborate

People with a positive mindset tend to seek opportunities to collaborate with others. This is because collaboration can open the door to alternative or different perspectives, which is an opportunity to learn and develop. People with a positive mindset do not fear that engaging with a group will result in others taking "credit" for their

The Data Hero Superpower: A Positive Mindset

work, because achieving the best possible outcomes through an environment that promotes growth is a key motivator.

They are more open to working on tasks with a collective objective and tend to be highly effective in team settings, as they will also tend to have a more positive attitude toward the success of others – which they will see as an inspiration rather than a threat. In pursuit of a common goal, people with a positive mindset will be more willing to share knowledge, especially if the exchange is reciprocal. Together, these things make people with more positive mindsets great collaborators and great team members – characteristics of people whom any team leader would be ecstatic to have in their organization.

The CEO of Microsoft, Satya Nadella, has said that the key to Microsoft's spectacular growth since he's been the CEO is the widespread embrace of a growth mindset. Under previous leaders, including Steve Ballmer and Bill Gates, the culture at Microsoft was a high-pressure environment where employees were often pitted in competition against each other, which stifled collaboration and created significant internal rivalries. Microsoft embraced a stack ranking approach to rate (and retain) employees, which promoted even fiercer competition between employees. These forces led to the creation of a high-anxiety, stress-filled environment that stifled collaboration and slowed the company's ability to respond to market changes.[12]

The transition of Microsoft to a more positive, growth-oriented organization is chronicled by Nadella in his 2017 book *Hit Refresh*, a must-read for any business executive seeking to better understand the power that mindsets play in an organization. In his book, Nadella openly acknowledges that the adoption of a growth mindset within Microsoft, citing the work of Dweck directly, is a critical dependency to deliver on their corporate transformation. Transforming the company from a group of "know it alls" to "learn it alls" is a goal

---

[12] Ex-Microsoft executive Paul Allen once described working with Bill Gates as "being in hell." See https://www.businessinsider.com/working-with-bill-gates-was-sometimes-like-being-in-hell-2011-4.

of his cultural shift, and several years into the effort, it's producing some major improvements at the company, and their bottom line.

These include significant changes in how Microsoft collaborates with other companies, including some of its fiercest competitors. Collaboration is a defining attribute of people with a growth mindset, so it should be no surprise that, under Nadella, Microsoft is taking a drastically different approach to working with other companies and software platforms than in the past. In helping to explain his perspective on collaborating with competitors, in his book Nadella noted, "Our partnership with Red Hat may not be as surprising to some as our work with Apple and Google, but when I stood on stage with a slide just over my shoulder proclaiming 'Microsoft ♥ Linux', one analyst concluded that hell must have frozen over."

Prior to Nadella taking the CEO reigns in 2014, Microsoft was the ultimate walled-garden ecosystem, where company efforts to get their clients and partners to adopt their internal proprietary software and platforms were fierce. This insular focus and lack of collaboration led to many claims of anticompetitive behavior, but it also put Microsoft at a significant market disadvantage. This was particularly the case in the rapidly evolving mobile computing space – which by 2016 accounted for more Internet usage than desktop computers and more Google searches.[13] Microsoft's unwillingness to develop applications for either the Android or iPhone platform opened the door for competitors like Google to dominate markets that benefitted from increased software sales on mobile phones but, more importantly, lucrative advertising revenues. By 2018 advertising on mobile phones had become a $100B market, which was only $10B shy of Microsoft's total revenue for that year.

Collaborating with other companies, while also creating an internal culture focused on collaboration over competition, is a critical aspect of Nadella's transformation strategy – which is clearly

---

[13] https://gs.statcounter.com/press/mobile-and-tablet-internet-usage-exceeds-desktop-for-first-time-worldwide

working. Perhaps the greatest proof of the positive impacts from the culture shift at Microsoft is within the market for cloud computing infrastructure, where the Microsoft Azure platform has made significant gains over the last several years in a market experiencing meteoric growth. In 2015 Microsoft had 9% of a $16B market, and in 2023 this number had increased to 23% of a $160B market – taking significant market share from several established players, including IBM and Alibaba.[14]

There are clearly many influences on Microsoft's broader corporate transformation, but the benefits of improved collaboration are well documented, and data suggests it's likely playing an outsized role at Microsoft. A Deloitte study showed that among employes who collaborate in the workplace, 73% do better work, and 60% are more innovative.[15] A study of more than 1,100 companies by the Institute of Corporate Productivity found that high-performing companies are up to 5.5 × more likely than lower performers to incentivize individual, team, and leader effectiveness in collaboration.[16] A study of more than 1,400 people in 2011 showed that 86% of respondents blamed a lack of effective communication or a lack of collaboration for workplace failures.[17]

Thanks to the explosive growth for computing infrastructure to support the widespread deployment of GenAI-based solutions, Gartner is forecasting that the total spending on all cloud-based solutions (which includes infrastructure, software, and services) will hit a whopping $1.8T by 2025. Had Microsoft employees continued to embrace the mindsets that defined the corporate culture established prior to Nadella's ascent to CEO, it's entirely conceivable

---

[14]https://techcrunch.com/2023/02/06/even-as-cloud-infrastructure-market-growth-slows-microsoft-continues-to-gain-on-amazon
[15]https://www.deloitte.com/au/en/services/consulting/blogs/delivering-on-promise-digital-collaboration.html
[16]https://www.i4cp.com/productivity-blog/top-employers-are-5-5x-more-likely-to-reward-collaboration#:~:text=A%20new%20study%20from%20the,and%20leader%20effectiveness%20in%20collaboration
[17]https://fierceinc.com/employees-cite-lack-of-collaboration-for-workplace-failures/?utm_source=chatgpt.com

the company would still be floundering in the cloud infrastructure market – a foundational component of the AI revolution that's only just beginning.

The impact that the mindset of any individual, or group, can have on the performance of any organization is profound. The successes realized from a focus on growth at Purina and candid feedback at Profisee are two great examples of this. We've likely all worked in teams at some point in our career with people who embody the traits of a positive mindset, and it's also likely they've made a lasting impact on both their company and those around them. When that person is in a position of authority, like Sol Rashidi or Satya Nadella, the impacts can be even more magnified and more impactful. Thinking back over my career, I can thankfully say I've been able to work with (and for) two or three of these people, and they've all had outsized influences on my professional development.

Being a resilient collaborator who innovates, seeks feedback, and is willing to change will most certainly make you both a productive employee and a great leader, but more importantly, embracing these traits will make you happier to be at work. Time will go by more quickly, and others will want to be around you. You'll be more likely to return home feeling refreshed and accomplished, and the idea of returning the next day will invigorate you. This means choosing a positive mindset is the ultimate win-win for any leader or employee, and later in Chapters 6–10, I'll share some specific actions you can take to put you on a path to positivity. The choice is yours.

Chapter 3
The Anti-hero: Limiting Mindsets

In stark contrast to positive mindsets, more limiting mindsets are those that stifle collaboration, innovation, and a willingness to embrace change. Limiting mindsets not only help to reinforce the status quo but also act as a corrosive force that undercut efforts designed specifically to improve a data function. This means even in situations where a data leader or practitioner has a stated goal of improving their data products – or their processes – if enough people in the organization approach their jobs with an overly limiting mindset, the efforts to implement a positive change are more likely to fail.

It's taken me a lifetime to be able to fully appreciate the role that limiting and often counterproductive mindsets have played across both my personal and professional development – and to get to the point where I can now clearly see when these mindsets are likely at play. But it wasn't always this way, and at times I've struggled to make sense of situations where those around me were embracing a mindset that actively hinders growth.

All-or-Nothing Thinking

Looking back, there's no better example of this than my experiences within the first few years of moving from Canada to the United States to attend graduate school in the mid-1990s. By some miracle I convinced my father to bankroll me on this escapade to the Sunshine State, which seemed like a downright magical option given I had spent the entirety of my first 25 years in Edmonton, Canada, where I can vividly recall situations where I was forced to shovel significant amounts of snow off our driveway as a young lad in every calendar month but one.[1]

I came to the United States at age 25 with a thirst for discourse and a desire to learn more about the things I was observing in my new home of Gainesville, Florida. I wanted to learn more about the history of the south and of race relations, I wanted to learn more about the political system and the views of my classmates and professors. I wanted to learn why some of the things I took for granted in Canada, like a wide diversity of political and social views on a given issue, didn't seem to have a place in American discourse.

I started asking questions to friends and classmates, and often, those questions were greeted with something to the effect of "we don't talk about that" or with a quick subject change. This was especially the case on issues related to race, when it was common for some people to just completely walk away.

On issues of politics, I was stunned by how quickly my classmates would galvanize into one of two camps and how rapidly the discussion could escalate into flared tempers and shouting matches. My inability to stimulate a conversation, or quickly kill one, got to the point where I became seriously concerned about my likeability – which is a real problem for somebody in a new country with no friends or family. Then one day, a wonderful human named Myles took me under his wing.

---

[1] July. I have vivid memories of massive snowstorms in both June and August, leaving only a single month of the year where snow wasn't a distinct possibility.

Myles was a classmate from Maryland, and he's African American. During one of my failed attempts to stimulate a discussion about one of the three forbidden subjects, Myles pulled me aside and gave me the lay of the land. In private, Myles was happy to share his experiences in growing up as an African American in the south and helped answer many of the burning questions I had about the state of race relations in my new home. Growing up in Canada I was not exposed to many of the insights that Myles shared, and I was incredibly humbled that he would be willing to share his experiences with me. As I learned to temper my public inquiries around the three forbidden subjects, I also learned that it took great bravery for anyone to break free from the "either/or" perspectives that permeated these issues, particularly politics.

My experiences in Gainesville were a glaring example of the first key trait of people with more limiting mindsets – and that is they *tend to embrace all-or-nothing thinking*. This is a very binary, "either/or" way to look at the world that requires complex situations to be reduced to choice between two opposites. When evaluating alternatives, people with a limiting mindset will struggle to see the many nuances that exist between competing options. Rather than a spectrum of possibilities, people with a more limiting mindset will often see only two.

> "(Let's) look at the way data scientists are taught and acculturated. The 95% confidence score is a great example of this. The problem is that the minute you start dealing with data that represents a predominantly human behavior, which is most of business, the 95% becomes a moot point. Then, data scientists will do one of two things: they will either say the data is worthless, or they will over-fit the model to get to the 95% confidence score, thus introducing their own set of bias into the outcome."
> *Mark Stouse, CEO of ProofAnalytics.ai;*
> CDO Matters, *Episode #38*

This perspective is a simplification of reality that enables one to skirt the often-difficult work needed to unravel the complexities of a situation. By eliminating ambiguity, taking an "all-or-nothing" approach also helps to reduce the fear of the unknown, which is often an effective defense mechanism. It can help to provide a justification for inaction, because adopting an extreme perspective will typically require far more drastic action than an iterative approach enabled by breaking big tasks into smaller pieces.

This "all-or-nothing" mindset also helps to promote confirmation bias, in that people with this mindset tend to seek information that supports their perspectives and does not challenge them. Unlike those with a positive mindset who seek feedback and to learn, an "all-or-nothing" worldview is inherently resistant to change, given the enormity of the change needed to operationalize an extreme perspective.

In group situations, when evaluating competing options, a widespread embrace of "all-or-nothing" thinking will quickly galvanize a group into two warring factions – not unlike the current political environment in the United States. Either you are with us or you are against us, and there's very little room for more nuanced perspectives between the two extremes. This serves to dissuade collaboration, as those with competing opposite perspectives are seen as a threat.

Growing up in Canada there were three major political parties, with a handful of other minor parties across a wide spectrum of political perspectives. This means I was taught from a very early age that there are always more than two views on any issues and that it's our responsibility as informed citizens to try to seek all of them out. There is most certainly party tribalism in Canada like there is in the United States, but there isn't nearly as much bipolar thinking on key issues. So as a new immigrant in 1995, the idea that you could reduce complex economic or social issues to either "red" or "blue" seemed to me, at the time, entirely foreign.

In Canada, at least in my schools and in the homes of my friends and family, it's common to talk openly about the issues of the day, even if they include ethnicity or politics or faith. Some of the best political discussions I've ever had occurred while at my Uncle Dave's house, where we would go most years for a Passover seder and for Hanukkah. I'm a Scottish/English/Irish protestant who never goes to church, but my Aunt Irene married a devout Jew, so out of respect for my aunt and uncle, we would attend all their major Jewish celebrations – as they would attend many of our secular celebrations.

As a little boy sitting at seder, I didn't quite understand why I would need to wear a yarmulke, why I would eat horrible gefilte fish, or what the significance of those annual dinners were. I was just doing my best to recite each blessing, answer the four questions, and buy my time before receiving gelt (kids got gelt after every meal at Uncle Dave's, seder or not). As I aged, I began to better appreciate the significance of those dinners and their influence on my perspectives, not the least of which included a hefty appetite for deep political discourse at family dinners. In time, I even learned to appreciate gefilte fish and horseradish.

Later aided (and ultimately impeded) by four ceremonial cups of seder wine after turning 18, discussions of politics, economics, religion, and anything else a family could argue about at Uncle Dave's were not without their share of tumult. But as much as we passionately disagreed (I'm conservative, with many family members proud socialists), we could walk away from the table with a deeper understanding and appreciation for the view of the other. If anything, the family bonds would grow stronger from those disagreements, not weaker. And they didn't just happen at my Uncle Dave's, they would happen in the home of every one of my aunts and uncles, at every major family gathering. To me, arguing about the biggest social or political issues of the day was a normal thing at all family and social gatherings, and they were amazing opportunities to connect on a meaningful level with the people who matter the most.

Lack of Accountability

Once I graduated with my master's degree from the University of Florida in 1995, I was lucky to land a job at a small but rapidly growing Internet company known as America Online (AOL). I started at

AOL as a phone-based technical support call center agent making $7.50 an hour. I knew my graduate degree was worth more way than $7.50 an hour, but I found an opportunity at an exciting company in an exciting industry willing to hire an immigrant on a temporary work visa that would expire less than a year after my hiring. In my last two months as a grad student, I sent out over 400 résumés to more "reputable" companies with reasonable starting salaries for somebody with my education and experience, but none was willing to even give me an interview – I assumed because of my tenuous immigration status.

I saw a ton of potential with AOL, but more than anything, me taking a job in a call center was an act of necessity more than an act of desire. I needed an opportunity – any opportunity – to establish myself at a reputable company that would be willing to sponsor me for a three-year "H1-B" visa, which is a significant investment for a company to make – and certainly not one they would make for a call center agent. I wish I could say my choice to go to work for AOL in 1995 was purely a function of my ability to see the potential in the company and the inevitable rise of the Internet, but that would be a lie. I needed a job to stay in the country, and they offered me one, and that was good enough. They also offered me these things called "stock options," which at the time, I didn't think would amount to much of anything – but eventually they did.

After taking the call center job, I knew that I needed to move up the ladder as quickly as I could and get into a position where the company would be willing to sponsor my H1-B visa. Staying an agent in a call center in Jacksonville wasn't an option, so I started doing everything I could to get noticed and gain experience. I signed up for every possible "special project" offered by management. I worked double shifts. I worked on holidays. I mentored new agents. I helped build and write training documents. I showed up early. I stayed late.

In time, and before my year-long temporary work visa expired, I was offered a job at AOL's headquarters in northern Virginia, just outside of Washington, DC. After eight months in the call center and the constant fear that I could be tossed out of the country at any moment, I was to become the new "technical project manager" for the Telecom team of AOL's Customer Support division, making $35,000 a year, which, at the time when compared to $7.50 an hour, seemed like a king's ransom. I was elated.

Over the next several years I would slowly work my way up the ladder at AOL, eventually managing a team of about 20 software engineers responsible for building significant portions of AOL's online advertising systems – a key piece of infrastructure that would eventually find its way into news stories published around the globe.

The late 90s were the peak of the dot-com bubble, and the early 2000s were the valley of its subsequent collapse. This was also a time that would become synonymous with corporate greed and excesses, fueled in part by several glaring examples of poor corporate governance and accountability.

There is no greater example in US corporate history about the negative impacts of a widespread lack of accountability than the collapse of Enron Corporation in 2001, a massive financial fraud that led to thousands of people losing their jobs and the elimination of $60B in assets. Around the same time, other companies were also getting into hot water with federal oversight agencies for similar lapses in oversight and accountability, most notably WorldCom, Tyco, and my old employer, America Online. Together, the governance and accounting shenanigans of these companies ultimately led to the US Congress passing the Sarbanes-Oxley Act, which established a public accounting oversight board and required CEOs and Chief Financial Officers (CFOs) to sign and certify financial reports.

AOL's time in the news came because of a Securities and Exchange Commission (SEC) investigation that ultimately culminated in the company paying $300M in files for misleading accounting practices. The accounting systems at the heart of the SEC investigation were built and managed by software engineers who worked for me.

The accounting practices in question were related to the valuations given to barter transactions between AOL and its online advertisers. In exchange for receiving online ads across AOL's online properties, advertisers would "pay" for those ads using something called a "barter," where instead of paying with cash, they would pay through the exchange of goods, services, and equity stakes in other companies. At the time, the business of online advertising was nascent, and many advertisers were reluctant to spend on an unproven medium. To keep fueling the insane revenue growth AOL had experienced throughout the late 90s despite slowing new customer acquisitions, the company was taking creative paths to build its online advertising business. During the heyday of these transactions, I recall being at AOL and hearing stories about highly "creative" deals sold by overly aggressive salespeople, including one unfounded rumor of a sales executive allegedly receiving a "dream bed" as part of a complex business relationship with a well-known hotel chain.

The SEC claimed that AOL inaccurately inflated the value of these barter transactions, thereby misleading investors and overvaluing its assets in the acquisition of Time Warner. The contracts and associated revenues for these barter transactions were booked and managed in the very same software systems my team built. I was thankfully not subpoenaed as a part of this SEC investigation, but I know many people, including most of my upper management chain, who were. Hearing stories of their depositions to federal investigators was chilling, to say the least – especially since we were all just software nerds hunkered in our cubicles in AOL's Virginia headquarters, entirely divorced from the high-wheeling advertising execs on Park Avenue in New York City.

What I witnessed firsthand at AOL was a rather brazen *lack of accountability* at a group level, which is a hallmark of trait of those who embrace a more limiting mindset. People who embrace such a mindset will tend not to admit mistakes and could perceive such an action as one that would threaten their self-image. Avoiding accountability enables one with a limiting mindset to project an image of competence, and it allows them to avoid the vulnerability associated with admitting they were wrong.

In her book *Mindset*, Carol Dweck specifically called out the leadership at AOL as a glaring example of what can happen when you put CEOs with a fixed mindset in charge of a large company:

> "Resident geniuses almost brought down AOL and Time Warner, too. Steve Case of AOL and Jerry Levin of Time Warner were two CDOs with a fixed mindset who merged their companies... Case and Levin had a lot in common. Both of them cultivated an aura of supreme intelligence. Both tried to intimidate people with their brilliance. And both were known to take more credit than they deserved... . Because of the (Case and Levin), AOL Time Warner ended the year 2002 with a loss of almost 100 billion Dollars. It was the largest yearly loss in American history."

Looking back, I feel incredibly lucky to have been a part of a pivotal time in the evolution of the Internet and global commerce. I was with AOL for 10 years, and I joined right at the start of the Internet explosion, riding the wave to the pinnacle of the dot-com bubble, only to see it all crash down a couple years later. My experience at AOL taught me some important lessons about what can happen when a group of senior leaders in a company embraces a mindset that fails to promote accountability for their actions. Even if 95% of the people in the company are acting with integrity and are fully accountable, all it takes is for a small group to have a completely outsized, negative impact on the entire enterprise.

Blaming Others

Over the years, managing teams of people has taught me much about human behavior, including my own. For whatever reason I've yet to fully appreciate, one behavior that I find the most difficult to have patience for is when people blame others for situations they clearly have agency over. Avoiding responsibility by looking at others, instead of looking at oneself, is another characteristic of somebody with a highly limiting mindset.

I suspect my disdain for those who blame others is likely a function of how I was raised. My parents consistently reinforced the importance of independence and self-reliance, and they were forever pushing my boundaries toward greater levels of self-determination. Even as a young boy I had complete freedom in the summertime to roam free in my neighborhood and the surrounding parkland from morning to night – so long as I returned in time for 6 p.m. dinner. And this was at a time before cellular phones.

I suspect this value and focus on self-reliance is what makes me so intently focused on the idea of self-agency, and perhaps what I see is a lack of agency in the corporate world has partially led to the creation of this book. A lack of agency and a tendency to blame others, thanks to an embrace of more limiting mindsets, are widespread in my industry, and more awareness of these issues is critical.

A tendency to blame others is partially a function of people with limiting mindsets having what is known as an "external locus of control." Coined in the 1960s by psychologist Julian Rotter, somebody with external locus control is one who tends to believe that life's outcomes and experiences are primarily determined by factors outside of their individual control.[2] When you embrace an external locus of control, you're less likely to accept responsibility for any negative situation you find yourself in, and you are more likely to minimize the role of personal effort and agency.[3]

The opposite is an internal locus of control, which is a belief that our individual decisions primarily guide our lives and our outcomes. Research has shown a correlation between people with an internal local of control and a growth mindset, which should be no surprise given people with a growth mindset believe their individual growth and development will determine their outcomes.

---

[2]Rotter, J.B. (1966). Generalized expectancies for internal versus external control of reinforcement. *Psychological Monographs: General and Applied* 80 (1): 1–28.
[3]https://www.psychologytoday.com/us/blog/automatic-you/202211/how-your-locus-control-affects-your-life

This means those with an internal locus of control will tend to view failures as opportunities for learning. Conversely, those with an external locus of control will tend to see failures as a confirmation of their inability to influence outcomes.

Rotter posited that one's locus of control is largely learned through experiences and that while it's a relatively stable trait, it could be expressed differently by the same person across different scenarios. This means it's conceivable that somebody could have an external locus in a work scenario but an internal locus in a more personal situation.

The following quote from Jordan Morrow's book *Be Data Literate* tells a great story that epitomizes an example of an external locus of control:

> "Imagine to yourself you are a statistician who has built a strong predictive model on the upcoming holiday season shopping schedule. In this model, you were able to source the correct data (which can be hard at times, we know) that helped drive a smart decision. Through the model, you build a presentation and start to share the message around. Unfortunately, as you start to talk about your analysis and share the results, the people you are speaking to are looking at you with blank stares. You get frustrated as you share more and more, as very few are accepting and understanding the message. You start to wonder why no one is getting the message? This big issue does not lie in your model, analysis, or the technology; *the problem lies within the data culture that exists in the organization and the lack of data skills.*"

In this fictional story, the success of the statistician depends on the ability of others to have a level of mathematical expertise equal to theirs, not on their individual ability to communicate effectively with the audience or to deliver a model that's easy to understand. It's not even suggested that the communication breakdown could be a function of the message or the messenger – in this story the problem is assumed to be the recipient. This is a fantastic example of an external locus of control, and it's a perspective that is widespread in the world of data and analytics. This is also a strong indication of the role that limiting mindsets are having on the relationship between data producers and consumers.

Beyond an external locus of control, there are many other factors that may be contributing to the tendencies of people to blame others, including "all-or-nothing" thinking, a fear of failure (and related defense mechanisms), and perfectionism. Perfectionists will set entirely unrealistic expectations for themselves and others, and when they aren't met, those with a limiting mindset will tend to blame others rather than acknowledge any individual role in the failure. Research suggests there are generally two forms of perfectionism: one involving goal setting that can generally be seen as motivational and empowering and another seen as unhealthy and demotivational.[4]

When these behaviors such as these are widely embraced or endorsed within a group setting, the impacts are significant. Accountability is a cornerstone of organizational health, and without it, companies will struggle to develop an environment of high trust, employee engagement, and ethical actions. The limiting mindsets that promote a failure to accept responsibility by laying blame on others run counter to creating a healthy and productive team dynamic and organizational culture.

Avoid Challenges, Reluctance to Take Risks

Another incredibly valuable lesson I learned during my 10-year tenure with AOL was the debilitating role that risk aversion can have on your career progression. My time with AOL provided some incredible opportunities (and it allowed me to immigrate to the United States), but once I started working in the corporate headquarters, my tenuous immigration status played an outsized role in every major career choice at the company. Being under a work visa, and not having permanent residence, meant that my ability to stay

---

[4]Stoeber, J. (2018). The psychology of perfectionism: An introduction. In: *The Psychology of Perfectionism: Theory, Research, Applications* (ed. J. Stoeber), 3–16. London: Routledge.

in the United States was entirely a function of me maintaining my job. When I made the huge leap to leave my family and my comfort zone in Canada to seek greener pastures in the United States, I committed to taking my best shot at building a life and a career – and to me, that meant there was no turning back.

It's difficult to explain the stress that comes from being in a situation where the potential loss of a job would mean the life you're building could come to an end. I suppose this is somewhat like how an entrepreneur might feel after investing their life savings into a business, but in my case, the difference is that my fate was not necessarily completely in my own hands – at least I didn't think it was. AOL embraced a draconian policy of downsizing 10% of their employee base every year, and the annual employee cull was not always based purely on performance. Changing priorities or a shift in AOL's business strategy (something that happened frequently, especially once the Internet bubble burst) could lead to even the best performers being laid off.

For me, these annual layoffs induced a lot of fear – which in retrospect I'm convinced was a desired outcome. I always considered myself a "top performer," and my annual reviews reflected as much. Still, the fact that even some of the best employees were consistently impacted every year had a chilling effect on my choices.

As much as it pained me to do it, I believed at the time that, given the stakes at play, I had no choice but to manage my career in a highly defensive posture, which means I was very reluctant to take risks. Rather than managing my job, my job managed me – as I had convinced myself that I was, for all intents and purposes, indentured. I had adopted an external locus of control around my career, where my employer (and not me) was in the driver's seat. At the time, I considered this an entirely logical outcome because my immigration visa was with AOL, and that I was bound to the company.

For years I was acting completely out of synch with my true character, which ultimately ended up creating more stress on a day-to-day basis than all those annual layoffs combined. I'm typically growth oriented, so the cognitive dissonance caused by me acting out of sync with my character became a massive burden. After all, I left my family and my friends and took a major risk moving to a new country – so my embrace of a risk-averse posture at work was a significant change.

As a result, by my seventh year at AOL I had become extremely bitter, and I was angry at the company for not recognizing my sizeable contributions and for consistently promoting others over me. I did not feel adequately compensated, as new hires with half my experience were making significantly more than I was. I felt like AOL was taking complete advantage of me and my situation, which only made me work harder and ultimately feel less appreciated. Three years away from receiving my green card, I had become a completely disgruntled employee who often verbalized his displeasure, particularly around how I was being poorly "treated" by management – so it was a miracle I managed to keep my job. With every day that passed, I was becoming more stressed, more miserable, and more at risk of being laid off.

In my eighth year I was able to change my career trajectory with some healthy doses of introspection and soul-searching, where one night on a Caribbean island I was provided a moment of clarity I'll never forget. I came to the realization that it was me who was responsible for my misery at my job and that it was my choices that resulted in my bitterness. This was not an easy realization, but it was necessary. Over a span of eight years I had become somebody who deeply embraced a more limiting mindset in their work and in their personal life. I perfectly described many of the traits of one with a limiting mindset, including an aversion to risk.

In avoiding risk, those with a limiting mindset tend to feel less of a need to innovate or change, as they will see any potential failure as a negative reflection in their innate skills, since their skills are not something that can be meaningfully improved from learning and hard work. Seeing failure as either an opportunity to learn or an attack on your self-esteem will have obvious impacts on your willingness to embark on tasks with either an uncertain or ambiguous outcome.

People with more limiting mindsets also seek to avoid criticism, since any negative feedback would be seen as an indictment of their intelligence, and not an opportunity to improve. Given that all risks come with the possibility of failure, the prospect of facing criticism and being judged as a likely outcome of that failure are sufficient motivators to avoid risks altogether.

In the workplace, hearing sentiments such as "this sounds like a disaster waiting to happen" or "I don't see the point of all this" are examples of what somebody with a more limiting mindset could say in reaction to being asked to take on a risk – and while at AOL these are slogans I used often. These perspectives are rooted in fear and signal a behavior known as "loss aversion," which can trigger disproportionate responses given we tend to feel the pain of losses two times more intensely than the pleasure of equivalent gains.[5] Loss aversion is closely linked to the status quo bias, which makes all of us naturally resistant to change and to disproportionately stick with the status quo.[6]

The connection between a desire to avoid failure and a lack of innovation is well documented in research. McKinsey noted that 85% of executives state that fear holds back innovation often or always in their organizations, and average or below average innovators are three times more likely to experience this phenomenon.[7] Building a corporate culture that promotes innovation and risk-taking is a top priority for many companies, especially given that a Boston Consulting Group study showed that companies with a strong innovation culture are 60% more likely to be innovators.[8] The Nike case study shared earlier is a perfect example of how a company can leverage innovation – even in a time of massive turmoil – to deliver outsized returns and competitively differentiate.

---

[5] https://www.psychologytoday.com/us/blog/science-choice/201803/what-is-loss-aversion
[6] Samuelson, W. and Zeckhauser, R. (1988). Status Quo Bias in decision making. *Journal of Risk and Uncertainty* 1 (1): 7-59.
[7] https://www.mckinsey.com/capabilities/strategy-and-corporate-finance/our-insights/fear-factor-overcoming-human-barriers-to-innovation
[8] https://www.bcg.com/publications/2023/innovation-culture-strategy-that-gets-results

In retrospect, given how negative and bitter an employee I had become and given the toxic impact I was surely having on others around me, I suspect my productivity and work ethic were the only things that kept me employed at AOL for as long as I was. My fervent desire to avoid losing my job enabled on overly limiting mindset that put me on the razor's edge of termination. How ironic.

Embrace the Status Quo, Resist Change

Avoiding risk and embracing the status quo will often create the same outcomes (which is often doing nothing), but the motivations for each are distinct. The root cause of somebody who is risk averse is typically based in fear (my fear of being booted out of the United States was the reason I was so risk averse early in my career), whereas the cause of embracing the status quo can often be based more on mundane drivers such as comfort with existing practices, laziness, or a lack of urgency to change. All, however, are traits of people with more limiting mindsets.

Those with a highly limiting mindset tend to resist change and, as a result, embrace the status quo. They tend to fear that change could lead to worse outcomes, which makes the familiar a generally more attractive option. Since people with a more limiting mindset see their skills as something that cannot be fundamentally changed, a focus on change, especially as it related to their own individual growth and development, would likely be seen as a waste of time.

As you'll read in the following chapter, I firmly believe that an *excessive embrace of the status quo* is perhaps the biggest challenge (and opportunity!) for all people in the field of data and analytics. Repeated and prolonged observations of data professionals making choices that ultimately reinforce the status quo is exactly what drove me to write this book, and the specific examples to justify my perspective are the topic of the entire next chapter.

There are many factors that promote an unwillingness to change in all people, and in the world of data, those forces are magnified by a complex web of players (as highlighted in Chapter 5), many of which have a financial interest in creating the illusion of change – but without delivering meaningful change. A pivot away from a limiting mindset to a positive, growth-centric mindset is what will break this pattern at both an individual and group level.

> "Randy Bean and NewVantage Partners have been doing their CDO survey, I think, for 8 years now...and the number-one challenge (for CDOs) is people, behaviors, and culture. And throughout the 8 years they've been doing it, that's the number-one challenge, by at least 80%. The technology part is 20%, and the people and behavior part are 80%, which is four times a bigger problem. But when you go and look at people's data strategy, 1% of the data strategy is around people, and it's really mostly about how do we set up some processes and how do we train people, but it's nothing about the real reasons why people aren't changing."
> *Dan Everett, Owner of Insightful Research;*
> CDO Matters, *Episode #37*

One behavior that helps to reinforce the status quo is something called "learned helplessness," where repeated exposure to uncontrollable negative events can lead one to believe they have no control over outcomes, even when the opportunity to influence them arises. This will often lead people to stop trying to influence outcomes in the future.[9] To some, this may appear as a "defeatist" attitude and will lead people to resignation or a lack of motivation. When you add the effects of confirmation bias, where people favor information that affirms a previous belief, there can often be extremely powerful forces within many of us that make the idea of change entirely uncomfortable.

As an industry analyst supporting MDM and data governance inquiries at Gartner, I experienced plenty of situations where my clients appeared to be embracing learned helplessness.

---
[9] https://www.simplypsychology.org/learned-helplessness.html

When discussing their challenges related to a lack of MDM (including things like inaccurate or untrustworthy reports) and what's required to overcome those challenges, I would consistently hear data leaders and practitioners express highly defeatist attitudes like "we've tried that before, and it won't work."

Learned helplessness is one reason why we repeat the same behaviors and expect different results (not changing even when opportunities to change present themselves), as can the sunk cost fallacy, which is a mental shortcut that motivates us to stick with a given behavior because we've already invested time and effort in it. Many large-scale corporate and governmental debacles have been at least partially attributed to the sunk cost fallacy (including the length of the war in Vietnam), and based on my experiences, the world of data and analytics is often impacted by the ill-effects of a combination of learned helplessness and the sunk cost fallacy.[10]

Anyone who has spent any time in the workforce has surely worked with somebody who is resistant to change and is familiar with the demotivational impact these people can have on a team dynamic – especially when it comes to creativity and innovation. There's no shortage of books available to help leaders be better motivators and to overcome situations where their teams are reluctant to change, and over the years I've read many of them.

One of the more refreshing perspectives I recently read was in Sol Rashidi's book *Your AI Survival Guide*. Rashidi recommends that leaders should actively limit the engagement of those work archetypes who are more likely to resist change, most notably what she called "curmudgeons" and "naysayers," on AI project teams. I found Sol's perspective entirely refreshing and provocative but also a bit impractical given leaders often have no choice but to engage people who may be highly change resistant. Looking back on many situations where I was leading teams of people resistant to change, I simply didn't have the luxury of excluding everyone who preferred

---

[10]https://hbr.org/2021/07/how-susceptible-are-you-to-the-sunk-cost-fallacy

the status quo – or I wouldn't have had anyone available to do any of the work. As much as I may have preferred to just sideline all of the change resistors I've encountered as a leader over the years, I've instead been forced to find ways to get them involved and get them motivated. It should be no surprise that, by this point, I believe a shift in mindset is the most important tool in every data leader's playbook.

Failure to See Positive Intent

Another factor that runs counter to creating healthy teams is distrust. I've twice worked in what I would call extremely low-trust environments, but I've also had the privilege of working in higher-trust environments – including one where I played a major role in helping to create it.

After departing AOL in 2005, I relocated from Virginia to Austin, Texas, to go to work leading the product management function at a company called Hoover's. Hoover's was the brainchild of a man named Gary Hoover, and it was a service that provided deep company and financial profiles of businesses. Hoover's first sold its insights on industries, companies, and key executives via print and CD-ROM, but would transition in the late 90s to an entirely online service, and I was hired to lead a team of product managers in the development of Hoover's Online.

In 2006 I was given the opportunity to lead a cross-functional team at Hoover's chartered to build one of the first applications deployed on the "App Exchange" of the goliath customer relationship management (CRM) vendor Salesforce.com (SFDC) – which at the time – was still a relative newcomer. The App Exchange allowed third-party software vendors to integrate their solutions into the SFDC ecosystem, which provided access to a potentially massive, and growing, body of new users and customers. My team was to build the software needed to expose Hoover's data within SFDC.

The team I inherited to build this software was a talented yet dysfunctional group that was clearly suffering major trust issues.

Previous grievances and grudges between several team members were abundantly obvious, and any time there was a disagreement on any issue, even relatively trivial ones, those disagreements were immediately escalated to leaders outside the project team. This would undercut my efforts to resolve those issues and further erode the trust others had in my leadership – not to mention the trust leadership had in me to lead the team. The *assumption of negative intent* was the norm, and open and candid communications within the group had become nonexistent. As a result, we had a team that didn't trust each other, and our project was well behind schedule and at risk of falling off the rails completely.

Turning that team around and creating an environment focused on open communication and trust is something I'm proud to say is one of my bigger professional accomplishments. By bringing people together and having candid exchanges about our situation and by creating spaces where people could feel safe to share their opinions without fear of retribution, we slowly started to resolve some of the interpersonal baggage people had brought from previous situations into the new team. Part of the transformation also required me to be both vulnerable and firm – where the former most certainly helped enable the latter. Over a span of a few months, my team members started trusting me and each other – after which point the project really started to hum. A few weeks later we successfully launched the software, and within months it was a blockbuster hit for my company.

One of the many things I learned in that experience is that when you believe others have positive intentions, it opens the door for trust, communication, and collaboration. If you think they are trying to subvert you or that they don't have your best interests at heart, you'll do whatever necessary to protect yourself – and the needs of the company will take a back seat.

Success in a data and analytics role requires high levels of communication and collaboration, often with people from extremely diverse parts of the business. When you assume others you work with (or for) have a negative intention for you, you'll create a situation of distrust that opens the door to a myriad of dysfunctions that will harm your ability to deliver value. More specific examples of these highly limiting mindsets in action are discussed in the following chapter.

People with limiting mindsets are less likely to see others as having a positive intent. This is because people in a more limiting mindset are likely to take a more defensive posture, which leads to a perception that others' actions may be competitive or threatening. Given the tendency for more rigid, "all-or-nothing" thinking, people with a limiting mindset will have difficulty in seeing the nuance in complex situations, making it harder to empathize with others' perspectives or to imagine the possible motivations behind an action. Their fear of being judged may be projected onto others, which may lead them to feel like they are constantly under a microscope – leading them to be less inclined to assume other's intentions are positive.

If you don't see people you work with as having positive intent, it's a sure sign you don't trust them. A lack of trust in your coworkers or your leaders is a hallmark of a low-functioning team, and there's no shortage of academic research to show that when employees don't trust each other, companies struggle. A Gallup study showed there is only a 1 in 12 chance that employees who don't trust their leaders will be fully engaged in the workplace, while a separate Gallup study showed that disengaged workers cost companies $450–$550B a year in lost productivity.[11] Organizations with high levels of trust will have higher revenues, customer satisfaction, reduced turnover, and increased job performance.[12]

In *The Speed of Trust*, Stephen Covey argues that a lack of trust in an organization creates a "trust tax," which slows processes and adds costs.[13] Thankfully, Covey sees trust as a competency that can be developed in any organization – a solid foundation from which to pivot away from a situation where everyone doubts the intentions of others to one where they believe those intentions are positive. My experiences at Hoover's suggest Covey was right.

---

[11] https://news.gallup.com/opinion/gallup/170570/gallup-releases-new-findings-state-american-workplace.aspx
[12] Dirks, K.T. and Ferrin, D.L. (2002). Trust in leadership: meta-analytic findings and implications for research and practice. *Journal of Applied Psychology* 87 (4): 611–628. https://doi.org/10.1037/0021-9010.87.4.611.
[13] Covey, S.M.R. (2006). *The Speed of Trust: The One Thing That Changes Everything*. Free Press.

Chapter 4
The Wrath of the Anti-Hero in Data and Analytics

In this chapter we will explore some concrete examples of just some of the many limiting mindsets plaguing the field of data and analytics. I'll share my perspectives on why some of these perspectives are so widely held and highlight some of the destructive and counterproductive impacts they have, as well as the role they play to reinforce the status quo.

The behaviors motivated by these mindsets are embraced by people at every level within a data function, at companies large and small, and across every conceivable industry. These mindsets are at the root of why so many companies, and people, have been working so hard to realize the transformative value of data and analytics but have been unable to do so – even when embracing so-called best practices. Limiting mindsets serve a massive anchor in our industry and many of the hard-working professionals within it.

When talking with many of the people I believe are inflicted with these mindsets, I am reminded often of the person I had become in my later years at AOL. I hear a lot of frustration, a lot of blame, and a whole lot of learned helplessness. And I hear expressions of these limiting mindsets from practitioners, vendors, analysts, and consultants. Many examples of these mindsets are expressed so often, and are so widely and deeply embraced, they've become dogma. They often run counter to our stated missions and have the exact opposite effect on our businesses from their stated intention. They disempower us, and they hinder our ability to be effective business partners.

What's perhaps the most curious thing about these highly limiting mindsets is that they hide in plain sight, generally on display for everyone to see or experience daily. The following sections are a just few examples of the limiting mindsets that are hindering our careers in the field of data and analytics.

The Unwillingness to Quantify the Value of Data

Imagine a scenario where the CEO of a major corporation decided that she wasn't going to report any data on the profits of a company to anyone. Not to her shareholders, not to her employees, and not to her customers. Can you imagine how completely chaotic that business would be, and what impacts it would have on the organization if nobody really understood if the things they were doing to improve the business were working or not? More than likely, that business would quickly cease to exist.

If this sounds like a completely unbelievable and ridiculous scenario, then think again. This is how most CDOs run their organizations – with no way to quantify the impact their efforts are having on business outcomes. A CDO unwillingness to quantify the impact of data is a result of a limiting mindset that seeks to avoid accountability and risk and embrace the status quo.

> "Most executives claim data is an asset but their companies don't measure its value like one. They might track data quality metrics, but that's not the same as valuing data as a true business asset. As the old adage goes, 'You can't manage what you don't measure.' It's as true for data as for financial, physical, or other

assets. This creates a vicious cycle where organizations that fail to measure their data as an asset then fail to manage it with necessary discipline, which ultimately leads to under-utilizing it and squandering its value. A CDO who cannot transform their data center into a profit-center will have a limited tenure."

Doug Laney, author of Infonomics*;*
CDO Matters, *Episode #5*

If I were able to give only a single answer to the question "What is the biggest single obstacle hindering the advancement of the data and analytics function?" (and my answer couldn't be "mindsets that limit growth"), that answer would be the following: *an unwillingness of data leaders to quantify the value of their data.* Just about every major roadblock encountered by CDOs can be traced back to the fact that most data leaders have no data on the value of their data. These major barriers include the following:

- A lack of stakeholder engagement
- A lack of sufficient resources or funding
- Insufficient support for the data governance function
- Lack of a focus on data quality within business units
- Lack of a "data culture"
- An inability to effectively prioritize efforts or allocate resources
- Poor user adoption
- And on, and on, and on...

All the biggest barriers faced by a data leader in the execution of their function could be overcome if they would take the time to develop metrics to show the value of their insights provided to their businesses, but time and time again, they consistently choose not to.

I have used the punch line "Data people have no data on the value of data" many times over the last year in many of my conference presentations and – quite honestly – it tends to land flat. This doesn't surprise me, because there is a widely held belief by many in the world of data and analytics that measuring the business value of data is impossible, which couldn't be further from the truth. Literally *anything* can be measured, yet somehow, the very people who are responsible for measuring things at companies choose not to measure the value of their services. It would be like operating a retail store with no price tags on anything, but that's exactly what we do.

Why is this the case? Especially when doing so would solve so many problems and make the job of a CDO infinitely easier and more satisfying?

There is no one answer here – but I know limiting mindsets are playing an outsized role here, particularly learned helplessness associated with the misguided belief that it's too hard, or practically impossible, to measure the business value of data.

In my conversations with data leaders, I encounter this mindset over and over again. I heard it while a Gartner analyst on a near daily basis. I hear it in comments to LinkedIn posts talking about the need to measure our value. I hear it sitting at lunch tables and at cocktail hours at industry events. There are many CDOs who embrace this perspective in both their words and, by not producing these metrics, their deeds.

I typically hear data leader's express sentiments like "It's impossible to do," "It's too difficult," or "The benefits are all indirect, so what's the point?" In my conversations I will *never* hear anything like "That's a great idea – I could learn so much about what needed to improve in my organization" or "I'm concerned we may be prioritizing the wrong things, but having data to show which efforts drive the most value would help us improve our prioritization." Time and time again in my conversations on these issues with data leaders, what I hear are perspectives that align to more limiting mindsets and none that align to more growth-oriented mindsets.

> "It still surprises me how many people in conversations I hear, and am privy to, of people saying, 'It's not possible to (pinpoint tangible commercial benefits out of (CDO) activities),' but ultimately if you want to sit at the top table, then that's the job."
> *Kyle Winterbottom, CEO of Orbition Group;*
> CDO Matters, *Episode #19*

At best, data leaders may be measuring the quality of the data under their watch, but not how that quality impacts business performance. When I asked my Gartner clients if they were measuring the business outcomes driven by their data, the answer was sometimes "Yes, we produce quality dashboards," which is not an answer to the question. Data quality metrics measure the state of the data, not the business. This means the answer to my question was almost always "no," because my clients could not tell me the degree to which the data they provide their customers is helping to increase revenues, lower costs, or mitigate business risks.

Data quality metrics are important, but "better data quality" is not a business outcome. Better data quality can drive improvements in the business, but simply producing a quality dashboard is a weak proxy for business value, if at all.

The concept of "value" is a two-sided coin: one side is the cost to manage and govern data, and the other side is the business benefit of data. And most data leaders are typically measuring neither.

The most common excuse used by data leaders to not measure the value of data is that the measures would be "indirect," given there is typically no causal relationship between data and business outcomes. While it may be true that developing bulletproof metrics that show a causal relationship between data and business outcomes would be difficult and costly, there are other metrics that could be built around statistical regressions and attribution models, which would be far easier to develop and, arguably, nearly as effective.

One could argue the entire marketing function is justified, and measured on, indirect metrics to show the impact of marketing spending on buyer behaviors. It may be costly and inefficient to develop metrics to show a hard causal relationship between a given marketing activity and a customer purchase, but modeled metrics using a regression analysis that correlate (attribute) multiple marketing activities to customer actions are widely used and accepted – however imperfect they may be.

Somehow these modeled metrics are good enough to justify the billions of dollars spent every year on marketing, but data leaders have convinced themselves those modeled metrics wouldn't be good enough for a data function. Modeled metrics are also used in HR, Finance, Procurement, and just about every other business function, yet in the world of data we've somehow convinced ourselves that building metrics to track both the cost and the benefit of the data and services we provide is unnecessary or somehow foolhardy.

Choosing not to measure the value of data is a classic example of "all-or-nothing" thinking, and it's also a signal of serious risk aversion. When you combine the two, a paralysis is created that results in nothing happening, even when doing so could have massive benefits.

In my many conversations with CDOs and CIOs on this topic while an analyst, I developed some theories as to why this was such a widespread problem – hypotheses that I was never able to fully validate and have not been tested in any research I've read on the topic. One of those hypotheses is that producing metrics on the value of data could potentially lead to unfavorable results. If yes, then it makes sense a data leader – particularly one with a more limiting mindset – would seek to avoid publishing them for fear doing so could lead to judgment and an indictment of their capabilities.

Another hypothesis is that producing these metrics could increase the likelihood that data leaders would be made accountable for improving them. If true, it would not be unreasonable to assume that some data leaders are choosing not to develop these metrics specifically out of a fear that what they would learn would cause them to be viewed in a negative light, further supporting the belief that a limiting mindset is at the root of this issue.

Another explanation here is that they are not being asked, or forced, to build these metrics. If you're a CEO reading this book, I strongly urge you to consider making these metrics part of your mandate for any CDO you may employ or consider employing in the future. If they won't, then I suggest moving the data function temporarily under your CFO, which in my experience is the reality for about 10–15% of all data teams.

The ultimate irony of this situation is that CDOs and other data leaders are the biggest advocates for their organizations to become more "data driven" and will often blame a lack of data culture as a major reason they are unable to deliver value to the organization.

Yet, when it comes to producing data to justify their very existence, they choose to not be data driven. Do you see a problem here?

The problem is that the words and the actions of many data leaders do not align. Put another way, many are failing to act with integrity, which is an unfortunate by-product of this ongoing avoidance of creating data to justify the data function. CDOs say they want their organizations to be data driven, yet they don't produce data to measure their value. This is a massive problem for many reasons, not the least of which is the degree to which it degrades the credibility of the entire data industry. CEOs and others in the C-suite see that the words and deeds of CDOs do not align and it impacts CDO credibility. *The greatest irony here is that by choosing not to measure the value of data, CDOs actively hinder the ability to deliver it.*

> "When you think about data from a financial perspective, not being an asset, when you think about it, you are using data to understand the hard assets that you have... If data is not an asset, then the hard assets you have, how are you keeping track of them? And the answer always comes back to data."
>
> Lawrence Young, *Value Consultant at Profisee;*
> CDO Matters, *Episode #32*

Data Literacy and Blaming Customers for Product Failures

The data literacy movement was born from the idea that people and forces outside the data function are primarily to blame for an inability of data leaders to provide business value. This strongly suggests that a focus on data literacy promotes a mindset with highly corrosive impacts.

My old employer Gartner defines data literacy as "The ability to read, write and communicate data in context, with an understanding of the data sources and constructs, analytical methods and techniques applied, and the ability to describe the use case application and resulting business value or outcome."[1] That's a mouthful.

Jordan Morrow, my friend and the "godfather of data literacy," defines data literacy as the ability to read, work with, analyze, and communicate with data.[2] In his 2021 book *Be Data Literate*, Morrow cites research that states 32% of business executives say they have confidence in their ability to use data and that 24% of decision-makers are confident in their data skills. Morrow suggests it's this lack of "data skills" that is causing the inability of companies to realize value from data, where he says:

> "Surely organizations and individuals are capitalizing on this amazing asset of data, right? Obviously, organizations are not falling short and are able to find insight to make smart, data informed decisions, aren't they? The reality says quite differently, and studies and data show us the truth: there is a large skills gap in the world of data that is hurting organizations' ability to succeed with their own valuable assets of data and analytical investments."

The connection between a failure of an organization to realize value from data and the skill levels of the users of data is the underlying premise of the data literacy movement. This focus on the skills of those consuming analytical insights, and not those producing them, is a perfect example of an external locus of control – which is a hallmark of a more limiting mindset.

Over the last year that I've had the opportunity to get to know Jordan, I know him to be an extremely supportive and passionate professional who believes in the power of data. He's been on my podcast, and we've spoken in person and online many times. He's extremely smart and well spoken, and he's gone out of his way to be helpful to me and many others – even when I've been an outspoken and public critic of data literacy. This speaks volumes about the

---

[1] https://www.gartner.com/en/information-technology/glossary/data-literacy
[2] Morrow, J. (2021). *Be Data Literate*. Kogan Page.

quality of Jordan's character, and I know he cares deeply about the industry of data.

As you'll quickly learn, I have concerns about how data literacy is being implemented at many companies. Still, Jordan and I are united in doing what we can to advance the careers of CDOs, and I sincerely hope that Jordan – and any other firm believer in data literacy – will see positive intentions in my criticisms of the movement he helped to create.

Data literacy became a hype-worthy movement starting in 2017, when Gartner first included a "lack of data literacy" as an option for CDOs to choose in its annual CDO survey asking about the biggest roadblocks to CDO success. The first time Gartner asked the question, a whopping 35% of CDOs blamed a lack of data literacy as a major roadblock to success, ranking as the second biggest impediment in the first year the question was asked.

In their annual "Chief Data Officer Year End Review" in 2016, when discussing the issue of short CDO tenures, the CDO Club noted a litany of reasons for CDO churn – and not one of them was data literacy.[3] This is likely because earlier that year Gartner noted eight major roadblocks in its very first CDO survey, and data literacy wasn't one of them.[4] Yet, just a few months later, because Gartner started asking the question about literacy in its survey, it became a huge issue. The ability of analyst firms to drive market perceptions and CDO agendas – often to the detriment of the industry – is something I will discuss in more detail in Chapter 5.

On the surface, especially to more technically inclined data leaders, data literacy may seem to many like a wonderful idea. This is likely a big reason why data literacy is so popular – going from a "new" concept in 2017 to the top of the Gartner hype cycle just three years later.[5] Data is complicated, so people need to understand data to get any value from it. If I don't understand the data, then I probably

---

[3] https://cdoclub.com/chief-data-officer-jobs-update-for-november-2016/#Review
[4] Gartner, "How to Overcome Critical Roadblocks to Succeed as Chief Data Officer," January 27, 2016.
[5] https://www.gartner.com/en/documents/3987607

won't use it, and the data function will be for naught, and we'll fail to become the data-driven organizations we aspire to be. For those of us more growth oriented, the idea of learning new things sounds like a great idea – and even if you're not, the idea of data training to improve customer adoption sounds completely reasonable.

The problems start to arise in the implementation of the program, its intent, and the mindsets of the people doing the implementation. A common theme of many examples of limiting mindsets gone amuck in the world of data is that the actions being taken to improve the data function often *sound* like a great idea – in theory. But when you integrate these concepts into operating environments rife with limiting mindsets and suboptimal cultures, you'll quickly observe these concepts having the exact opposite impacts as their stated intentions.

Data literacy is a great example of this. It sounds reasonable, but when you consider the state of the data function at most companies and the prevalence of limiting mindsets, you can quickly see how a focus on data literacy could become highly problematic.

To answer the question of "What's wrong with data literacy?" let's return to that fictional bakery I told you about at the beginning of Chapter 1. If you recall, it's the only bakery in town, on a busy street with plenty of foot and vehicle traffic. Many in the town have tried the artisanal breads being offered and baked fresh every day, but you are having difficulty keeping any of your customers, and your business is struggling.

If you were that baker and your business was in peril, what would you do? Unfortunately, the answer to this metaphoric question for struggling CDOs in the world of data and analytics is "We will impose mandatory training to our customers on how to eat bread and the processes used to make it."

I first shared my perspectives on the corrosive impacts of how data literacy is being implemented in many companies in an article I wrote for *Forbes* in early 2023 titled "The Problems with Data Literacy."[6] This article was a reaction to the hundreds of conversations I

---

[6] https://www.forbes.com/sites/forbestechcouncil/2023/02/10/the-problems-with-data-literacy

had with data leaders from 2019 to now, who were struggling to deliver value to their organizations, many of whom were (or are) aggressively embarking on data literacy programs to solve that problem.

In those conversations I would consistently hear a *lot* of frustration being expressed in phrases such as "you can lead a horse to water" or "they business doesn't get it" or "I have hundreds of dashboards nobody is using." The frustration was evident in their voices, and often, they expressed downright animosity to the very people they were chartered to support.

When I asked what they were doing to, improve their customer satisfaction and product adoption, many responded with "We're implementing a data literacy program." I would ask other questions like "Are you able to articulate the value of your services?" or "Are you working to better understand the customer needs and reluctance to use your reports?" or "Are you confident the problem of low adoption of data isn't the quality of the data?" Typically, the answer I would hear to these questions was "no."

Whether we want to admit it or not, data leaders are in the business of selling products. These products should solve customer problems and do it in a way that drives meaningful business value. What I would hear in my conversations with these frustrated data leaders, time and time again, was that many who were struggling with their business were viewing their customers as the root cause of the problem – *and not the quality or usability of their products.*

Having deep roots in product management, the answers I was hearing from many of my clients who were embarking on literacy programs were troubling. In my mind, the problem here is simple: *if people are not buying your product, then the problem is most likely your product.* But in the case of many CDOs struggling to deliver value, a drastically different perspective is common. For those focused primarily on data literacy, instead of looking internally at what would need to improve to make the customers happy, they were instead looking externally at their customers, in the hopes that making them smarter, or more "literate," would be the key to providing them value from data.

If you recall from the previous chapter, the tendency to see others as the problem is known as an external locus of control, and it's a common trait of people with more fixed or limiting mindsets. Blaming forces outside of the data team for what may well be a massive failure to understand data consumer needs is a perfect example of this.

Like that baker who runs the only bakery in town, many data leaders are blaming a lack of customer skill as the core reason for a failure to deliver value. Instead of revisiting their strategies, their delivery models, or the quality or usability of the products they were delivering, they were forcing their customers into mandatory training. This creates three big problems:

- **Literacy programs with an emphasis on methods and techniques will negatively impact productivity.** If there is one reality that most data leaders quickly determine early in their careers, it's that their customers really don't care, or need to care, "how the data sausage is made." You can be an amazing driver without knowing how cars are made, and forcing your customers into training on the "methods and techniques" of data means precious time will be taken from their primary jobs. That's assuming the training will even have the desired impacts.
- **Assuming data literacy is the only reason companies fail to realize value will create a toxic divide between producers and consumers of data.** A 2020 study by Gartner found that only 25% of companies measure the impact of their key information assets. In absence of data to prove otherwise, this data suggests that even if you force mandatory data training, there's no way to ensure that the training will result in the business realizing value from data. In three out of every four companies, if anyone asked, "How will you know the business value of data will be realized from user training?" they could not confidently answer the question, because data does not exist to prove the value of training one way or the other.

Worse yet, that same Gartner survey noted that 27% of respondents are reluctant to share data due to quality concerns. This suggests many people have significant concerns about the

The Wrath of the Anti-Hero in Data and Analytics 75

quality of the data products being offered by their CDOs – yet many CDOs believe that forcing mandatory training on products their customers perceive as low quality is the right thing to do.

If you're not measuring the value of data and there are significant concerns about the quality of the data provided, what makes CDOs conclude that mandatory training on that data will improve their relationships with their customers?

Imagine any scenario where you've had a bad customer experience and you've lost confidence or trust in a specific company or brand for a product you rely on day to day. Do you honestly believe that taking time to get trained in that product, or how it was made, would be what you need to rebuild your trust?

If you had taken the time to express your concerns about the usability or quality of the products coming from the data team, would you feel like your CDO was listening to your concerns if, rather than improving their product, their response was to require you to be trained on it?

Probably not. Many of you would feel like your concerns are being ignored and that the training you would receive would only make a bad situation worse. This is exactly what I mean by a "toxic divide," and lack of confidence in data teams, as articulated through short CDO tenures (and plenty of research data), is clearly playing a role.

- **If most companies are not measuring the business value of data or the current "data skills" of their employees, how can CDOs be so sure of the effectiveness of any literacy program?** The correct answer here is they can't, and that's because there's never been any quantitative research, to my knowledge, which proves a meaningful relationship between better data skills and the realization of business value from data. Most data leaders are asking their customers to take a leap of faith in the value of a literacy program, which is the exact opposite of being "data driven." This need for business customers to take leaps of faith, in absence of being provided any data to prove the benefits of that leap, is a common theme across many data programs we'll touch on throughout this book.

The rampant embrace of limiting mindsets in many data organizations will help to ensure the implementation of a data literacy program is doomed to fail or – best case – reinforce the status quo. In the worst case, the implementation of these programs will have the *exact opposite effect* from their stated intentions. Data leaders want to increase data usage, but data customers will feel alienated or not listened to and may likely rebel.

After all, who wants to be called "illiterate"? I don't know many producer/consumer relationships where the sellers of a product think their buyers are illiterate (and where they widely advertise it), but somehow, highly limiting mindsets have convinced us that blaming and judging the very people we are chartered to serve is completely acceptable. It's not, and we can (and will) do better.

Extreme Forms of "Data First" or "Data Driven"

In theory, creating a corporate culture where a shared value prioritizes data over intuition is a good thing. This is typically what most people would define as a "data-driven" culture – although detailed perspectives on this issue do vary. Still, a good baseline is a belief that all else being equal, facts should be used to make decisions – not gut instincts.

The idea of being "data first" is largely the same as being data driven, and these concepts are often used as synonyms. A consensus is that "data first" is more about putting data at the heart of the operating model of your entire business – and not just at the forefront of a given decision.[7]

This means being data driven is an outcome of taking a data first business strategy where – again – the core concepts of analyzing data to make decisions, with a priority on facts over feelings, are difficult to argue. As shared values our organizations can aspire to, the platitudes of "data driven" and "data first" are relatively benign and, on the surface, entirely reasonable.

---

[7] https://www.forbes.com/sites/rhettpower/2023/02/12/what-will-it-actually-take-to-lead-a-modern-data-first-organization

In practice, however, many data and analytics teams that I've worked with have taken these benign perspectives to the extreme, where the data has become the primary focus of those organizations, and not the business functions supported by the data. Here again we have another situation where a reasonable concept, when implemented into an organization rife with highly limiting mindsets, can become a corrosive force. Let me explain.

All businesses are a collection of individual specialized functions like sales, marketing, procurement, manufacturing, and others. For businesses to operate efficiently, each of these functions must find a way to collaborate with each other. This is especially the case for functions that play a support role (e.g., marketing supports sales, finance supports everyone), and it's especially the case at the connection points between complex cross-functional business processes (like "quote to cash" or "procure to pay").

As there must be some degree of collaboration across functions in the management of a business process, so too must there be collaboration in the management of the data that spans those processes. A lack of collaboration with their customers is one of the many reasons why so many CDOs struggle to deliver value, and overcoming this issue is something discussed in far greater detail later in Chapter 6.

It's worth noting that the power dynamics within these collaborative efforts are not equal, nor should they be. Data and analytics teams play a supporting role for their customers, which are the business functions. In this producer/consumer dynamic, the needs and the priorities of the consumer should always take precedence over those of the producer. In collaborative situations, this means that the incentives underlying a shared goal should not equally align. The incentives for the producer should be a happy customer who sees value in what they are consuming, and the incentives for the consumer are profits. When weighing the priorities of these outcomes, the latter should always "win."

This means that a mindset that sees the priorities of a data function as equal, or greater than, the priorities of the business function is most certainly a limiting one – given that a prolonged focus on data, and not customers, would have disastrous long-term impacts to the business.[8] Yet, this is exactly the mindset of many in the world of data. Many I've spoken with have put data on a pedestal and used the idea of being "data first" to justify a lack of a customer focus. In doing so, they inverted the producer/consumer dynamic and made the raw material more important than the process that consumes that raw material.

I generally disagree with the assertion that data is only the "exhaust" of a business, because it's not. It's both exhaust and a mission-critical input. However, there are many in the data world who believe that data is more important than the processes that create or consume it, and they actively promote the idea that being data driven requires all systems and business processes to be designed around the data.

Extreme forms of this "data-first" perspective help to explain why so many data teams are so insular, why so many are focused primarily on technology, and why so many struggle to build meaningful and prolonged relationships with their customers. It also helps to explain why so many are focused on data literacy instead of business literacy. These teams have operating models that are excessively focused on their internal processes, and not sufficiently focused on customer enablement and success.

In my roles as a consultant, an analyst, and a vendor, I've been consistently amazed by how infrequently data professionals can articulate the business needs that are driving the acquisition of new technology. Often, they can articulate none – and are able to articulate only how the internal data management process will improve as a result.

Sometimes, making our internal processes more efficient is necessary, but having no idea what the connection between making those data processes more effective and downstream business impacts is commonplace – if not the norm. This is even the case where customers within the business are asking for a specific data solution, like MDM. They may ask for a solution to eliminate

---

[8] Unless your business is the business of selling data – which certainly happens but is not entirely common.

rampant duplication of customer records – and the data team will seek solutions – but still be unable to articulate how the business will benefit.

This inward focus on technology and data, and not customer success, is a massive problem for CDOs and I would argue has largely represented the status quo since the data function was born. Yet, when discussing the issue of a lack of understanding of customer needs and a more inward focus on technology and data, the issue is almost always framed from the perspective of the data customer failing to engage with the data function, not the other way around. For example, a "lack of business stakeholder involvement and support" is the number-four roadblock to the success of data and analytics initiatives from the Gartner 2023 CDO survey.

The idea that the customers, and not data teams, must better engage is yet another example of CDOs embracing an external locus of control. This is a perspective I hear often in my conversations with CDOs, where the belief that major dependencies for their success are a function of what others outside the data function must do, and not themselves.

Unfortunately, this perspective is the exact opposite of a growth mindset, and it's the exact opposite of a customer focus. Could you imagine a situation where the leadership of any major organization cited a "lack of customer engagement" as a major reason for a significant product failure? Do you think Coors management believed that a lack of customer engagement with the Coors brand was the reason Coors Rocky Mountain Spring Water was a colossal failure, or that Sony executives blamed their customers for the failure of the Betamax? An excessive focus from data leaders on tools and technology in lieu of a focus on customer success is a well-known and commonly discussed problem in the world of data and analytics. While I was an industry analyst, an excessive focus on technology and data was consistently something Gartner research repeatedly cited, over a period of many years, as a top reason for both MDM and data governance program failures. The tendency for data leaders to see data and new technologies as "silver bullets" is well established and will help to reinforce the status quo of a failure of data functions to realize full benefit of data, which is yet another reason why a focus on being "data first" is symptomatic of a limiting mindset.

> "What's changed is that businesses are now driving the conversation. It used to be that IT folks would come back from conferences and tell the business things like, 'there is a new graph database,' or 'there's a new indexing technique, and I can improve this query performance,' or 'I have a new BI tool with some caching.' The business response was typically apathetic, boiling down to: 'So what? Am I getting my data, high-quality data, on time without breaking the bank? All this mumbo-jumbo is not important.'"
>
> Sanjeev Mohan, Founder of Sanjmo Consulting;
> CDO Matters, *Episode #54*

When I've had the opportunity to challenge some data leaders on this inward perspective, particularly the issues of a "lack of business engagement" or a "lack of support for data," the justifications typically come back to the idea of the data teams and business teams being in an equal partnership. There must certainly be an active collaboration for an optimal relationship between the two groups, but the responsibility to build and maintain that partnership falls to the producer, not the consumer. If the partnership is lacking, CDOs must be the ones to bridge the divide and do the work necessary to create whatever engagement is needed for a fruitful relationship. This is true with every customer relationship in an organization.

In the world of business we all have customers, and we all exist to serve them. If that dynamic gets inverted, everything breaks. This is exactly what's happening when data teams embrace an insular and limiting "data-first" mindset that believes their customers are responsible for driving better engagement with a data team and where the primary focus is on deploying data technologies.

Data Culture Is a Dependency to Deliver Value and Is Somebody Else's Problem

A fourth example of limiting mindsets in action within data teams today are the ideas that the adoption of a data culture is a hard dependency for a CDO to deliver business value and that the changes needed to adapt a data culture are for those outside the data function. Both are examples of learned helplessness and an external locus of control, and both are indicative of the mindsets that are deeply ingrained in many data teams.

The perception that organizations lack a data culture, and that a CDO must change the way people feel and behave toward data as a key deliverable, leads 70% of CDOs to spend more than 20% of their time on driving culture change, with 55% saying a lack of a data culture is their top roadblock.[9] Across a variety of research firms tracking this data, the belief there is a pervasive cultural resistance to data-driven decision-making within organizations across the world is widespread – at least when CDOs are asked the question.

In Chapter 2, I touched on the phenomenon I've heard expressed by many CDOs, which is the idea that changing their corporate cultures depends on their ability to provide value from data – when research suggests the *exact opposite* is true (driving outcomes can influence culture). As an industry analyst I would consistently hear CDOs express frustration about their relationships with their clients, where the situations that prompted those frustrations were cited as evidence of their customers, and their companies, not embracing a data culture.

Business stakeholders not showing up for data governance council meetings. Ongoing issues with data quality in various source systems. Low adoption for self-service analytics platforms. Poor data literacy. Data entry errors. Insufficient funding of the data function. These CDO frustrations, and many others like them, are commonly used by CDOs as evidence that their companies are not data driven, and if they were to get any value from data, they must change their attitude and behaviors toward data.

Yet, having worked within many product and business functions and having been a data leader myself, I know the reality at many organizations is more nuanced. Even if all those behaviors

---

[9] https://mitsloan.mit.edu/ideas-made-to-matter/survey-details-data-officers-priorities-challenges-2023

frustrating CDOs are true, it can still also be true that leaders in those organizations desperately want and need accurate and insightful data. All the business leaders I've worked with (or supported) have voracious appetites for data, and if they can't get it from a central IT team, they'll get it some other way – which helps to explain why so many companies have data teams within business functions outside the control of IT and why there are countless "shadow IT" groups developing data teams and solutions.

When pondering many of the CDO frustrations I would hear daily while an analyst, I reached the conclusion that when CDO's would say "We don't have a data culture," what they were really saying is "My business partners aren't doing what I want them to do." CDOs need collaboration and investments to succeed, and when they don't get them – regardless of the reason – a lack of a data culture is high on their list of reasons to explain why.

This perception that companies don't care about data, or "lack a data culture," is a major reason why CDO turnover is high, at least for those voluntarily choosing to leave. What I have observed is that a CDO will spend one or two years trying to change the culture, often because they believe doing so is necessary for them to deliver value, and when they fail to do so, they'll move to the next opportunity. I have seen this very scenario play out many, many times.

When being recruited for the next company, those CDOs who believed their old company did not have a data culture will use that to justify why they left, or as a justification for why they didn't make any major headway in the position. For many CEOs or CIOs evaluating the hire of that CDO, the justification for a lack of significant victories will not be questioned given that all the top research firms continually cite a "lack of a data culture" as a huge problem at many companies. Over and over this cycle repeats. The lack of a data culture makes it impossible for CDOs to succeed, and the pattern of learned helplessness that puts those CDOs in a victim position is repeatedly reinforced.

As I noted in Chapter 2, this habit of limiting mindsets to have reinforcing properties makes them especially pernicious, and this example of failing CDOs being repeatedly hired by those who accept the misguided belief that CDOs lack agency of their own success is a perfect example of this. Rather than look internally at what data organizations could be doing differently to drive culture change from within and lead by example, many CDOs are instead looking externally and expecting others outside the data organization to grow and develop as a dependency for their success. This is another situation where limiting mindsets have taken root in many data teams – as I've witnessed the ongoing frustrations of CDOs trickle down to many within and outside their organizations.

This emotional contagion caused by prolonged frustrations associated with the belief a company lacks a data culture is highly problematic. In many of my conversations with data practitioners, I'm struck by how often many seem completely disempowered, and even seem somewhat victimized by the environments they are in.

The idea that the entire data function is some form of perennial underdog, fighting the good fight, doing the hard work needed to make potable lemonade from the constant stream of lemons they're forced to process, is a sentiment I hear expressed often. For many, this mindset comes right from the top of the data organization and is visible for all to see – since year after year everything and everyone *but* the CDO is cited as the biggest roadblock to the success of the data function.

According to some of the most trustworthy research in the space, the entire data organization is beholden to the behaviors and attitudes of the rest of the company for their success, so it's no wonder why so many in data teams express feelings of powerlessness that characterize a limiting mindset – but it doesn't have to be this way. As we'll explore in the next chapter, there are things we can all do, today, to embrace more positive mindsets about our roles, our customers, and our data.

Garbage In, Garbage Out

Examples of a limiting mindset are rampant across all aspects of data and analytics – even to the point of dogma. There's no better example of this than the "all-or-nothing" axiom of *garbage in, garbage out (GIGO)*, an utterly meaningless yet completely toxic sound bite that poisons our industry and allows any data professional who embraces it to instantly avoid accountability, all for the small price of negating the entire reason for their jobs in the first place.

Put another way, if you're a data professional and a regular user of the phrase "garbage in, garbage out," then you're essentially asserting that you're powerless to improve the data or analytics you're providing your customers. You're also suggesting that all those expensive pieces of software between the source systems and your reports are simply dumb conduits that move data from one place to the other. If your customers or your C-suite executives heard you repeatedly using this phrase, could you blame them for questioning what you're getting paid for? Or for wondering about the purpose of all that expensive data management and analytics software?

This may sound dire, but I disagree. The goal of the data and analytics function is to provide actionable and meaningful insights to their customers. If data professionals say they cannot provide those insights because of what somebody outside the data team is doing to make their jobs harder, they are basically saying they are powerless to effect any change at all.

When a data professional asserts that they are essentially powerless and that others outside the data have the ultimate power, they are embracing an external locus of control – to the extreme. A widespread embrace of the sentiment "garbage in, garbage out" is a great example of this, and it's also a perfect example of "all-or-nothing" thinking. It also supports a warped perspective that positions the data team as a beleaguered and underappreciated group that's doing its best to fight the onslaught of incoming "garbage," which also just happens to be the lifeblood of the company.

The great irony here is that the idea of GIGO is itself meaningless because data quality is entirely subjective and in the context of GIGO can include anything from complete inaccuracies to simple (and *intentional*) variances in source data structures – and everything in between. The generalization of any data that does not conform to a global analytical standard, which usually isn't even defined, as *garbage* is a perfect example of a mindset focused on the negative aspects of data over the positive. Not only does GIGO see the raw materials negatively, but it also justifies a victim mentality, reducing data professionals to digital trash collectors who are completely powerless to the vagaries of all upstream people, processes, and technologies.

The definition of "data quality" is subjective, and it's both a noun and a verb. It refers to the state of data, and it also refers to the processes used to "clean" data. When referring to the state of the data, there are anywhere from 4 to 12 (or more) dimensions of data quality, where the "rules" used to assess and remediate quality can also vary between functional, cross-functional, and enterprise-wide use cases (see Figure 4.1). This means the definition of "truth" (or accuracy) is contextually bound, where there are many valid contexts within a single business. In layperson's terms, this means that what's accurate to Marketing could be inaccurate to Finance. And what is accurate for an analytical use case may not be accurate for an operational use case. In other words, the concept of data quality is both murky and nuanced and highly dependent on where and when the data is created and how it's intended to be used.

This means the idea of a highly deterministic, binary perspective to data quality that asserts quality is either 100% good or 100% bad (and, by association, garbage or not garbage) is a drastic oversimplification and a completely meaningless distinction. It's a shining example of "all-or-nothing" thinking, yet another glaring indication that limiting mindsets are playing a huge role here.

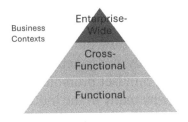

Figure 4.1 Business contexts

To facilitate accurate and efficient aggregation of data into analytical outputs, one of the more common data quality tasks is to transform data coming from multiple systems and processes into a common structure and format within downstream analytical systems. When data is in multiple structures and formats, it's still generally considered to suffer from poor quality.

The requirement to transform data into a common structure is a result of the fact data resides in business applications in different structures – which is by design. The fact data "looks" different in a CRM than in an ERP system reflects the different requirements of the users and processes supported by those systems. To suggest the need to standardize data is a function of the quality of data is both disingenuous and inaccurate – yet data transformations are still considered a quality function.

The processes to identify and remediate quality issues can get complicated and, often, labor intensive. A failure to address these issues will reflect negatively on the accuracy of the insights provided and can therefore cause data customers to lose confidence in the data team, so it's easy to understand why data quality is a touchy subject for most data professionals.

However, if human beings remain responsible for entering, reviewing, or governing data, there will always be errors in data because people are fallible. Rather than see data quality as an opportunity to highlight the capabilities of a data team, given the limiting mindset of many in the data function, data quality issues are instead positioned as a massive burden. One could argue that data people have jobs specifically because of quality-related challenges, yet still, data quality challenges are something that data professionals complain about all the time. In their complaints, it's common for the GIGO platitude to be used to justify their frustration with "the business" for creating such a heavy burden, even while that business may be operating efficiently and generating a healthy profit.

The highly limiting mindset promoted by "garbage in, garbage out" helps to explain why many in the industry believe data quality issues are so widespread. It also helps to explain why we're regularly exposed to headlines like "80% of data scientist time is wasted due to poor data quality"[10] or "only 3% of companies' data meets basic quality standards."[11] These sweeping assessments of the state of data quality within companies are commonplace, are widely quoted in books and research articles from industry thought leaders, and are generally regarded as accurate.

But are they? If data quality is subjective and a function of the context in which it was created or will be used, then any statistic that reduces any assessment of the "state" of data quality at all companies to a single number should be treated with great skepticism.

The proliferation of a very limiting, "all-or-nothing" perspective on data quality continues to justify and reinforce unproductive mindsets in the world of data. Data quality is subjective, and there is simply no such thing as all bad or all good. There is often a very good and very justifiable reason why data may lack consistency or have variable quality by source. Even if human error or laziness is to blame, data quality issues give data professionals a reason to justify their jobs.

Yet, when we widely repeat and embrace "garbage in, garbage out," we help to promote a deterministic perspective that suggests data leaders either are failing miserably or are held hostage by hopelessly broken business processes, run by business leaders who clearly don't care about data. These sentiments fuel more learned helplessness, more frustration, and more negative emotional contagion within data teams, which continue to reinforce negative thought patterns. Here is yet another situation where an effort supported by positive intentions (a desire to help, inform, and motivate change), when released into an environment dominated by very limiting mindsets, can drive outcomes that are in direct opposition to the original intent.

Don't get me wrong – data quality issues are very real; they negatively impact our business productivity and efficiency, and they negatively impact the quality of the insights data professionals

---

[10] https://www.dataversity.net/survey-shows-data-scientists-spend-time-cleaning-data
[11] https://hbr.org/2017/09/only-3-of-companies-data-meets-basic-quality-standards

are able to provide. This is simply a matter of fact, and data quality problems are a driver of significant inefficiencies at companies plagued by them. So I am most certainly not suggesting we stop caring about data quality – as addressing those issues are a critical part of any CDO's operations.

What I'm asserting is that everyone in the world of data needs to start thinking differently about data quality and be more mindful of the words and phrases we use to describe it. The more we talk about how bad data is, the more we think it's bad – and the more those limiting mindsets reinforce themselves. Garbage in, garbage out is a platitude that reduces a nuanced and complex situation into an all-or-nothing proposition, and when used repeatedly and flippantly by data professionals to reinforce the idea we are constantly burdened by it (and not employed because if it), it disempowers us and fuels a negative feedback loop that's hindering our growth.

Seeing Negative Intentions in Others

Data leaders and professionals find a myriad of very subtle and insidious ways to suggest that their customers have less than positive intentions when it comes to the creation and management of business data assets. And when they suggest their customers do not have positive intentions, they embrace a limiting mindset that hinders growth.

While I've not heard many data professionals directly assert that their customers are intentionally trying to subvert their ability to get their jobs done, I've lost track of how many times I've heard them passively suggest it. Repeatedly suggesting their data supply chains are full of "garbage" is a great example of such a passive assertion.

Another example of a data leader suggesting their customers have negative intentions is articulated through a phrase I've heard many times, where an exasperated data leader expresses some variant of the idea that "the business doesn't care about data quality." While at Gartner, data leaders would consistently share their frustrations in having to deal with low-quality data coming out of CRM systems, ERP systems, and many other software applications that are helping to automate critical business processes. This frustration would lead data leaders to suggest that a lack of caring or empathy from their business users were at the root of many of their biggest data problems, adding even more fuel to the belief their company didn't have a data culture.

Here again we see another external locus of control, where it's being suggested users outside the data team are making the jobs of data professionals harder or that external forces are to blame for suboptimal data or analytical insights. We also see another drastic reduction of a complex problem, where it's asserted a major reason why data quality issues exist is the flagrant indifference of business professionals to the plight of hardworking data people.

Why is the problem complex? We touched on the complexity of the issue of data quality, but there are also many complexities in the decisions all business professionals must make about what data to capture and how to capture it. The same is true with how and when to use or apply it.

In situations where human beings are required to enter data into a software-based system (on a web page, a registration form, an account record in a CRM, etc.), there exists a complex web of trade-offs between speed and accuracy that all process owners and managers must balance.[12] So, while it may be factually accurate for a data professional to assert that a data quality problem could be solved by making a data field required on a data input form or that inputted data be validated/verified at the time it's captured, the reality is far more complicated and nuanced.

Every step that slows a user or adds a complication in a process designed to move a user to a specific goal could yield suboptimal results for that business process. Having managed teams that design and build marketing software, I can say with complete certainty that in a perfect world *every* marketer I've ever worked with

---

[12]The trade-off between speed and accuracy isn't a platitude, it's a fact. See: Maolin, Y. (2024). Speed-accuracy tradeoff. In: *The ECPH Encyclopedia of Psychology.* Springer, Singapore: https://doi.org/10.1007/978-981-99-6000-2_859-1.

would love to capture every possible nugget of 100% accurate data on every prospective customer that they encounter. However, marketers also know that capturing that highly accurate data comes at a cost – where the more data that's captured and the more validation processes are added, the more likely that customer will abandon the process before they complete it.

In the case where internal stakeholders, like salespeople, are entering data into business applications, the trade-offs are less obvious but still play a significant role. All producers of data within a company have specific throughput expectations, often managed via some form of production quota. They also have limited time and, often, are using suboptimal technologies. More important, their incentives may generally have little, or sometimes nothing, to do with the quality of data they create.

Noted billionaire and business partner to Warren Buffett, Charlie Munger once said, "Show me the incentives and I'll show you the outcome."[13] It's often the case that business professionals are not incentivized to ensure the data they input into internal systems is accurate – where often the only incentives they have are around speed and quantity, where accuracy necessarily must be sacrificed. This is often the case in situations where information is being captured about people in a sales process, where the incentives may lean more toward quantity over quality. In this situation, the lack of "caring" about data is not being expressed by the individual employee but by the incentives they are given by senior leadership.

The objective and subjective quality of data captured by people or systems within a company is a nuanced and complicated matter. Still, a data leader perspective of business creators of consumers not caring about data is commonplace, and it helps to fuel a limiting mindset that helps to disempower data people and create a divide between data teams and their customers.

Another way that data leaders passively suggest that their customers do not operate with positive intentions is when they express

---

[13] https://www.forbes.com/sites/jackkelly/2023/08/18/follow-the-incentives-and-that-will-tell-you-everything-you-need-to-know-about-a-companys-culture

frustrations around their inability to get their business partners to "own" data. Many data professionals, especially those who ascribe to the teachings of the Data Management Association (DAMA), which publishes the gold standard for data practices known as the DMBOK (Data Management Book of Knowledge), firmly believe that success in the governance of data hinges on business leaders "owning" data.

According to DAMA, a data owner "is a businessperson who is accountable for decisions about data within their domain."[14] More broadly, the concept of data ownership is roughly tied to having accountability for the quality of data in each business context (domain) and the management of governance policies that establish the quality rules and enforcement mechanisms.

The frustrations expressed by data leaders unable to get business partners to "own" data are often cited as a major roadblock in many data governance initiatives. Over the past three years I've facilitated many data governance roundtables, including one the week prior to writing this, where frustrations resulting from an inability to get business to accept "ownership" of data has been a common theme. CDOs are following DAMA's advice and are pushing their customers to own data as a critical dependency for executing on a data governance program, and many are struggling to get traction.

There are many reasons for this – especially the fact most data leaders cannot quantify the value of data governance – but regardless, the concept of data ownership itself is problematic. This is because the data that matters the most to the organization, typically known as *master data*, is data that is widely shared across the organization. In the world of data, the Pareto principle applies, where 20% of the data is responsible for driving 80% of the value organizations realize from data – and that data is master data.

Master data is that which describes customers, products, assets, employees, locations, and all the other business critical "nouns" that quite literally act as the connective tissue within business processes that cross functional lines. Examples of these processes

---

[14] DAMA International (2024). *Data Management Book of Knowledge*, 2e. Technics Publications.

include "quote to cash" or "procure to pay" and where master data is created in one group but used "downstream" by another.

In simple terms, the management and governance of all data can happen at one of three levels in every organization: local, regional, or global (see Figure 4.2).

Local data is created or consumed only within a given system, process, or business function/domain – and does not cross into other functions. Regional data is created and/or consumed across one or more business functions, and global data is created or consumed everywhere. Master data is both regional and global and, as such, requires some degree of consistency and commonality for both operational and analytical processes to be optimized. This is known as master data management (MDM), and I am one of the foremost experts in this field.

MDM exists because individual business functions operate differently and have different analytical requirements for data, yet the data used within those functions is widely shared across the organization. Ensuring each business function can continue to operate with some degree of autonomy, while still using data that is widely shared across functions, requires high degrees of collaboration in the management and governance of that data. This is the genesis for MDM.

Given that the most important data within any company is widely shared and critical for cross-functional efficiencies, the idea that any one businessperson could own it, as DAMA suggests as an industry best practice, is entirely misguided. Here again we have a highly deterministic, "all-or-nothing" perspective on a complex issue that simply cannot be reduced to a binary yes or no situation – but that's exactly the approach many companies, analysts, and consultants attempt to take.

Figure 4.2 Levels of data governance

When CDOs seek to enforce the ownership of data on their business partners, either via edict or through consensus, the results are subpar, fleeting, and frustration-inducing. The reasons are many, but at the top of the list of reasons is a repeating theme throughout this book: the harsh reality that most CDOs cannot tell their customers in the business what the quantifiable benefits of "owning" data will be.

Even if a business leader takes a leap of faith and assigns a person to "own" to a given data entity (take customer data, for example), typically to an early or mid-career analyst without any organizational clout, that person will quickly hit some major roadblocks. These roadblocks include the fact that the data requirements of their individual function will not always align to the data requirements of another function, and friction will inevitably ensue. That data "owner" will soon learn that their authority largely ends at the boundary of their business function and that any meaningful progress on the definition, enforcement, or management of data governance policies for shared data must occur in highly collaborative environments. That data owner role will necessarily need to morph into one that looks more like a functional data steward – that's assuming the business leader is willing to continue supporting a role that they are unable to financially justify. Many do not.

Here again we have another situation where an otherwise reasonable idea (which is to ensure there is a person accountable for ensuring appropriate controls, governance policies, and management of data) when implemented into an environment dominated by limiting mindsets and all-or-nothing thinking is potentially causing more problems than it solves. Having a single person in one business function assume the role of "owning" data that crosses functional lines is a recipe for failure, a situation I've seen play out time after time after time.

A major failing of data leaders in their attempts to force or coerce their business partners to "own" data is that they do not recognize the misaligned incentives that are responsible for ensuring the concept of data ownership is dead on arrival for many business units.

The governance of any data that is widely shared must be a shared responsibility but one where the costs of supporting it are disproportionately borne within functional levels of the organization. The benefits, however, are disproportionately realized at higher, more cross-functional or enterprise-wide levels, as illustrated in Figure 4.3.

In a hypothetical situation where data governance policies were widely embraced across every group and department in a company, salespeople would adhere to policies related to accurate customer data in a CRM, and customer service agents would ensure every nugget of data created for a new support ticket was accurate and timely.

Representatives from every business function would regularly attend data governance council meetings and would play an active role in "owning" their data. Business users would actively monitor data quality, and they would take steps to remediate quality issues before they could become problematic to downstream processes – including analytics.

In this hypothetical scenario, the costs to ensure well-governed data are greatest at the functional level of an organization, but the benefits are realized elsewhere. Cross-functional processes, including

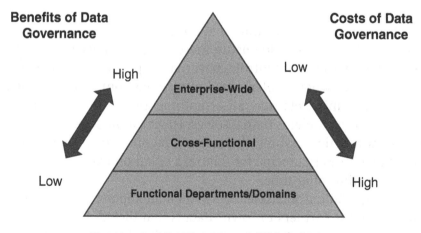

Figure 4.3 Data governance cost/benefit paradox

downstream analytical insights, are the biggest beneficiaries of having well-governed data at the source. Procure-to-pay, quote-to-cash, and other end-to-end business processes flow smoothly, and the analytics for these processes are accurate and consistent.

The benefits of data governance are less material at a functional level, because many of the policies are specifically designed to ensure cross-functional and enterprise-wide uses of the data. Ensuring that the revenue from a sales contract in a CRM can be accurately recognized without manual intervention in an ERP benefits the finance organization, but the cost to ensure that the contract data was entered correctly (and completely) at the beginning of the process is borne by sales.

Sales may successfully execute a contract without capturing all the data finance needs to recognize revenue – and capturing (and governing) all the data needed to execute the end-to-end process at the beginning of the process comes at a cost, a cost that sales may often not be willing to pay. When the hypothetical scenario described doesn't happen and functional units pay little attention to data governance, the costs are often pushed to data teams, causing those teams to assume that their business partners have negative intentions, or are completely ambivalent about the quality of data. This scenario is common and helps to reinforce limiting mindsets and the belief that people outside the data function do not have positive intentions.

The root of this problem is that the data requirements of one functional unit are not the same as the data requirements of another, yet where the same data is used across them. This creates something known as a "collective action problem," not unlike any public good where one group pays but another group benefits – an incredibly difficult problem to solve for even the most skilled leader. This means that CDOs who embrace the negative perspective that their business partners don't care about data (or don't care to own it) are taking a highly simplified view of a complex situation that's a function of many factors, many of which *have nothing to do with data.*

When they express frustrations and allow for a contagion of negative emotions within their organizations caused by the perception their customers don't care, they promote a limiting mindset that fails to see positive intent. When they try to enforce the concept of "ownership" of data that is widely shared, even with good intentions, it will create friction between all different business functions, which naturally have different incentives and requirements. All these things together help to create or exacerbate a divide between data producers and consumers, and instead of increasing the likelihood their business uses data to drive value, they will often have the *exact opposite effect*.

Deterministic, "All-or-Nothing" Thinking in a Probabilistic World

A final example of how limiting mindsets are dominating many data and analytics functions is something I've highlighted many times in six examples of limiting thought patterns in this chapter, which is a tendency to embrace highly deterministic approaches on complex issues. Data quality is complex. Data governance is complex. Managing business processes is complex. AI is complex. Yet, an embrace of negative perspectives about our data, our roles, and our customers leads many to reduce these complexities down to binary, all-or-nothing choices that help to reinforce the status quo and limit our ability to drive business value.

There is no greater example of the limiting force that a widespread embrace of deterministic thinking is having in the world of data and analytics than what I've witnessed over the last two years since the consumer launch of ChatGPT. Excessive support for highly deterministic thinking has been liberally applied in all the considerations needed to operationalize GenAI-based solutions, much to the detriment of many in our field.

Launched in November 2022, the explosion of ChatGPT, and the AI-fueled mania that followed, took many data leaders – especially the roughly 50% of companies with little experience in data science – completely by surprise. I can confidently make this assertion based on all the reactions I've witnessed since, which have been extremely slow to materialize – even for those companies that have made GenAI a board-level priority.

The near-immediate reaction from most consultants, analysts, software vendors, and CDOs to the meteoric adoption of ChatGPT was the widespread promotion of the idea that for companies to realize the transformational value of AI, they must first establish a strong foundation of data governance and management. This idea of "focusing on foundations" as a key dependency for companies to operationalize GenAI at scale was widely communicated across industry events, analyst insights, and vendor promotions throughout 2023 and continues to this day – as many data leaders have concluded the dismal state of their enterprise data prohibits them from using their data to train GenAI models. The cautionary sentiment of "I can't use my data to train AI" (often followed by a reference to garbage in, garbage out) was something I heard frequently expressed by data leaders in 2023, and it's something I continue to hear to this day.

The belief that drastic and significant improvements must be made in data governance and quality before AI can be used to drive business value within their companies is a perspective of a majority of CDOs. A 2024 study performed by the Harvard Business Review (HBR) for my company Profisee, in partnership with Microsoft, found that 59% of data leaders cite the establishment of data governance policies and standards as the biggest dependency for the successful adoption of AI, with 65% of companies focused on data governance in the next year as a key AI enabler.

As it is with all platitudes, the idea that CDOs must "focus on data foundations" is impossible to argue. It's also impossible to argue that improving your data quality will not have positive impacts on the AI-based systems that consume that data. The problem here is not the belief we can all do better in how we manage and govern data (we most certainly can). The problem is that when you reduce a complex situation to a binary choice of being "ready" or "not ready" for the adoption of AI within an environment heavily influenced by limiting mindsets, the "not ready" perspective can have a paralyzing impact. And for many, that's exactly what has happened – at least insofar as using their internal data to build custom GenAI solutions.

More than a year after the ChatGPT launch, two studies showed that only 5–6% of companies had any production application of GenAI.[15] However, in their "State of AI" report published in May 2024, McKinsey noted that 65% of companies said they were using some form of GenAI, and a similar report from PwC cited a figure of 73%.[16] This means for 94–95% of companies, the usage of GenAI is not coming from any custom solution built by a data and analytics, or data science, function. GenAI usage comes from individual users using commercially available GenAI solutions (like Bard and ChatGPT), particularly in marketing, sales, and software engineering functions, to drive significant gains in individual productivity.

In its "2024 AI Business Predictions" report, PwC noted that while many companies will find attractive ROI in GenAI, "only a few will succeed in achieving transformative value from it."[17] This means the greatest value of GenAI will not come from companies simply letting employes use commercial GenAI chatbots and applications like ChatGPT, it will come from "taking advantage of GenAI's capacity to be customized."[18] Here again we see evidence of the incredible opportunity being provided to data leaders but only 5% of them taking advantage of it.

For well over a year, I repeatedly heard CDOs and other data leaders express concerns about using their data to train GenAI models. Even though the "P" in ChatGPT stands for "pre-trained," there was a widely held belief within the data community – which is only now starting to slowly dissipate – that most data teams would be using their own internal data to train their own large language models (LLMs).

---

[15]Article citing studies that show low GenAI adoption: https://sloanreview.mit.edu/article/five-key-trends-in-ai-and-data-science-for-2024/; link to Amazon study: https://aws.amazon.com/data/cdo-report

[16]https://www.mckinsey.com/capabilities/quantumblack/our-insights/the-state-of-aihttps://www.pwc.com/us/en/tech-effect/ai-analytics/ai-predictions.html

[17]https://www.pwc.com/us/en/tech-effect/ai-analytics/ai-predictions.html

[18]Ibid.

The first version of Meta's LlaMa LLM, with 405 billion parameters, required thousands of GPUs to be running for three weeks straight, at an estimated hardware cost of $25M.[19] The training of the LlaMa 3 model required over 16,000 GPUs, represents a hardware cost alone of over $500M.[20] The cost and compute power needed to build custom LLMs means that most companies will not be building them from scratch, yet for well over a year, this was a commonly held belief by many data professionals. Many still hold this belief.

Moreover, the data required to build these models is not highly structured, well-curated, and governed source data sitting in the data warehouses of companies across the globe. The data used to train commercially available LLMs is unstructured text data from the Internet – a source not widely known for its integrity or high quality.

As out of reach as it is for most companies to build their own LLMs, the option to fine-tune open-source language models has always been an option. So too has the option of using software to integrate what's known as a retrieval-augmented generation (RAG) pattern, which is a way of injecting a known fact set into the prompt given an LLM to improve the accuracy and consistency of the response. So, while building custom LLMs may not be an option for most, using software and tools to "ground" the responses of commercial LLMs most certainly is and has been since the hype around GenAI all started.

Yet, it took more than a year for most of the data industry to widely acknowledge that a more pragmatic, practical approach to operationalizing GenAI, which could help limit hallucinations and produce more predictable and accurate responses, was available. Instead of exploring these options, most were widely citing concerns about an inability to use their data to train LLMs, all the while embracing legacy approaches to try to address their "foundational" issues, which for many have gone unaddressed for years.

---

[19]https://arxiv.org/pdf/2302.13971
[20]https://www.datacenterdynamics.com/en/news/meta-report-details-hundreds-of-gpu-and-hbm3-related-interruptions-to-llama-3-training-run

Rather than a rush to innovate, what we've seen in the world of data and analytics is a widespread embrace of the status quo, even at a time when a significant number of companies have a stated business priority of finding ways to leverage value from AI. Instead of data leaders driving the GenAI agenda in their companies, individual users, business functions, and software engineering teams are the ones in the driver's seat – putting many CDOs in a highly defensive and tenuous position.

How is it that nearly two years after the explosion of ChatGPT that only 5% of data and analytics organizations appear to have taken the lead on deploying customized GenAI technologies within their organizations?

There are many answers here, but the widespread embrace of highly limiting mindsets that ignore more practical, middle-ground approaches to GenAI in favor of "all-or-nothing" perspectives are certainly playing an outsized role. Instead of working to identify use cases or business problems more immune to the limitations of GenAI that could be significantly improved with it, many data leaders quickly concluded their data, or their governance capabilities, weren't "ready" for GenAI. Instead of working to close significant knowledge gaps around how GenAI solutions work and can be best optimized using existing capabilities, many data leaders continue to advance the misguided idea that they needed to improve their legacy approaches to data management and governance to realize value from GenAI. In short, many shunned GenAI-based innovations in favor of the status quo – even while others in the organization, outside the data function, were finding ways to use GenAI in safe and effective ways.

Had more data leaders embraced a growth mindset around GenAI, they would have quickly learned that a focus on their legacy approaches to data governance and management would yield very little in terms of their company's ability to drive value from GenAI. This is because GenAI-based solutions are fundamentally different than the other systems that data leaders extract data from or provide data as inputs to.

The biggest difference is that software and analytics tools process *data* and AI systems process *information*. The delta between these two worlds is the notion of context: an entry in a table or an Excel spreadsheet has practically none, while a string of several sentences has plenty.

GenAI-based systems are created, tuned, and optimized by unstructured data – mostly in the form of text. To optimize the output from a model, users will input text via prompts, where that text is entered as a natural language query.

The problem for CDOs is that most governance processes today are focused only on data being consumed through business software applications and business intelligence platforms. These systems act like machines, while AI-based systems are designed to mimic people.

Governance processes are not optimized to ensure large swaths of text data, often scattered across the organization in unaccounted-for systems and tools, are managed with anywhere near the rigor as data sitting in their data management and analytical platforms – like data warehouses, MDM Hubs, or data quality tools. Typically, unstructured text is completely ungoverned in most companies – and will often only have basic access and security controls assigned from whatever software application was used to create them.

This phenomenon is something I called the "AI governance elephant in the room," which I described in an article I published in Forbes in May 2024.[21] Data consumed by AI-based systems must be accurate, consistent, and explainable to mitigate any suboptimal behaviors of AI, yet the scope of data governance processes at most companies does not encompass the very data these AI systems prefer to consume.

Examples of this disconnect likely play out hundreds of times a day at most large organizations. New pieces of text content are

---

[21]https://www.forbes.com/councils/forbestechcouncil/2024/05/07/the-ai-governance-elephant-in-the-room

created and posted by contributors across every corporate function to a combination of internal- and external-facing systems. HR professionals update an employee handbook. Marketers post new material to a company website. Procurement specialists post new supplier guidelines to third-party agents. Customer service representatives post FAQs and other support documents on a SharePoint site managed by an outsourcing company. Brand managers share product descriptions with an external advertising agency. And on and on. And at most companies, all this data is almost entirely outside the scope of the data governance program.

At the start of the GenAI hype, many CDOs, prominent thought leaders, and consultants were all saying that the ability to leverage value from GenAI was dependent on a focus of data governance foundations. While this may be factually true, given that those foundations would optimally span *all* data in an organization, the fact practically nobody in the industry was talking about the importance of expanding the focus of governance programs into the world of unstructured data is highly problematic.

An excessive reliance on overly limiting and deterministic mindsets caused many data leaders to frame the issue of their "AI Readiness" as a binary, yes–no proposition. This caused many to take an extremely conservative approach that embraced a status quo incapable of helping them to make any meaningful progress toward implementing this transformative technical innovation. GenAI systems are far from perfect, and there is much work needed to make them applicable for all possible uses in a company – but the fact that 70% of companies are using them suggest there are plenty of use cases that GenAI systems are good enough to support.

Chapter 5
Reinforcement Mechanisms in Data and Analytics

In this chapter, we will explore the complex web of interactions between data professionals, consultants, industry analysts, and software vendors that help to reinforce the status quo and overly limiting mindsets in the data industry. Over the years I've been a consultant, a software vendor, and an industry analyst, so I come by my observations honestly. Having been on the front lines of all fields, I can say with confidence that nobody in these positions is even aware of the role they play in helping reinforce mindsets that hinder the true potential of data – I believe the exact opposite is closer to reality.

I am confident that all the participants in this complex web firmly believe they're working to promote and advance the field of data and analytics – which makes having conversations to suggest the contrary difficult, to say the least. Unfortunately, the lack of dialogue around the ongoing failure of leaders in our field to drive meaningful changes in their organizations is a big part of why the status quo is so deeply entrenched. It's not easy to challenge our current realities in a way that doesn't come across as preachy or accusatory. After all, nobody wants to be told they're doing a bad job – most especially when they've convinced themselves they have nothing but positive intentions and that it's primarily external forces that are to blame. If you truly believe yourself to be a victim of all these outside forces, having somebody suggest that *your* behaviors are the root of the problem is a message not likely to be well received.

The belief that everyone in the data world is doing their absolute best, despite a litany of ongoing external forces that consistently undercut data leaders' ability to succeed, is a dominant perspective in the industry. A lack of executive support, an insufficient data culture, data illiterate customers, and low stakeholder engagement are just some of the many outside forces that data leaders must battle every day as they nobly fight for the advancement of data-driven decision-making in their organizations. These perspectives, and the limiting mindset at their root, are widely embraced by data practitioners, consultants, analysts, and vendors.

This means that taking a strong position that asserts all of these parties must assume more agency over their individual behaviors would necessarily come with a certain degree of risk. Challenging the norms of any culture comes with the possibility one could be ostracized from that culture, so the idea that anyone who depends on CDOs and other data leaders for their very paycheck would openly challenge the accepted norms of that group is a tall order – and it's a position few are taking.

I believe all the key participants in this ecosystem have positive intentions and truly want companies and their data leaders to realize the transformative power of better data. That's been my goal for many years now, and that's a big reason I've written this book. It's with that knowledge that I hope my message is received by everyone in the data industry in the spirit in which its being delivered. For CDOs and other data leaders to break free from the mindsets that paralyze their industry, they'll need help from everyone who plays a supporting role.

Market Realities

Consultants, analysts, and software vendors are all dependent on data professionals to give them business – especially repeat business. Each of these parties makes money because they've successfully convinced data leaders that they need to partner with them to help solve the most difficult problem faced by data leaders. One could argue that the ongoing presence of these problems is a strong motivator for the problems to persist, but in the spirit of assuming positive intentions, that's a perspective I'm not willing to embrace.

That said, there exist few reasons why a consultant, an analyst, or a software vendor would want to accept the risks that are associated with trying to convince their clients to challenge the status quo. Conversely, there are plenty of reasons why any of these parties would seek to reinforce the status quo, maintain positive working relationships, and not rock the boat. It also happens that in doing so, the problems caused by overly limiting mindsets persist, and few changes are realized.

Each party in the data ecosystem plays a unique role, and each helps in their way to reinforce the status quo and not challenge negative these limiting mindsets. Together, their actions combine into a framework I'm calling the "Information Technology Ecosystem Feedback Loop."

Information Technology Ecosystem Feedback Loop

The first version of this framework was something I created to help explain why people in the world of data and analytics seem to be consistently inventing new words to describe old phenomenon. First introduced via a post on LinkedIn, the "Semantic Pedanticism Feedback Loop" was my tongue-in-cheek attempt to get data people to better understand the role that all the players in the data ecosystem play in creating and reinforcing certain narratives (more specifically, making new words to describe old things that don't need new words). After spending time analyzing what was initially supposed to be equal parts humor and insight, I realized I had created a reasonably robust model that helps explain a lot of things in the world of information technology, and not just the creation of new words but also the creation or reinforcement of any narrative or perspective, including industry best practices.

The more scenarios I fed into my model, the more it seemed to help explain those scenarios – including the proliferation hype around new things and of overly limiting mindsets and the behaviors they support. In the case of the latter, there is perhaps no better example of this than data literacy, so for the remainder of the chapter I'll use it as a case study when referring to the model in Figure 5.1 and the interactions it helps to explain.

At a high level, the model suggests that analysts and thought leaders play an outsized role in helping to drive the zeitgeist of whatever industry or field they are covering, as well as the adoption of new technologies and approaches. In the case of data and analytics, these analyst firms include Gartner, Forrester, IDC, and a long list of individual thought leaders and pundits who all help to shape the perspectives and trends that become widely embraced by

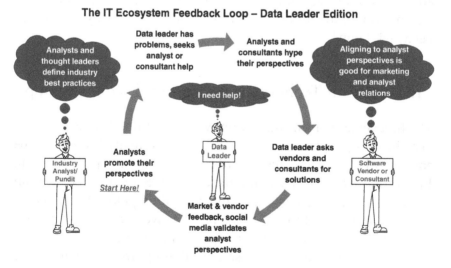

Figure 5.1 The IT Ecosystem Feedback Loop

data professionals – which can also include higher-level executives at consulting firms.

As analysts and thought leaders promote certain perspectives (which could include technologies, practices, roles, and, yes, mindsets), those perspectives are absorbed by data professionals, software vendors, and consultants through several channels, spanning industry events, webinars, whitepapers, LinkedIn posts, and individual analyst client consultations – just to name a few. In the case of my old employer Gartner, the new perspectives (what Gartner calls "practices") and technologies are typically added to their annual hype cycle or promoted through inquiries and written research as best practices. As analysts and thought leaders repeatedly promote these ideas, they gain traction in the market, and data professionals start taking greater and greater interest.

As data professionals start taking interest in these perspectives and technologies, and the more they are promoted by analysts, the more consultants and software vendors start to also take interest – to the point where those things will be integrated into the software or services offerings of both consultants and vendors. Even if the new perspectives are more aligned to a management or governance practice or role (and not a specific technical capability), vendors will still look to align their messaging around that new perspective. For example, becoming more "AI ready" would primarily require a focus on people and processes, but there's no shortage of technology providers in the data space that aren't taking the opportunity to position their solution as one to help companies become more "AI ready."

As consultants and technology vendors integrate the hyped perspectives into their software and service offerings as a response to growing customer demand, the more the analyst's original perspective on the importance of that perspective is validated by market feedback. As the hyped perspective takes root within the industry, analysts continue to trumpet it through all their various communication channels – but now they are armed with the data to provide quantifiable proof that the perspective is something their customers are demanding. However, the reality is often that the initial demand was created by the analysts and thought leaders themselves, not data leaders. By telling the market that a given perspective is important or valid, analysts and other thought leaders create a self-fulfilling prophecy whereby that perspective will almost always end up becoming important – simply because they said it was.

> "There is this cycle and somewhat self-fulfilling thing in our space that creates, in most cases, this froth and mayhem and buzzwordiness, and the search for the latest and greatest thing, which plays into my thesis. I think one of the biggest things holding us back in the entire data community is how we talk about data. Adding more effluvia to that vocabulary is in total counterproductive. You get all these different kinds of techniques that people use. They try to coin stuff. They try to get cute about it...I'll pick one: lakehouse. I think that's a silly name. Is that where my data goes on vacation?"
>
> *Scott Taylor, The Data Whisperer;*
> CDO Matters, *Episode #20*

When talking about the generation and promotion of any perspective in the data world, it's important to separate ideas (or approaches or frameworks or plans) from mindsets. You can have a fantastic and truly innovative idea, but if you try to integrate that into an organization that embraces all the core characteristics of a limiting mindset I reviewed in the previous chapter, in the long run that idea will likely fail. The IT Ecosystem Feedback Loop helps to ensure any idea or perspective, good or bad, will be quickly disseminated across a wide field of highly influential people and forces. These perspectives can help to reinforce limiting mindsets, or they can challenge them. In the case of the former, they will find incredibly fertile ground within most data teams and spread like wildfire. In the case of the latter, they will struggle to gain a foothold, for many reasons I'll outline here.

Let's remember we're not just talking about things on an analyst's hype cycle. We're also talking about the best practices and perspectives that are promoted through inquiries and published research, like those outlined in the annual CDO survey. The major roadblocks to CDO success, for example, are an example of the perspectives that act as the genesis for the recommendations that their analysts will make to thousands of data leaders on the specific behaviors needed to overcome those roadblocks. We discussed many of these perspectives in the previous chapter, including a perceived lack of a data culture, lack of executive support, and data illiterate customers. These perspectives are promoted, and thanks to the IT Ecosystem Feedback Loop, they are quickly magnified and validated.

As an industry analyst, I had front-row seats in watching this feedback loop play out in real life. Concepts that had little market traction would be promoted by analysts – typically because the analyst believed in that concept – and within six months, data leaders would seek to gain more information on that concept. Once this happened, it was a validation that the concept was important to the market, and the more data leaders asked about it, the more consultants and vendors paid attention.

This cycle continues until it reaches the point where either data leaders or analysts no longer see any utility in it. This process can be accelerated or contracted by any of the major players based on the degree to which it's being operationalized or extolled by their clientele. For example, if a significant number of CDOs stop asking for consulting services for a given practice being promoted by an analyst, the consultants will communicate that back to analysts, and the process could stop. This is exactly the fate experienced by the data mesh, where the entire boom and bust cycle played out in under two years.

The interesting thing about the data mesh is that it was not originally aggressively promoted by an analyst firm – it was promoted primarily through a book written by a data and analytics consultant. This is not entirely uncommon, as other phenomenon, including data literacy, have also benefitted greatly from hype created by the publication of a book. Heck, many even the concepts I'm promoting in this book will work their way on to a hype cycle. It wouldn't be the first time.

Sometimes perspectives pushed through this cycle become legitimate data management practices, but sometimes, they are massive distractions that have as much to do with forwarding the career of the analyst, consultant, or software vendor – and not necessarily those they are supposed to serve.

There is no better recent example of this feedback loop in action than data literacy. As discussed earlier, data literacy was brought into the mainstream of the world of data when it was added to the second annual Gartner CDO survey in 2017, when it became one of the options for data leaders to choose in their pick list in a survey to measure the major roadblocks to CDO success.

Data literacy was offered as a choice as a CDO roadblock likely as a response to ongoing CDO frustrations related to struggling data democratization and self-service analytics efforts, thanks to the mass market adoption of self-service analytics tools like Power BI (launched in 2015), Tableau, Qlik, and many others. According to Dresner, analytics "self-service" was the third highest priority for business intelligence leaders in 2018, so it stands to reason that finding ways to drive end-user adoption of those platforms would be a key to their success.[1]

As a result of Gartner and other analysts focusing on promoting data literacy and analytics self-service, consultants and software vendors quickly followed suit. In late 2018 the analytics software vendor Qlik created the Data Literacy Project, which is consortium of five different organizations, including Qlik, a major data consultant (Cognizant), and a major data provider (Experian).[2] Chartered to create "a community dedicated to making society more fluent in data," the project provides users the ability to take a data literacy self-assessment and provides tools and training to improve data literacy.

In 2018 the business intelligence software vendor Qlik published a survey that was used to provide quantifiable proof of the problem caused by illiterate data consumers and in 2020 Accenture, in partnership with the Data Literacy Project, published similar

---

[1] https://www.forbes.com/sites/louiscolumbus/2018/06/08/the-state-of-business-intelligence-2018
[2] https://www.qlik.com/us/company/press-room/press-releases/global-organizations-launch-data-literacy-project

data to show the crippling effects of a data illiterate workforce.[3] This survey included an often-cited statistic to assert that 48% of people "frequently defer to a 'gut feeling' rather than using data-driven insights when making decisions."[4]

In early 2021 Jordan Morrow published his book *Be Data Literate*, and by late 2021 Google Trends data shows the phrase "data literacy" was significantly increasing. All the while, from 2017 onward, Gartner and other analysts had continued to promote the idea, with "data literacy" still relatively high on the hype cycle in 2024.[5] There is no shortage of software vendors claiming their solutions help to enable a business priority on improving data literacy. It should be no surprise that many of those promoting data literacy are also focused on promoting data self-service tools. The more data skills that users in marketing, finance, and HR have, the more they will use self-service analytical tools, and the more money the vendors of those tools will make.

In the span of just five years, data literacy had progressed from something not widely discussed to an industry best practice. The fervor and speed at which the idea of providing the consumers of data products training on how to use those products is truly startling and is a testament to how powerful the feedback loops in the IT ecosystem are. The idea that a relatively mundane and widely accepted part of any product go-to-market process, *end-user training*, can attain the same level of perceived criticality for data leaders as defining a data strategy or governance program is truly remarkable.

What's perhaps more remarkable is the level of bias and profiteering that is clearly playing a role in the agendas of all the players in this complex ecosystem. I will touch on these motivations individually in the following sections, but it should be no surprise

---

[3] Qlik (2018). How to Drive Data Literacy in the Enterprise, White Paper. https://bigsquid.ai/us/bi/-/media/08F37D711A58406E83BA818EB1D58C9.ashx?ga-link=datlitreport_resource-library (Accessed: 13 January 2024).
[4] https://newsroom.accenture.com/news/2020/new-research-from-accenture-and-qlik-shows-the-data-skills-gap-is-costing-organizations-billions-in-lost-productivity
[5] https://www.gartner.com/interactive/hc/5516495

that the perspectives promoted and aggressively hyped by analysts, consultants, and vendors are all those that will make them more money. For this reason, I suspect we'll likely never see "fire your software vendor" at the top of any hype cycle anytime soon.

Analyst Influences

For nearly three years I was a Gartner analyst – and I am extremely grateful for having had the opportunity to work for a great company and to have supported so many passionate data leaders during my time. It would be impossible for me to put a value on all the lessons I've learned, the relationships I've built, and the companies I've influenced. My time as an analyst was a massive blessing, and it's something I'll always remember in fondness.

Rating software products is just one small part of being a Gartner analyst. Most of my time was spent supporting what are known as "client inquiries," which is where executives from companies that subscribe to Gartner services can have one-on-one conversations with analysts on any topic related to that analysts' area of coverage.

My main coverage areas were data governance and master data management, but I also supported many questions related to data strategy, data quality, and general data management questions. Answers analysts provide on client questions comes from published analyst research, and the insights provided in that research is a function of previous research, the expertise of the analyst (and the broader analyst community), and what the analyst is hearing (and learning) in those client inquiries.

The things I heard from data leaders, the stories they shared, and the many frustrations they vented to me over a three-year span all helped me better understand the broader ethos of a mindset less focused on growth and more focused on the status quo. Like most analysts, I was – and remain – dedicated to helping those leaders overcome their biggest challenges.

I can say with complete confidence that every analyst I've worked with sincerely wants to see their clients succeed using the insights they provide and that they firmly stand behind the insights they offer in their research. After all, many of those insights come from customers who have said they're realizing some benefit from previous advice or they're provided via the many qualitative or secondary research surveys that Gartner publishes, like its annual CDO survey.

There is positive intention in the analyst and thought leader community, and there is a strong desire to help clients. Unfortunately, the limiting mindsets embraced by many data leaders are also embraced by many in the analyst community. I believe the root of the negativity in the analyst community is frustration – largely a result from providing insights and recommendations to some of the biggest companies in the world, sometimes over a period of years, but where those recommendations are failing to make a material difference for the client.

I witnessed this frustration firsthand, and it tended to be most acute within the analysts with the longest tenures. I witnessed analysts express what could, at times, be considered disdain for their clients who – for whatever reason – were unwilling or unable to implement the suggestions being provided to them. I also witnessed the frustration that comes when you continually push the same agenda, year over year, only to continually have that agenda marginalized or even outright ignored within your client base.

There is no better example of this than repeated analyst efforts to get their clients to measure the business value of the data and analytics insights and services they provide. Time after time, year over year, analysts from across the broader team supporting data and analytics leaders would stress the need to quantify the business benefits from investments in data. Despite this, little progress would be made to that end. This message of the dire necessity to measure the business value of data would be delivered repeatedly in keynote speeches, during one-on-one client inquiries, and within published research.

In my three years at Gartner, I was involved in helping to promote three different frameworks that could be used to measure the business value of data, with each iteration designed to address some perceived shortcoming of its predecessor, with each iteration largely falling on deaf ears within the client base. Having been a Gartner client prior to becoming an analyst, I was aware the message of "measure the value of the solutions you provide" had been an often-repeated best practice for well over a decade. Yet, year after year, Gartner's own data would consistently show that data leaders were choosing not to follow this advice.

The Sisyphean task of repeatedly pushing a new business value framework rock up the metaphoric hill, only to have it roll back down, is just one example of a situation that would replay daily for many Gartner analysts – and I think it's a big reason why some of them also suffer from limiting mindsets or fail to see the impacts they have on data leaders.

The evidence of highly limiting mindsets in the analyst community can be found in the concepts and programs they promote, the questions they ask in research surveys, and words they use in public forums. When looking specifically at the CDO survey and the top barriers to CDOs (see Figure 5.2), all the six top roadblocks for success in data and analytics initiatives are *external to the CDO*. None of those top barriers speaks to the limitations of the leadership, knowledge, or management style of the CDO themselves. The top roadblocks are all framed to promote a perspective that the CDO is largely a victim to outside forces, and not in control of them.

These roadblocks, which are hand-picked by analysts within their survey design, all highlight just how deeply engrained these extremely limiting mindsets are within the data industry and how the analyst community is helping to reinforce them. Through their publication and dissemination across a myriad of printed research,

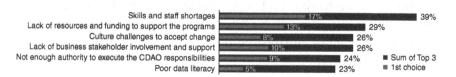

Figure 5.2 Top roadblocks to data and analytics initiatives
SOURCE: Gartner (March 2023).

one-on-one inquiries, and expensive in-person events, these perspectives – which promote the idea that forces outside the data organization are largely to blame for CDO ineffectiveness – are validated and become accepted as an accurate representation of the state of the data nation.

Unfortunately, the questions asked in these surveys are rife with leading question bias and are the genesis of a self-fulfilling prophecy that's a courtesy of the IT Ecosystem Feedback Loop. As we've seen with data literacy, the simple act of an analyst firm asking a question entirely validates the concept in question – and that's because what's being asked by the analysts reflects what's being heard in those client inquiries. CDOs express frustration that their users are not adopting self-service analytical tools, and then that frustration is carried forward into a negatively framed question about the skills of their users. CDOs express frustration because they believe their organizations are incapable of change, so a question about a dysfunctional organizational culture is asked in the next survey.

Arguably the greatest value of any analyst is the fact they are talking to hundreds of top data executives. The fact they are deeply plugged into the data community is what leads analysts to adopt many of the perspectives they subsequently promote. So, it should be no surprise that when a CDO who embraces a limiting mindset tells their analyst that other people are the problem, that analyst will then turn around and ask questions in their surveys to validate if what they are hearing is indicative of reality. CDOs assert something is true, then in surveys analyst firms ask CDOs to validate their own assertions. This is exactly how the IT Ecosystem Feedback Loop starts and how it gains momentum.

This is not to suggest that the perspectives promoted in the Gartner CDO survey (and many others) aren't indicative of the actual perspectives shared by most data leaders – in my experience they accurately reflect their perspectives. I am suggesting that what's being measured in these surveys is not the root cause of CDO challenges. They are measuring symptoms, but not the disease, and as long as CDOs are able to claim they lack agency over their own success, little will change.

It's far easier for a CDO to say "My company doesn't value data" than it is to acknowledge that you may be playing an outsized role in helping to promote that perspective. This means to get at the heart of the biggest challenges faced by CDOs, analyst firms would need to start asking survey questions that get to the root cause of CDO problems, instead of just validating them. Questions like "How do you feel about your job?" or "To what degree do you feel personally responsible for the inability of your organization to get value from data?" would need to be included in their surveys, but unfortunately, they aren't.

Instead, the questions being asked in most surveys of data leaders are the ones analysts already know the answer to. The most logical reason to explain why these more difficult questions aren't being asked is because analysts do not want to alienate their clientele. The power dynamic between analysts and their clients is most certainly not an equal one, so it's reasonable to assume that the dependency that analysts have on their clients is significantly constricting their ability to provide the candid and constructive feedback or research insights that are more likely to have meaningful, and potentially discomforting, impacts.

Individual analysts play a huge role in deciding what perspectives or technologies are promoted and which are not – within certain limitations. However, if an analyst wanted to create an entirely new insight or perspective, based on their expertise or what they were hearing every day from clients, they have the freedom to do so. While certainly not a new phenomenon, one of the practices I actively promoted while an analyst was the concept of data sharing – because I believe strongly in its potential to fundamentally change how companies govern and manage significant portions of their data estate. I was not asked to cover this but was instead given the freedom to research and promote the idea given my belief in its value for my clients. This freedom is a good thing in that it promotes innovation and new ways of thinking.

Beyond individual analysts, there are several important roles within Gartner that also influence research agendas, where the justifications for those agendas are rightfully more economically driven. The core business model of most analyst firms is rather simple – a recurring annual subscription. This means there are strong incentives for all analyst firms to innovate in their research and to create new research "products" that would motivate their subscribers to renew. If the research didn't change much year over year, then fewer incentives would exist for customers to renew, which would pose a huge problem for the company in the long term.

The business model of analyst firms creates incentives for analysts to create new "things," like frameworks, methodologies, perspectives, or disciplines. In essence, these are new products that will help incentivize data professionals to renew their subscriptions, since that would be the only way to stay abreast of all the new things. This is another reason why old models or frameworks, even ones that work and are well adopted by the clientele, are constantly being changed and tweaked, even if the market isn't asking for it. I suppose this is no different than any other consumer good – people like shiny new things, and new sells.

There are additional motivations to innovate that extend beyond the business model and individual analyst passions – including the rewards that analysts can realize if one of their ideas gets hyped and drives a lot of client inquiries and demand for research. If a topic you research (or create) is extremely popular, then you're far more likely to get invited to speak at remote conference locations around the globe – as opposed to just the conference located in your home country.

The need for the clients of analysts to be happy, provide good feedback, and renew their subscriptions could most certainly be compromised if clients perceived that their analyst was being overly combative or accusatory. Therefore, it's highly unlikely you would ever encounter a situation where an analyst would tell a data leader that they are actively choosing to disempower themselves through an excessive embrace of negative perspectives. With the current incentives and analyst business model, that's highly unlikely to happen. Instead, a safer route for an analyst to take is embrace the same mindsets, the same perspectives, and the same frustrations.

When you add up all these forces, it becomes easy to understand why analyst firms would be the first to create new hype-worthy phenomenon or to avoid asking questions that may be uncomfortable to answer and why many of those hyped perspectives serve to reinforce the status quo. The combination of these forces also helps to explain why most analysts would be completely unaware that they, like their clients, are stuck in a pattern of repeating behaviors that are not helping to fundamentally advance their trade.

Don't get me wrong – I am not suggesting that *all* the recommendations made by analysts promote a very limiting mindset within their clients or that the recommendations from analysts don't have value. Quite the contrary. I think *most* of the recommendations from analysts are extremely worthy of consideration. When I review the available research related to improving CDO performance, created by highly intelligent and passionate professionals, I generally agree with what I see. A huge issue is that the recommendations are being implemented into data organizations that are crippled by an embrace of overly limiting thought patterns focused on the status quo.

The same is true with most of the perspectives on the Gartner hype cycle, a process that is designed to allow data leaders to understand and monitor what Gartner believes are innovative ideas in the world of data and analytics. Most of what is hyped is innovative, but in many situations, those ideas fail to deliver the transformative benefits you would expect from truly innovative ideas because they're being integrated into environments rife with negative mindsets.

Not only are those hyped concepts being implemented into organizations crippled by counterproductive mindsets, they are also being created within analyst organizations similarly encumbered. I can vividly recall a conversation I had recently with an extremely influential industry analyst, where I was sharing my concerns about the potential negative impacts of calling the customers of a data team "illiterate." His response was direct: "That's exactly what they are." I wouldn't expect most analysts to be as blunt as this, but the mindset underpinning the response, which is one where the customers are viewed as the problem, is common. This is a direct result of hearing clients express, over and over, that they believe a lack of customer skill is a massive roadblock to their success.

I think this level of negativity is not the norm in the broader analyst community, but it's shared by enough analysts, particularly those with the most tenure, to where it's a significant problem. However, having a handful of grouchy analysts who freely verbalize their frustrations and mirror (but don't challenge) the extremely limiting mindsets of their clients is not the biggest problem for that community.

The biggest problem fostered by the limiting mindsets in the analyst community, when coupled with other inhibitors such as their core business model, is a reluctance (or inability?) to take the risks required to promote the disruptive perspectives that are needed for their clients to take more agency. At some point, data and analytics analysts and thought leaders must take a step back and start asking some difficult questions about issues they desperately need to address. The first question to ask is why, when they have been saying many of the same things repeatedly, through a countless number of forms and frameworks, have many of those recommendations largely been ignored? If you stand behind your recommendations, then why are so many CDOs continuing to fail, and why does CDO tenure remain so low?

Doing the same things and expecting a different result is not a recipe for success, and my hope is that analysts and thought leaders figure out that new perspectives, and new approaches, are needed. Here's one big suggestion that I think would help to drastically improve the quality of the insights about CDO performance and significantly reduce bias in the data: include the customers of CDOs in the CDO survey sample. If the CDO organization is supposed to serve its internal customers, why wouldn't you ask those internal customers how the CDO is doing? Why not ask them about their perceptions of the quality of the data, the usability of the products, and their relationships with their data providers? I suspect this would provide some highly actionable, highly insightful results that aren't subject to all the biases that go along with having what is essentially an annual self-assessment of their performance.

There is recent evidence to suggest that Gartner is aware of the dire situation facing many data leaders and that perhaps they are open to considering some new approaches. At the 2024 Gartner Data and Analytics summit in London I heard some of the strongest language I've ever heard yet from Gartner around the state of the data industry, where it was suggested on the keynote stage that CDOs need to reinvent themselves lest they become irrelevant, with their organizations assimilated into other technology functions.[6]

This suggests that Gartner, like me, believes it's a "make-or-break" time for CDOs, yet a continued focus on the same messages, over the same media, by the same messengers is unlikely to solve the problem. Analysts must find ways to have more meaningful and provocative conversations with their clients about what's needed to become better leaders and how the individual behaviors and mindsets of data leaders are hindering that goal. They must also start having conversations with the customers of those data leaders and include them in their evaluation of CDO performance and in making suggestions to improve it. If those conversations don't happen on their own, then maybe this book will be successful enough to motivate everyone in this complex ecosystem to start having more of them. I sincerely hope it is.

Consultant Influences

Consultants play an important and influential role in the data and analytics ecosystem. I have interacted with well over 1,000 companies in some way over the last five years, and a significant majority of those companies leverage consultants to help implement new technologies, optimize data management or governance processes, or make strategic recommendations. This means the things that consultants say, the perspectives they promote, or the work they do all have a significant role in enabling their clients to realize value from data and the perspectives they embrace. This includes both

---

[6]https://www.gartner.com/en/newsroom/press-releases/2024-05-13-gartner-data-and-analytics-summit-london-2024-day-1-highlights

creating and fueling hype and helping to reinforce mindsets which embrace the status quo.

A great example of consultants fueling the hype machine was the recent mania around the data mesh. The data mesh skyrocketed in 2022 within a year of Zhamak Dehghani, a consultant for Thought-Works, writing the book *Data Mesh*. Having a consultant create this much hype within the world of data and analytics is atypical – as it's far more common that consultants will repeat or promote the perspectives being advanced by analysts and other thought leaders. This is due to the important role that analysts and thought leaders play in helping consultants, especially smaller, more boutique firms, to gain extremely valuable market and competitive insights. Through their relationships with thought leaders and analysts, consultants can realize extreme economies of scale within their operations that they could never generate on their own.

For example, the cost for a smaller consulting shop to execute an ongoing survey of hundreds of CDOs from across the globe would most certainly be drastically higher than the cost of a subscription to Gartner or any other analyst firm – so there are valid economic reasons why consultants would have a heavy reliance on analysts for their insights and market perspectives. The same is true for the creation of any statistically relevant quantitative or secondary research highly focused on market trends or competitive intelligence, endeavors that would be well beyond the grasp of any small to midsize consultancy.[7] Having worked for several years in a small consulting shop with fewer than five full-time employees, so I know this world well.

While an analyst, I spoke often and regularly with consultants, sometimes through inquiries and sometimes through what are known as "briefings" – where the consultant would introduce their team members, give their perspectives on the market, and share insights on their various offerings. However, most of the interactions with consultants occurred through inquiries, where the consultants

---

[7] I can't provide specific numbers (and I hope you can understand why), but my company recently commissioned a relatively small survey of about 300 data leaders from Harvard Business Review, and it was a major financial investment.

would get information on market trends, major challenges, and vendor insights from the analysts. Again, the quality and depth of these insights would be way beyond what those consultants could likely generate on their own, making sure that consulting companies are a significant source of revenue for analyst firms.

I'm not suggesting all consultants have direct client relationships with analyst firms – I suspect only a fraction of all consultants do. Subscriptions to analyst firms are expensive and would be cost prohibitive for many small consulting companies. Still, the insights and perspectives promoted by analysts and other thought leaders create a zeitgeist that consultants are more likely to promote than challenge, especially given consultants are likely hearing those exact perspectives directly from their clients.

Data leaders say their companies lack a data culture, and analysts and thought leaders repeat and amplify this through a wide array of media including published research, industry events, white papers, and so on. By the time a consultant is engaged to help solve a problem, what they hear from clients will be a common problem, given it's what they're hearing everywhere else.

In my role as a thought leader and CDO with Profisee, I continue to have ongoing interactions with many consultants – for the same reasons I had them while at Gartner. I am extremely active in industry events, on social media, and through all the channels that Profisee uses to distribute my published content – including YouTube, my live monthly "ask me anything" events, and my podcast, *CDO Matters*. I don't have nearly as many interactions with CDOs and CIOs that I did while at Gartner, yet I'm confident that I have more interactions with potential clients than the average consultant who is billing 40 hours a week – which means I'm a useful and extremely cost-effective tool to help them stay plugged into the data and analytics market. Roughly 50% of the growing community of data professionals who consume my content are consultants, and I greatly value the trust they put in me as a thought leader in our industry.

Over my many years in IT, I've worked with (or hired) every conceivable type and size of consultant, from one-person shops to every one of the biggest players in the space, like Accenture, Deloitte, and PwC. I've worked with strategic consultants, software specialists, and staff augmentation generalists. I've also been a consultant working in a small boutique, so I know firsthand the rigors of running a services business, managing client satisfaction, and successfully executing statements of work. Consulting can be a tough job, especially for the smaller shops, and the need to differentiate through subject matter expertise, successful (and on time) projects, and happy clients can the difference between building a successful business and living paycheck to paycheck.

The consulting business is all about optimizing available resources, so the pressures to have everyone billing 80% or more of their time is high – while at the same time ensuring that everyone continues their professional development and hones their skills through vendor and industry certifications, attending industry events, and consistent uptraining. Profit margins can be thin, especially if external, subcontracted resources are needed, putting even more pressure on consultants to minimize downtime and keep all resources fully engaged on client engagements. The smaller the consultancy, the harder it is to devote the needed time to market and competitive intelligence and to individual professional development.

This means the motivations for consultants to rely on analysts and other thought leaders to help them augment their views on the market, the sentiments of their potential clients, and advancements in new technologies are many. There simply isn't enough time in the day for most consultants do that they need to get done, while also doing their own research on all the newest trends, CDO challenges, and evolving technologies. Bigger consulting firms most certainly have an advantage here, but they are the minority. This explains why so many consultants are highly dependent on analysts' insights and why they are more likely to reflect analyst perspectives – particularly those of Gartner – than they are to develop "net new" perspectives on the market that are potentially out of sync with what the rest of the market is saying.

If Gartner and other analysts are hyping "new" things, are promoting approaches or frameworks that reinforce the status quo, or are embracing perspectives that promote behaviors which hinder growth, then it's likely most consultants will be doing the same. Analyst perspectives are well known and well promoted and, in the case of Gartner's beloved Magic Quadrant, are often considered the "gold standard." This means the likelihood of a consultant recommending a "best practice," or a software solution, that's drastically out of step with any of the major analyst firms recommends is highly unlikely.

The frameworks and approaches used by consultants to solve problems in the data and analytics space are remarkably like the frameworks and approaches recommended by Gartner. Both will have data governance frameworks, approaches for data strategy, data and analytics operating models, and, of course, business value frameworks – just to name a few. These approaches will be leveraged within consulting services engagements and will help to validate the legitimacy and perceived value of the concepts that both the consultants and the analysts are promoting. It's a highly symbiotic and self-reinforcing relationship.

Consulting engagements in the data world all follow a similar and highly predictable pattern of some form of an "as-is" assessment (which may include a maturity assessment), followed by a gap assessment, followed by an implementation/remediation plan, followed by ongoing monitoring. Most consulting engagements often start with an "Phase 1" engagement where the scope and cost of a secondary engagement is defined. The "Phase 2" engagement will typically have a fixed cost but rarely ends up finishing on time or on budget – often because the initial scope or requirements were not fully understood or anticipated. Along the way, the frameworks recommended to address a specific challenge – like data governance or MDM – will closely resemble the "best-practices" approaches that have been followed within the data space for the last two decades.

I could write an entire book on the effectiveness of consultants in the data and analytics space, focused on some of the many changes I think are needed within that industry. So many of the approaches we have come to believe are best practices are of dubious benefit and, in many ways, seem designed specifically to extend the length of these engagements. A great example of this are maturity assessments – which are generally considered an important tool in understanding where a client is "starting from" and where clients need to most improve to close any gaps between where they are and where they need to be. In theory.

The maturity assessments of most data organizations reveal a remarkable similarity across all companies, where the average scores for each typically revert toward a mean (on a scale of 1–5), somewhere around 2–2.5. Most companies are extremely weak in governance, average on data management and analytics, average on technologies, and significantly lacking on data strategies and business alignment. There may be pockets of strength in certain capabilities (like ETL), but for the most part, the data and analytics maturity of the average company is below average.

There you have it. I just described the data and analytics maturity of 80% of all companies currently paying for a maturity assessment, which probably also accurately describes your maturity level. The cost you paid for this book just saved you six figures in consulting fees for a maturity assessment! But I digress... .

Another reason why consultants are likely to not stray too far from the perspectives embraced by analysts or other thought leaders, or the best practices they recommend, is that consultants are hired specifically to solve a client problem – where it's *the client* that typically defines what the problem is. If a consultant sits across a table from a CDO during a discovery session and says, "I need to improve our data literacy," the likelihood the consultant would say something akin to "No, you don't, you need to develop a growth mindset and focus on business literacy" is extremely unlikely and highly inconceivable.

> "When I was in KPMG, one of my things was risk and performance, which are two sides of the same coin. I was not a popular partner when I went into one bank and said, 'Why are we doing the same project five times?' to the lead partner. And he said, 'What do you mean?' I said, 'Well, we've got a program in the front office. We've got a program in compliance and risk. And

we have something in IT building stuff. They're all basically solving the same problem. . . . If we basically collapse these into one project, which will cost the equivalent of two of the five, we will do everything the customer needs.' Then [he says], 'But that's not what the customer wants; we're doing what the customer wants.' I said, 'We should be doing what the customer needs,' but this is not what they want to hear."

Eddie Short, former CDO and consultant;
CDO Matters, Episode #53

Clients express a problem, and those problems are likely to reflect what the analyst firms have validated are the root causes, and then consultants are asked to solve that problem. Given what the consultants are hearing from clients is consistent from what they're hearing from analysts, the consultants are even less likely to challenge what they're hearing from their clients. It's a recursive feedback loop with little room for different perspectives or different solutions.

If you remember the story where you're a baker running the only bakery in a small town – let's assume you conclude that a lack of customer knowledge on the nutritional value of artisanal breads is the main reason you're not selling more of it. Then imagine your local newspaper reports that a lack of general citizen knowledge on nutrition is a growing problem for the community, where you are cited as a source for the news article, and nobody else is interviewed for their perspectives. Anyone reading that newspaper, who trusts the reporting and doesn't have the time to do their own investigation of the situation, is highly likely to assume that solving the issue of providing more knowledge to the community on the nutritional superiority of artisanal bread is absolutely the key to your failing business – when the reality is most likely a suboptimal product.

In this metaphor, consultants are reading the analyst newspaper as a trusted source and acting based on what they read. Given all the demands of being a consultant, there's little time or opportunity to apply critical thought to what the analyst promotes since – after all – that's supposed to be the analyst's job. The analyst insights and perspectives are then woven into the service offerings and market messages of consultants, at which point there's a second validation of the original perspective from yet another trusted and highly paid source.

As analyst firms tend to behave in highly conservative and risk-averse ways, so do consulting firms – albeit for slightly different reasons. The consulting business is highly competitive, but it's also one significantly driven by the relationships that consultants have with individual data leaders. Consultants are hired often specifically because of those relationships, especially given that there's little to drastically differentiate the core competencies between any of the bigger firms – all of which will have significant data and analytics bench strength, with staff certified across most of the major software vendors.

Brand integrity and the strength of client relationships is everything to consulting companies, and the motivations to successfully execute on a given statement of work (SOW) – which will naturally tend to represent an incremental (or perhaps even MVP) advancement of a given management of governance discipline – means there are strong incentives to avoid taking any massive risks on a given engagement. The negative impacts on the reputation of the company (or the senior partner) for a high-profile failure, especially for a smaller consultancy, could be drastic.

Another reality in the world of data and analytics, which is true for both analysts and consultants, is that neither is typically paid for successful business outcomes. The overwhelming majority of engagements are billed by the hour, and even in the situation where a specific deliverable has been contracted within a statement of work (for example, the implementation of a new software solution), the incentives are tied to the deployment of technology and not the realization of business benefits from that software. There are certainly some limited situations of performance-based SOWs, but in the data world, they are practically nonexistent.

Consultants follow industry best practices and well-established frameworks and are paid regardless of whether those approaches drive true business value for their clients. There are few motivations to monitor if the recommendations they make, or the software they implement, are making a real difference. This is not to suggest consultants don't care about client success – I believe they all do. However, the consulting business model is one that constricts the ability for consultants to suggest entirely unproven or novel approaches to solving a problem or to implement performance-based compensation – both of which I believe are desperately needed in the world of data and analytics. It's far more likely consultants will stick with the existing corpus of industry best practices and billing practices, even if the dire state of value delivery within the data space strongly suggests those approaches are simply *not working*.

In total, the interconnections between consultants and analysts run deep. Even in situations where a consultancy has no direct client relationship with an analyst firm, the ability of analysts to significantly influence the narrative of the data and analytics ecosystem in which consultants operate has impacts that are unavoidable. These connections all act to reinforce, validate, and amplify the perspectives of the analyst community across the broader ecosystem of companies hiring consultants to help guide or implement their data management and governance strategies. Moreover, they often help to reinforce the same old and tired approaches to solving the problems that many data leaders have been unsuccessful in solving.

The dynamics inherent to the relationship between clients and consultants, where clients heavily influence the framing of both the problem and the proposed solution, also help to ensure that the output of consultant engagements most closely aligns to the client's worldview. When that worldview is one heavily influenced by overly limiting mindsets, the work product of consultants is more likely to reflect and reinforce the status quo than to meaningfully challenge it.

Vendor Influences

The implementation of new technology is often the first thing considered by data professionals seeking to solve a problem, so it's logical that software vendors also play an important role in helping to shape perspectives of data leaders – for better or worse. The products and the messages used by vendors to promote those products will often closely align to the perspectives of analyst firms given the incredible influence the analysts have in the data space. As analysts and consultants embrace these overly limiting mindsets bent on serving the status quo, so do software vendors. The reason here are many, but they start with the dependencies that vendors have on both analysts and consultants.

If you're a software company selling to IT leaders like CDOs or CIOs, the importance of being on the top right of the Gartner Magic Quadrant cannot be overstated. For better or worse, Gartner remains incredibly influential in the world of IT, and its insights are used extensively by buyers to evaluate potential software providers. If Gartner says you're a legitimate vendor with a good product, a good vision, and a high ability to execute, then you're going to be considered by most buyers as a leader in the space – even if they're completely unfamiliar with your company or your product. If you're not on the Magic Quadrant, then you're less likely to be considered by most software buyers in the data space. It's that simple.

This means there are significant incentives for software vendors to build and maintain positive relationships with analysts. This requires establishing a regular cadence of briefings and inquiries so that analysts are aware of a vendor's product and its capabilities. It also requires having the vendor's clientele provide feedback on their product through the analyst online communities and ratings platforms, which are often augmenting or even replacing the use of end-user surveys supporting the Magic Quadrant process. For the bigger software companies, there are often entire teams of people supporting an "analyst relations" (AR) role, where it's primary responsibility to ensure the analysts are seeing a given software vendor in a positive light.

The difference between being considered a "challenger" and a "leader" on a Magic Quadrant can be the difference between millions of dollars' worth of annual software sales for a vendor, which makes AR an incredibly important function in any software company. It also means that software companies, particularly the smaller ones, are far likely to fully endorse and support any of the perspectives being promoted by analysts in an effort to get in the "good graces" of the analyst companies. There is little downside for a software company to align with the perspectives of an analyst firm, but there is plenty of downside for any vendor not considered by an analyst as a legitimate contender in a given competency.

This means the dependency software companies have on analysts, especially those trying to establish themselves in a market, is significant. This is why Gartner is incredibly sensitive to creating any perception of being "pay to play," and the company goes out of its way to ensure it maintains a positive brand image and is seen as completely impartial. Ultimately Gartner, and all other analyst firms, are in the business of trust, and they all work diligently to ensure their clients view them as an impartial and trustworthy business partners.

As an analyst, the need to maintain impartiality is something we were trained on extensively and were constantly reminded of. This is why you'll rarely see analysts with significant social media footprints – since the diligence required to ensure you're not seen as favoring any one vendor or product over another can be daunting in an environment when simply hitting the "like" button on a post mentioning a vendor's product could be problematic. This is also why the water bottle sitting on my desk right now has a piece of duct tape across the middle of it, since that tape covers the letters "IBM" on the bottle – which I didn't want anyone to see on video calls while I was an analyst – lest they conclude I was recommending IBM products. So, when it comes to analyst perceptions of vendors, I can say with confidence that impartiality is well maintained (at least at Gartner), and for good reason.

The opposite is most certainly not true. Software vendors must do everything in their power to be seen in a positive light by analyst firms – the stakes are simply too high to do otherwise. This means it would be logical for all vendors to most closely align their perspectives to those of the analyst firms, and it also means the analyst firms have an outsized influence on the road maps and priorities of those firms.

If an analyst reports that a given vendor is weak on given capability, then that vendor will most likely prioritize resolving that weakness. If an analyst suggests that the market needs more of a focus on a given data management practice, then vendors will market their products as enabling or supporting that practice. If an analyst suggests the market would better respond to a given messaging, then vendors will embrace that messaging. If analysts suggest a software market is moving in a certain direction, many vendors will lean in that direction. The level of influence that analysts have in the IT software industry cannot be overstated.

Like many consultants, smaller vendors simply don't have the resources to generate meaningful market research on their own, which also makes many of them dependent on analysts and other thought leaders for insights on their customers' biggest challenges. Knowing those challenges is critical to developing software solutions to address them, and being able to access analyst insights at a cost significantly less than what it would take to build and staff a market and competitive intelligence function, has its advantages.

When product managers at software companies are able engage in direct market research, they are also likely to hear the exact perspectives that analysts are hearing in their inquiries. They will hear data leader challenges related to being unable to stem the flow of garbage in, disengaged executives, the problem of illiterate data customers, and frustrations caused by organizations unwilling to change. These perspectives will echo those published by analyst firms and will serve as a powerful reinforcement for the validity of the analysts' insights.

The marketing departments of software companies will also conduct customized market research – but often with a very different outcome in mind. Rather than only measuring the sentiment of the market or better understanding customer needs, sometimes the research initiated out of marketing departments is more designed to drive market sentiment and behaviors than measure it. This happens when product or marketing groups in software companies commission research from notable firms with respected brand names, including analyst firms, where the findings of the research are reasonably well known – or at least strongly hypothesized – in advance of conducting the research. Survey questions are designed to steer the responses toward the market perspective the research is designed to validate, which is a perspective that suggests data leaders need the products of those vendors. While these undertakings may follow some degree of statistical rigor, they are most certainly not without significant faults and are not always fully aligned to the scientific method.

The creation of "research" to advance a specific vendor agenda, like selling more software, using dubious methodologies, insignificant sample sizes, and zero peer review is the norm in the world of data and analytics. It's also a big reason why limiting mindsets are so pervasive, because much of the research in our space is framed in a way as to promote the idea that data leaders are not to blame for companies failing to realize the value of their investments in data. Once again, we see a situation where those beholden to data leaders to buy their products are far more likely to sympathize with or validate their customers perspectives than challenge them.

This is a big reason I'm highly skeptical of much of the research in our space and why I apply heavy doses of critical thought to most of what I read – given so much of what is published as "research" is essentially a marketing message. The irony of me quoting multiple research studies to advance my narrative in this book is not lost on me – but this is why I'm including citations so you can access the data yourself and reach your own conclusions.

The natural incentives for software vendors to attempt to bend the industry toward embracing perspectives that will help them sell more software means data leaders should most certainly be skeptical of what they hear and read. Vendors that find a way to exploit the tendencies of data leaders to embrace these limiting mindsets and the behaviors they promote are likely to find great success in their market messaging – because they add yet another layer of validation on top of the analysts and consultants taking the same approach. They also validate the data leaders' frustration, and even greater credence to the underlying beliefs, like learned helplessness and blaming others, that hinder growth and perpetuate the status quo.

Social Media Influences

Over the last few years social media has become an extremely influential force in the world of data and analytics. According to Gartner, 46% of B2B software buyers use social media, particularly LinkedIn, to support early-stage sales cycle efforts, such as learning about solutions that can help solve their problems.[8] A study published by LinkedIn in 2023 said that LinkedIn was the most used source of information for technology buyers for 37% of those buyers.[9] This means that what CDOs and other data leaders are reading on LinkedIn is most certainly having a huge impact on how they perceive their roles, their customers, and their data. It should be no surprise, therefore, that many of the influencers on LinkedIn can tend to strongly reinforce the limiting mindsets of data professionals across a variety of ways.

Beyond serving as an important source of information about technology options, LinkedIn plays an increasingly important role in supporting learning and development, where users are exposed to content from both vendors and peers that can help to keep data leaders up-to-date with current trends and industry best practices. According to a study of 125 learning and development professionals from Fortune 500 companies, 82% of them said they use social media to network and advance their professional skills.[10] This all means a significant number of CDOs and other data leaders are

---

[8]https://www.gartner.com/en/digital-markets/insights/social-media-best-practices-for-b2b-businesses-#:~:text=About%2046%25%20of%20B2B%20buyers,as%20identifying%20need%2Dto%2Dknow

[9]https://business.linkedin.com//content/dam/me/business/en-us/marketing-solutions/resources/pdfs/linkedin-tech-buyer-namer-jan-23.pdf

[10]https://smartcdn.gprod.postmedia.digital/vancouversun/wp-content/uploads/2011/01/cara_socialmediaimpact_pulsesurveyreport.pdf

heavily exposed to content on social media, particularly LinkedIn, on a frequent basis.

Over the past two years, LinkedIn has represented my biggest opportunity to interact with data leaders, and building a professional network on LinkedIn has been a top priority for me – consuming easily 30–40% of my time on any given day, with four to five content posts a week. In building my 16k+ followers since leaving Gartner, I've learned an immense amount about LinkedIn, the data and analytics content that seems to be in most demand, and the content that is most engaged with. As much as I consider myself a data expert, I am also becoming a LinkedIn expert – for better or worse.

Overall, my experience on LinkedIn has been an extremely positive one, and I am continually surprised by the quality and quantity of interactions I can have on any given day. I have met some incredible and smart people on LinkedIn, some of whom I now consider my friends – even though I've yet to meet many of them in person.

My mission on LinkedIn is simple: to share the insights gleaned after 30 years in the world of IT in the hopes that I help CDOs and other data leaders extend their tenures and drive value for their businesses. Yes, I work for a software company in Profisee, but thanks to the commitment of a forward-leaning and innovative chief marketing officer, Reed Gusmus, I remain razor focused on being a trusted advisor on LinkedIn, and not a salesperson.

Reed is a huge believer in what is known as "dark social," or the various influences in a marketing program that can't be measured, including the value of having a CDO on LinkedIn (me) who acts as a trusted advisor to anyone online, regardless if they want to buy from Profisee.[11] This means there is an expectation that my presence online will build brand awareness and goodwill, with the hopes that my acting as a trusted advisor will make buyers more likely to see Profisee in a positive light and to choose us when the time is right for MDM. Like all companies, we have a

---

[11] What exactly is "dark social"? See https://blog.hootsuite.com/dark-social/#What_is_dark_social.

corporate presence on LinkedIn where we are not shy about trying to promote the virtues of our product, but when it comes to my LinkedIn feed, I consciously avoid selling and stick only to sharing insights around industry best practices.

The approach I take on LinkedIn to avoid selling is most certainly not the norm. What's more normal is that people are creating and sharing content with the specific goal of directly influencing behaviors, like making you sign up for an online course or register for a webinar. While there are certainly some people active on LinkedIn who take the same approach I'm taking, it's a small minority. Only 1% of LinkedIn's 760 million users are actively posting content online, and by my non-scientific evaluation of those content creators, they tend to fall into one of four personas. In rank order, they are:

1. Influencers, who are dependent on LinkedIn for their income (35%)
2. Thought leaders with consulting businesses, or who work for consultants or recruiters (30%)
3. Data practitioners who have other day jobs (25%)
4. Thought leaders working for software companies (20%)
   a. Who actively sell/promote (15%)
   b. Who actively avoid trying to sell (5%)

Perhaps the most annoying cadre of LinkedIn users not listed here is "business development representatives," who are using the platform to relentlessly spam potential buyers to land a sales meeting in exchange for everything from Amazon gift cards to being featured on a billboard in Times Square in New York City (this was just offered to me, I'm not kidding). Thankfully, these users aren't creating any content, because if they did, it would make LinkedIn a difficult place to inhabit for more than a few minutes a day.

When looking at the four primary types of content creators, it should be easy to see there are commercial motivations at play that would hinder what could otherwise be considered editorial integrity. Most of the content creators are trying to motivate users on the platform to embrace a certain perspective or take a certain action – usually buying a certain product, including online training courses.

Influencers are in the business of monetizing their online communities to the brands willing to pay for the exposure – which for some influencers can be upward of 100k data professionals. Their content tends to have the most "production value" since they are dependent on clicks and engagement. Influencers will typically rely on lighter, more entertainment-focused content to build and maintain their communities and will not generally be known as experts or learned practitioners in the data world. This shouldn't be a huge surprise given the main skill of influencers is marketing, not data. There are some LinkedIn unicorns with legitimate data pedigrees who have become incredible influencers, but they are indeed rare.

The second type of content creator tends to be a data professional who is parlaying their expertise as a previous practitioner into the world of consulting – sometimes for a midsize firm but, more often, for themselves. The content they create tends to be far more insightful and actionable than anything you would see from an influencer, but ultimately, they are trying to sell their services to the 99% of people not creating content on LinkedIn.

Often these people will have written books covering their areas of expertise, which helps to build and maintain credibility and drive sales leads for consulting engagements. These people are also highly active speakers at industry events and will typically be invited over thoughts leaders with similar expertise but who happen to work for vendors, since those who work for vendors are expected to pay for the right to speak at conferences.

By my estimate, roughly 25% of the content creators I interact with on LinkedIn are people working in day jobs as data professionals and are creating content out of a desire to share what they know and learn from others. These tend to be mid-to-late career professionals, as it's rare to see significant online engagement from those at earlier phases of their data careers. For these people, I believe much of their motivation to post content also comes from a desire to build a personal brand, and a peer network.

Lastly, there are content creators who work for software companies – most of which are actively trying to promote and sell their products. The content of those thought leaders who actively sell tends to be rather predictable, where regardless of whatever data challenge is being discussed in each thread, the software of that person's company is almost always the cure.

Then there is the rare situation like mine, where somebody with deep industry experience is getting paid by a software company to share what they know, build a personal brand, and develop an online community focused on learning and development. Yes, I sincerely hope that people from my community will *eventually* buy our software, but my LinkedIn success metrics are not tied to software sales, they are tied to user engagement. I am aware of perhaps ten other people in the world of data and analytics with a similar approach to LinkedIn as my own and I've come to know most of them quite well over the last two years.

Given these four LinkedIn personas and their motivations, I would estimate that only about half of the content a data professional would see on any given day on LinkedIn could be considered as largely devoid of any obvious ulterior motive. The other half is essentially entertainment and meme-driven marketing, or user self-promotion. And unlike any other mass marketing media, there are some tactics utilized on LinkedIn that are proving to be highly effective in our modern era, and many of them are closely align to the examples of the mindsets shared in the previous chapter. The top three examples of behaviors endorsed in LinkedIn content about data and analytics which support mindsets that to not promote growth are:

- **All-or-nothing thinking:** As memes go, "garbage in, garbage out" is about as popular as they come in data-related content posts on LinkedIn, and rarely does a day pass where I don't see some mention of this toxic meme on the platform. The popularization of AI has only accelerated the use of highly deterministic positioning within LinkedIn posts, especially those related to data quality. It's a common occurrence to see several posts a day all advancing the idea that "AI built on bad data will produce bad results." On the contrary, it's extremely rare to see any posts that acknowledge the complexities and nuances inherent to things like probabilistic AI models, adaptive forms of data management and governance, or disparate business processes. Instead, what's most common is highly polarizing perspectives that rely heavily on platitudes – particularly if those posts are from influencers.

- **Blaming others:** A day cannot pass without encountering a data-related post on LinkedIn that promotes the idea that the biggest challenges faced by data leaders are external to the data function. Posts that suggest poor data quality is a function of indifferent or illiterate users or because business users will not "own" data governance appear on my feed regularly. Similarly, posts that promote the idea that low adoption of data-related products is a function of low user skill, and not poorly built products, are commonplace.

- **Assuming negative (or ambivalent) intent in others:** Posts that suggest data quality is somehow a function of indifferent or uncaring users within business functions are common and tend to get a lot of LinkedIn engagement. The same is true with posts that vent frustration for a lack of business engagement in supporting data governance functions, where sentiments that promote the idea that users outside the data function have a wanton disregard for the difficulty of the jobs faced by data people are common on LinkedIn. Often, the discussion threads for these posts seem to take the form of a group/mutual therapy session, where people commenting seem to take comfort in knowing they aren't the only ones doing the difficult but necessary work that they seem to believe their customers have a willful disdain for.

Even in situations where content creators avoid the promotion of behaviors that support anti-growth mindsets in their LinkedIn content, most of the "best practices" being shared on LinkedIn are repeating or recycling the same old and tired approaches we've been trying for years – most of which have proven ineffective in enabling data to become a truly transformational force.

In addition, it's quite common for the best practices in question to have been created by the very people promoting them today on LinkedIn, or at the least, they've been promoting them for multiple decades. If you're a noted thought leader in the data world who has actively contributed to the corpus of knowledge that's widely accepted as an industry standard for the last 20+ years, it stands to reason that you'll be far less likely to believe those insights are anything but a good idea – particularly if your career is in its latter stages. Change is difficult for everyone, but it's especially difficult if you've built an entire career around the very ideas that are being considered for revision.

There are other examples of limiting mindsets on LinkedIn that are surely helping to promote the status quo, including the behavior of the LinkedIn algorithm, which tends to create what could best be described as echo chambers of like-minded people. People who like and engage with the same content are likely to be presented with the same or similar content in the future and are more likely to connect with the purveyors of that content.

The echo chamber phenomenon on LinkedIn means I am totally open to the idea that there's an entirely different LinkedIn reality to my own – a LinkedIn community of growth-minded, optimistic, and change-ready data professionals who don't complain about their customers, their data, or their roles. However, I find this highly unlikely, given my active involvement in every major data-related industry conference on two continents. If this other reality existed, I would probably have met its members in real life and connected with them on LinkedIn long before now.

To be fair, more positive, growth-minded experts and thought leaders *do* exist on LinkedIn, and to a certain degree, many of us have already formed a miniature version of this alternative reality. I won't highlight all of these exceptional and intelligent people by name, but they are the same ones who make my LinkedIn experience a generally rewarding one, and for whom I am incredibly grateful. Interacting with them gives me hope, and their support was a big reason I'm writing this book. And if you're reading this and you're in this small cadre of people devoted to creating meaningful and growth-focused change, then you know who you are.

I am grateful for LinkedIn, the learning opportunities it provides, and the meaningful relationships I've built on the platform. However, it unfortunately plays a significant role in helping to reinforce the counterproductive mindsets that are running rampant in the world of data and analytics. A preponderance of posts promoting the idea that data customers are to blame for the inability of CDOs to deliver value, that "all-or-nothing" mindsets that reduce highly complex issues into binary choices, and that data consumers are ambivalent to the plight of hard-working data professionals, are all helping to hinder the growth of the data profession. Content creators who depend on the platform for their income are unlikely to challenge these perspectives, and only a select few "influencers" on the platform have the freedom to espouse any perspective that runs counter to those held in the majority.

Technology Influences

The last force that helps to reinforce overly limiting mindsets in data and analytics is technology – most notably GenAI and LLMs. As truly transformational as GenAI technologies are, they have limits when helping data leaders navigate the complex world of managing and governing data and leading data teams. Because GenAI solutions are typically using data and insights gleaned from the Internet, data professionals shouldn't expect them to suggest any new or innovative ideas on how to realize the value of data within companies.[12] On the contrary, any data leader or practitioner using an LLM to provide insights on how to best meet their customer needs should expect to see recommendations that reinforce the same old and tired approaches that are limiting the ability of data leaders to be the agents of change their organizations desperately need.

---

[12] If, by the time you are reading this, AI has found way to provide truly novel insights not based on data it was trained on, then we've crossed the AGI rubric, and we'll have much, much bigger issues to figure out that go well beyond the scope of this book.

A simple query to four of the most-used LLMs, including ChatGPT, Gemini, Claude, and Microsoft Copilot, using a prompt of "What are the biggest reasons for data governance programs to struggle?" yields some remarkably consistent responses, all of which have been cited and well known for nearly two decades.

Question: "What are the biggest reasons for data governance programs to struggle?"

Reason	ChatGPT 4.0	MS Copilot	Claude	Gemini
Lack of Executive Support or Buy-in	X	X	X	X
Unclear Goals or Role Definitions	X	X	X	X
Cultural Resistance / Resistance to Change	X	X	X	X
Insufficient Resources or Budget	X	X	X	X
Data Silos and/or Data Quality	X	X		X
Complex Regulatory Environments	X	X		X
Lack of Accountability or Data "Ownership"	X	X		X
Failure to Demonstrate Value	X			
Overly Complex Data Landscape	X		X	X
Inconsistent Data Definitions and Standards	X			X
Inadequate Communication			X	
Lack of Technology or Legacy Systems			X	X
Overambitious Scope			X	
Lack of Training			X	

There is absolutely nothing on this list that hasn't been well discussed in the data community for a long, long time. However, in reviewing the list, you can see just how the limiting mindsets of the data professionals creating the content that was used to train these LLMs has worked its way into their output. The idea that the very challenges that a data governance program is designed to solve are cited as the reasons they struggle, including things like data silos, data quality, or inconsistent data standards, are perfect examples of this.

The learned helplessness that many data teams feel around data quality and a lack of adoption of data governance is clearly being echoed by these LLMs. This helps explain why the AI chatbots are all essentially saying "Efforts to improve data quality struggle because there is no data quality." In essence, these chatbots are suggesting your governance efforts are doomed to fail before they even start – and if such a blatant display of defeatism isn't an example of a mindset that favors the status quo over growth, I don't know what is.

A consistent focus on "lack of executive support," "cultural resistance," "a lack of budget," or "lack of data ownership" all support the idea that forces outside the data organization are a big reason why data governance programs struggle, and all are examples of AI inheriting a mindset from the data it's been trained on. Meanwhile, only a single LLM notes "a failure to demonstrate value" as a reason governance programs struggle. This is unfortunate but a clear indication that the LLMs are simply repeating the beliefs most widely embraced by most CDOs and within most data governance content available online today.

Don't get me wrong – these answers from LLMs are entirely reasonable given the body of knowledge on data governance that exists within the data world today and is widely available across a wide variety of content channels. I was quite surprised by a lack of any overt hallucination in any of the LLM's answers, and every assertion from the LLMs I queried could be supported by content that is widely available today across any variety of analyst, vendor, consultant, or social media websites.

What's noteworthy is that these answers from LLMs all affirm what is already widely accepted and embraced. But that's the problem. We've been embracing these exact perspectives for years, and little has fundamentally changed in the tactics we use to overcome them.

When a variation of the same question is framed in the positive, where the same LLMs are asked "What are the keys to a successful data governance program?" the answers are highly consistent and are typically the inverse to the negatively framed question.

Question: "What are the keys to a successful data governance program?"

Reason	ChatGPT 4.0	MS Copilot	Claude	Gemini
Executive Sponsorship and Buy-In	X		X	X
Clear Vision and Objectives	X	X*	X	X
Resources and Budget			X	X
Data Stewardship/Ownership & Accountability	X	X		
Data Quality Management	X	X	X	X
Data Governance Framework	X	X	X	X
Cross Departmental Collaboration	X		X	X
Data Governance Technology	X	X	X	X
Ongoing Training and Education	X	X	X	X
Metrics and Continuous Improvement	X	X	X	X
Adaptability to Regulatory Changes	X			
Cultural Alignment			X	X
Phased Implementation			X	
Effective Communication			X	X
Clearly Defined Policies & Enforcement			X	X
Compliance and Security			X	X
Data Inventory / Catalog			X	X

Once again, only one LLM out of the four raised the issue of business value, where Microsoft Copilot suggested that having a clearly defined business case is a key to data governance success. Generally, even when framed in the positive, the answers to the question are largely consistent.

Across both queries I was rather surprised, at least on first glance, how prevalent and consistent the issue of technology is within the answers. Yes, technologies can be highly effective to help scale and automate a governance function, but across my many interactions with data leaders, the core challenges (and opportunities) are rarely associated to a lack of technology – they are typically people and process related. Even in situations where the LLM is recommending something that isn't technology (like continuous improvement), there is text in the answer that recommends using technology to enable it. When you drill into provided citations, it quickly becomes clear on why the LLMs are so focused on technology as an enabler of data governance success – they appear to be pulling much of their insights from content posted by data management and governance software vendors.

Another interesting phenomenon in the responses to the positively framed question is the ubiquity of the belief that end-user training is a key to data governance success, especially since a lack of training is cited by only a single LLM as a reason for governance programs struggling. I hypothesize that this is a function of the popularity of data literacy and the prevalence of online content related to it. The consistent promotion of the idea that the data skills of business users is a key dependency to the success of a data governance or management program from thought leaders, analysts, and vendors helps to explain why end-user training is something the LLMs see as a key to governance success. I find it interesting that the LLMs all use the word "training" and not the word "literacy." This is purely speculation, but it's entirely possible they avoid the word "literacy" given its highly judgmental tone. If true, then having an LLM express more empathy in how they describe the skill levels of data consumers as compared to data producers is quite remarkable.

Would a CDO who fully implements all the recommendations of these LLMs have a successful data governance program? Yes, I suspect they would. There are notable concerns with how many of the recommendations are framed in that they would validate any CDO who embraces an external locus of control (and therefore, an extremely limiting mindset), but the recommendations from the LLMs are not the problem. These recommendations are well known and have been widely communicated for years.

The problem is *how* CDOs are going about implementing these recommendations and that they are being implemented in data organizations that embrace a culture rife with mindsets that promote the status quo. There is plenty of data to suggest that even though these recommendations have not fundamentally changed in more than a decade, they still have merit. Yet, when many CDOs attempt to follow these recommendations, they do so within a culture that drastically limits their effectiveness. Behaviors of data leaders and team members who see negative intentions in others or blame others, or any other mindsets that prioritize the status quo, will ultimately sabotage any effort to deliver meaningful change and results.

There is a better way. There are tactics and perspectives that all data leaders can begin to integrate to their data teams – today – that will help to pivot their teams from limiting mindsets to more positive, growth-oriented mindsets. The example shared earlier of the drastic changes at Microsoft that are a result of an increased adoption of growth mindsets shows that if the biggest company in the world can do this, all companies can do this.

Are you ready to become the data hero of your organization? Let's do this!

Chapter 6
Putting Your Customer at the Center of Everything You Do

Since the creation of the data and analytics function in companies, data practitioners have battled with a tendency to focus on *how* they support their customers to justify their existence, and not why. As discussed earlier, this inward focus on the mechanics of managing and governing data in lieu of a focus on customer needs is a major contributor to the overly limiting mindsets which drastically hinder our data organizations today.

The most important thing for any CDO is not the data or how it's managed, *it's customers*. The first step that all data leaders must take in their migration toward becoming their company's data hero is to put the customer at the center of everything they do. In his book *Hit Refresh*, Microsoft CEO Satya Nadella highlighted the criticality of taking a customer-centric view when he said, "First, we needed to obsess about our customers. At the core of our business must be the curiosity and desire to meet a customers unarticulated and unmet needs with great technology."[1]

---
[1] Nadella, S. (2017). *Hit Refresh*. Harper Collins.

Nadella rightfully acknowledges that obsessing about customer needs is a dependency to drive a culture of growth. This focus opens the door to new ways of thinking about the data function. It enables a transition away from highly insular and outdated approaches to which disempower data leaders and reinforce suboptimal mindsets, to methods that are focused on growth, innovation, and the delivery of business value.

Throughout this book I've intentionally used the word "customer" to describe the consumers of data and analytical insights. The first step to putting customers at the center of everything is to start using the word "customer" to describe those who benefit from a data function. Yes, internal customers are also business stakeholders or users or beneficiaries, but using the label of customer helps to establish a producer–consumer dynamic that acknowledges the power dynamic in the relationships is not one of equals. It's one where the consumer has the ultimate say in what they need to optimize their processes, systems, and products. Using the word "customer" is also the recognition that if the customer is not happy (or not realizing value), then the data producer is failing, and changes must be made. How we use words is important, and as data people, we should know this as well as anyone.

A rabid focus on customer success will best position data leaders to break the negative feedback loop of feeling undervalued or underutilized. This will happen because of a focus on building solutions they know customers want to use and would otherwise happily pay for. If you're only building things you are confident your customers need, then there's little room to be building things that just sit on a digital shelf and never get implemented. This is all a function of embracing a mindset that puts the customer at the center of the data function.

Let's remember from Chapter 1 where you are a small-town baker with a struggling business. If you put the customer at the center of everything you did, the minute your business started to falter you would immediately turn to your customers to better understand why they were not buying your breads. You would survey your customers. You would actively seek feedback on every aspect of your business. You would have conversations with both previous customers and any prospective new ones. You would develop an intimate understanding of the needs and desires of all your customers, across all groups and types of potential buyers. You would learn what they want, and what they don't want – and you would adjust your business to best meet the needs of the customers which most closely align to your passions, your expertise, and your capabilities.

Most important, you would be constantly seeking candid feedback and deeply integrating it into your operations and your products. Embracing a growth mindset by actively listening to customers and putting their needs in front of your own is what will best position you to realize business success – and that's also what will best position a CDO for success – and it all starts with a focus on serving customers.

Let's dive a bit deeper into the different approaches and behaviors that CDOs must embrace to implement a customer-centric data organization.

Become Customer Driven, Not Data Driven

CDOs are in the business of managing and governing data and producing analytical insights, but these things describe *how* CDOs deliver value to their business, and not why. The "why" is ultimately about helping customers deliver more revenue, make their businesses more efficient, or mitigate business risks. An internal and insular focus on how data people provide value is a big reason why so many data teams struggle to escape the status quo.

Heroic data leaders see the notion of being "data driven" for what it is – a distraction that helps to support a very limiting mindset by promoting the misguided idea that data is more important to companies than business process excellence. It's an inward focus on how data gets used in a company, and not why. The key to breaking free of these mindsets is adopting a customer-first approach that acknowledges data is an enabler of customer and business success, and not the reason most companies exist in the first place.[2]

When you put the customer at the center of a data function, it quickly becomes clear that it's not for data leaders to try to push or enforce an agenda of the company to become more "data driven." When you are relentlessly focused on customer success, there is no need to expend excessive amounts of energy trying to promote or enforce the use of data within an organization or to try to shame customers into more widespread use of data. Instead, that energy can be focused on better understanding what customers want and how data or analytics can fulfill those needs. Customer-facing data leaders don't need to expend energy trying to persuade people across the organization that data is important. Yet, this mindset that efforts must be expended to push a data-driven agenda, and a data-driven culture, is exactly what drives many data organizations today.

> "The first thing a customer wants to know is what value do I get? Am I getting some return on my investment? Am I increasing revenue? Am I decreasing operating costs? What is the value? They want to start with the value first. . . for the products that do work out, they tend to work out partly because the Chief Data Officer or the head of Product is working directly in tandem with sales and marketing to create a narrative, to tell that story of value to the customer, and making sure the customer has a very simple and crystal clear understanding of how this dataset or this product is going to help them achieve the outcome they want to achieve".
> Saleem Khan, Chief Digital Product Officer at VettaFi;
> CDO Matters, Episode #18

Put another way, data leaders who are not focused on their customer's success are trying to "push" a data agenda in their organizations. CDOs need to push their companies to adopt data. Data managers

---

[2] The exception here is a company where the primary business is selling data. Even if this is the case, the focus of anyone in any product or analytics role should still be on customer success. Data is simply an enabler of that success.

must push the sales organization to stop taking data entry shortcuts. Governance teams need to push business users to "own" data.

So much of what many data leaders promote is the idea they need to actively promote a "data culture" in their organizations, and – over time – this has created a foundation where many are entirely focused on what others must do, and not what they must do. This is the definition of an external locus of control, and it's a hallmark behavior of those who embrace the status quo.

However, when you put the customer at the center of your data function, you will create an environment where the success of the customer will help to "pull" the data function along. This is not to say that there isn't some role for the promotion and marketing of a data function. Even companies that are extremely customer focused still have a marketing function. Yet, it's worth considering that most enterprise-wide data functions have very little internal competition – not unlike our baker friend from Chapter 1.

Individual business functions can (and often do) have their own data teams, but those teams are typically focused only on the needs of that individual domain. The domains of cross-functional and enterprise-wide data management and analytics are a monopoly at most companies, and it's a monopoly held by a centralized data team under a CDO.

This means there's less value to widely advertise or "push" the value of the products of a data team. What should be promoted within a data team is the idea that the success of customers matters more than anything else and that everyone in a data function is focused on the "why" of customer success. Instead of pushing others, data leaders must look inward and ask their teams to start focusing on customer success and enablement. Creating a culture that supports and enables customers, instead of one that is pushing them to act, will be a key outcome of a customer-first approach.

The first step toward creating this environment in a data team is to widely embrace using the word "customer" to describe the benefactors of a data function. In lieu of using the phrases "data driven" or "data first," heroic data leaders will instead use the phrase "customer driven" to describe their missions and their organizations. Over time, the notion of customer centricity will be baked into every aspect of a data strategy and supporting operating model.

Focus on Customers and Their Business Processes, Not Technology

A second step in the journey to focus on customer success is to deprioritize the role that technology plays in the support of a data function. Technology is critical to allow a data organization to scale, but it's another example of a focus on "how" and not "why."

I'm not suggesting technology isn't important. It most certainly is. What I am suggesting is that data teams today place far too much focus on technology as the first consideration when evaluating their key initiatives for a given year. Having less focus on technology will require heroic data leaders to first consider the needs of customers *before* jumping to any conclusions about the technology needed to solve those needs. This requires developing a deep and intimate understanding of the business processes and decisions that data are supporting. One could call this the improvement of the "business literacy" of a data team, but a more productive phrase to describe an increased focus on outcomes over technology is building better customer insights.

A good test to ensure less of an initial focus on technology is for a CDO or CIO to require everyone on the team involved in a major initiative to answer the question of "What business problem(s) are we trying to solve?" as a prerequisite to any serious consideration of a new technology. Understanding the business problem that is being solved should be the "north star" of every significant undertaking of the data function, all the way from the data strategy to every detail of the operating model – including the data governance program. If the CDO or any other leader involved in evaluating any new technology solution cannot articulate the business benefits of that technology, this is a clear indication that there's insufficient understanding of the customer's needs.

Creating a formalized process for answering this question can be accomplished by mandating that a business case must be created before there can be any serious considerations for new technologies. In the world of software development, such a document may often be called a "business requirements document" (BRD), and it helps to ensure there is a reasonable justification for building software in first place. Requiring a similar document within a data team is entirely reasonable, as it will help to ensure there is a valid business problem/opportunity and that the expected cost of any new technology is justified. The importance of this document will be touched on in greater detail in Chapter 7.

Assume Positive Intentions, Have Empathy

In their journey to put the customer at the center of everything they do, a third behavior that data leaders must individually adopt, and promote across their teams, is to start assuming that others have positive intentions. The best way to do this is to build meaningful connections between people in data roles and between those who consume data or analytical insights in a company.

An example here would be to promote programs such as job sharing or job shadowing. Heroic data leaders would create programs that require data team members to take an active role in understanding the motivations and needs of those who are reliant on data. The simple act of standing behind somebody and watching as they create a new record in a software application can go a long way to helping understand the many data and system-related roadblocks that people in an organization face every day. Even greater empathy will be promoted when there are personal relationships developed between people in data teams and everyone who creates or consumes data in their company. Creating programs to get data professionals out from behind their monitors and in front of their customers, where they can hear firsthand of how data is used or created, should be a top priority for any CDO who is looking to become more customer driven.

In addition to engaging customers in their work environments, CDOs could require all their teams to have once-a-month brown-bag sessions where people from across the organization come to give a presentation on the tools and processes they use in their daily jobs. They could come to show how they create new supplier or customer records, or they could come to provide insights on how they use dashboards. The goal would not necessarily be for the customer to come and provide specific requirements to the data team (although that would certainly be one side benefit). Instead, the goal is to provide insights on how the customers of data teams interact with the tools and systems they use every day.

In some situations, job exchange programs are also a potential opportunity – especially for those in more governance and data management roles. It is entirely conceivable that anyone in a data governance function could spend a day or two in the role of those people in business functions who are responsible for managing business processes where data is being created or consumed. For example, many sales organizations have some form of sales operations role, where a requirement for that role is to ensure sales opportunities are accurately captured and managed – typically using CRM software. There are equivalent operations-centric roles in Finance, Procurement, HR, and many other business functions – where data for employees, assets, vendors, suppliers, and a myriad of other data domains is being created, reviewed, or approved. Having data governors or managers doing these jobs, even if for a day or two a month, could go a long way to helping those within the data team to build more empathy with their customers.

There is no shortage of other tactics that data leaders can take to break their own functional silos and more directly engage their customers. The goal of these activities is to break the barriers between data teams and their consumers and to create personal relationships with data creators and customers. When people in data roles are better able to understand the travails of others, it's far more likely that they would see the actions of others as being generally positive. Data team members would come to learn that everyone is typically doing their best with the tools and constraints they are given and that inconsistent or lower-quality data often has nothing to do with the actions of individuals with ill intent. They would see that people are often making difficult trade-offs that put a premium on speed over quality, not because they don't care about data but because they believe they are doing what's in the best interests of the company and its customers.

Better Aligned Incentives and Success Metrics

For many data leaders, the transition toward more customer centricity will face significant hurdles, and one of the biggest is the fact that many CDOs lack incentives tied to customer success or satisfaction. Often, many data leaders have incentives that are tied specifically to the deployment of new technologies, including data management software or cloud computing infrastructures.

Moreover, even if there's a CDO who fully believes in the benefits of running her organization as a profit and loss center, the reality is that there would be significant changes needed in the operating models of most data teams to support such a transition. This means that heroic CDOs who are looking to become more customer centric must take progressive and incremental steps toward the adoption of incentives which more closely align to customer success.

The most critical step here is the implementation of a value engineering function within a data and analytics team, supported by skilled value engineers. If there was one role most critical to changing the overall trajectory of the data function in any company, it's the value engineer. I will go into greater detail on the criticality of this role in Chapter 7 when discussing data product management, but to get to a point of having incentives tied to successful customer outcomes, data leaders must be able to measure the value that their products provide.

Once CDOs are confident they can accurately measure the value they provide, even if those measures are only for a single business domain or function, they can then engage with leadership to begin having conversations about adjusting annual performance metrics more aligned to customer success. Many today have some form of variable compensation tied to overall company success, but in this case, the incentive would be specifically aligned to the KPIs of a given business function.

The same is true if the CDO was hired specifically to fulfill a given business mandate, like a digital transformation. The CDO would leverage their value engineers to understand and quantify how improvements in data management or governance would support the KPIs of the mandate for which the CDO is responsible, and their incentives could be aligned accordingly.

Beyond value engineering, significant other changes within the data team would also be needed over time, including many of the other recommendations noted in this chapter. Making one of the changes I'm recommending is certainly better than making none – but it's the combined impact of making all of them, over time, that will yield the greatest rewards. And making one change, like assuming positive intentions, will help support making other changes, like having incentives tied to customer success. All these recommendations will support and magnify each other.

> "One of the things that John Smale, who was the CEO of Proctor and Gamble, used to say back in the eighties was 'you are what you measure, and you measure what you reward.' This was his way of saying we are as a company what we pay our people to do. So, if we say we are all about environmental issues and diversity and social good and we pay our executives on quarterly profits, your message is a lie. Your charter is a lie.... We optimize the pay of our executives on short-term lagging indicators, and it's disastrous in the long term."
> *Bill Schmarzo, Author of* The Economics of Data, Analytics, and Digital Transformation*;*
> CDO Matters, *Episode #30*

Voluntarily abandoning performance incentives unlinked to customer success in lieu of metrics that many data leaders erroneously believe are impossible to generate requires courageous leadership. And it's that type of leadership that is needed for companies to realize, once and for all, the truly transformative value of data.

Proactive Engagement and Feedback Loops

Heroic data leaders who seek to put the customer at the center of everything they do must proactively engage with customers and build feedback loops so their input is captured and actioned. There are many ways to approach this critical need, one of which I'll go into significantly more detail in the following chapter.

One approach to engage customers that I don't always recommend – but one that is commonly used – is to take more of a service desk approach to managing customer requests. These efforts often follow ITSM standards, which are commonly used by IT support functions and help desks. Not unlike many bakeries where you walk in an take a number, "tickets" are given to customers who queue up for support, where each request is quickly triaged and assigned some sort of service level (with appropriate follow-up times, often based on service-level agreements). There may be *some* data products with support and cost models that justify a service desk approach, but these will most certainly not be the norm at most companies.

There are many problems with taking this type of service desk approach in a data function – the biggest one being it's clearly not proactive. Customers must come to you for help or with requests, which means the onus is on them, not you. This is highly problematic, and taking such an approach will likely only reinforce overly limiting mindsets and not break them.

> "Asking those questions of customers that stimulate thought, asking those questions that get people to turn that diamond over and to try to gain either a new concept or a new aspect of an existing concept – that opens the door for you to be able to gain their trust, to gain the credibility that is so necessary."
>
> Dr. Joe Perez, CTO CogniMind;
> CDO Matters, *Episode #56*

A critical aspect of developing more of a growth mindset is the ability to receive candid feedback, where that feedback is viewed as both a gift and an important dependency for guiding future efforts.

CDOs seeking to drive these improvements must adapt their processes and tools so that all feedback is systematically captured. It's important to note that feedback can take many forms and is not limited only to what you will hear directly from the mouths of your customers.

Customer feedback can also come indirectly, often through usage and adoption metrics. A lack of adoption of a given dashboard, especially one that has been requested by a customer, is a clear indication there's a need that dashboard is not meeting, there's a problem with the data, a requirement was missed, or that the product design was suboptimal. In many ways this type of feedback is as important as the feedback you'll get directly from customers, especially in organizations where the relationship between producers and consumers of analytical insights is highly dysfunctional.

> "I would recommend what is the most prevalent use case to get you the most exposure. If you've got a long list and somebody's given you a lot of money to do this, they are going to want to present some kind of early success story to say 'Look, this stuff is actually working.' My conversations are usually around what's going to get you the biggest bang for the buck. And then ensure whatever you're doing is also part of the same foundation you build for everything else."
>
> *Doug Kimball, former CMO of Ontotext;*
> CDO Matters, *Episode #26*

Revisit Organizational Structures, Roles, and Responsibilities

A final important step that heroic data leaders must take to become more customer focused is to revisit their legacy organizational structure, supporting roles, and core operating model. Changing the overall mindset of the organization is the top goal, but putting the right structures in place to allow more positive, growth-centric mindsets to blossom will drastically help accelerate the process.

When considering the operating model of a data team, there's been a tendency over the last several years for organizations to struggle to find the right balance between more centralized, IT-led data and analytics functions and less centralized functions. This has resulted in many companies oscillating between the two extremes, where an excessive pivot toward one end of the spectrum will eventually result in a reactionary pivot back to the other.

The battle between these extremes is easy to understand. Companies see the value of having some central control over data (especially given much of it is widely shared across functions), but they also see the benefits of allowing business functions some degree of autonomy over their own analytics. The popularity of the data mesh, which is very much a focus on hyper decentralization, is a testament to the widely held belief that centralized data teams are ill-suited to best support individual business functions.

An excessive focus on centralized data and analytics teams, often within an IT function under a CIO, without an equal focus on supporting business functions, will inevitably lead those functions to take matters into their own hands. Analytics teams will form in marketing, finance, supply chain, and other business functions, and they are increasingly commonplace.

The existence of "shadow" data teams is very much a function of the failure of more centralized data teams not having a customer focus, or a growth mindset. Created without the input or engagement from a central data team, the existence of these teams inevitably creates additional friction between the central team and data consumers within business functions and is a recipe for a highly inefficient approach to the discipline of data and analytics.

> "I'm a strong believer in centralized data management and decentralized analytics. I know there are situations where it's just not physically possible by sheer number of people, but I think they only way to truly standardize on the language of data, it has to have very strong guardrails... . Common definitions and conceptual models, this is what this thing means, and this is where you

can get data about it. As an analyst or a data scientist, you go to the same place to get the same data as everyone else."

Veronika Durgin, VP of Data;
CDO Matters, Episode #35

Data leaders seeking to optimize their organization around customer success will shun the see-saw oscillations and instead embrace a hybrid operating model that is both centralized and decentralized, typically what is known as a *federated approach*. The need for this approach is the recognition that not all data is created equally. Recalling the three-ring Venn diagram from Chapter 4 (see Figure 4.2), there is a strong business justification for the management of some data as a shared, cross-functional asset. There is also a strong business justification for the management of some data to be highly decentralized, with complete "ownership" at a business function level, given much of that data will never be used anywhere outside that function.

It's worth highlighting the differences between decentralization and federation. A federated approach to data management is one where there is autonomy over data management and governance at a local level, but there is also some notion of a more centralized management function to play a coordination role between the business units and local needs as compared to those at more of a regional or global level. Fully decentralized approaches lack any sort of global or regional coordination of data management and governance.

Company size will play a role here, where smaller companies will struggle to realize the full benefits of federation since they'll be unable to justify positions dedicated to data-related jobs when there is already a presence of a central data team within IT. I can't provide any magical insights that correctly estimate the size of company needed to justify having dedicated data roles within business functions, but in my experience, once a company starts to hit close to a hundred million dollars in sales, it's more likely they would be able to justify having an employee doing analytics outside of a centralized IT team. Often, this person comes out of some operational role within that group (like sales operations or marketing operations) and, at the beginning, will usually wear multiple hats.

Once data teams start to proliferate within business functions, the connection between the centralized data function and the various federated functions must be purposeful and managed. There must be roles within the federated data teams that report back into the central function, where those individuals are responsible for ensuring continuity and consistency in the management of data, the creation of data products, and the governance of data shared across business functions.

The effective management of the data governance function for data that is widely shared within an organization may be one of the more difficult yet critically important roles in a customer-centric data team, and it's something discussed in greater detail in Chapter 7. This is also where I detail my recommendations for all the changes needed within data organizations, including the various supporting roles that together will create an environment best-suited to foster more growth-centric mindsets across the organization.

Suboptimal data roles and responsibilities are not the root cause of the mindsets plaguing our organizations, but they certainly help to play a reinforcing role. This is why when considering the organizational structure and supporting roles needed to create a customer-centric data team, data leaders should be ready to take some bold steps. This is particularly the case for any role where direct customer interactions are required, such as data governance, business analysis, or project management. We'll discuss these changes in more detail in Chapter 7.

Chapter 7
Integrating Product Management as a Discipline Within Data and Analytics Teams

The second critical step for data leaders to take in the evolution of their teams toward more growth-centered mindsets is to deeply integrate the discipline of product management within their organizations. When it comes to my passion for product management and my fervent belief that's a critical ingredient for data leaders to build teams that embrace more positive mindsets, I come by my opinions honestly.

> "We've been talking to customers about data products and data product management, more specifically, for a number of years. And getting there was almost like trying to create an organization that uses agile in its deepest form – the methodology agile, not being agile. So it's quite a transformational thing that needs to happen to become fully agile in the same way it's quite a

transformational thing to become fully product led with how you think about building solutions to solve problems."

Jason Foster, CEO of Cynozure;
CDO Matters, episode #45

For the first half of my career, I was focused on a product management path, including most of my time at AOL and several years that followed. Working up the management ranks at AOL I stumbled into product management, where I quickly learned that I was both proficient and passionate. I absolutely love solving complex problems, and the harder the problems are, the more I'm motivated to solve them. This meant that product management, which involves deciphering a complex web of interconnected influences that are constantly changing, turned out to be a perfect fit for me.

I've held the title of "product manager" (or a leader of product managers) for more than a decade. I know the field extremely well and even have direct experience where the products I was managing, while at both Hoover's and Dun & Bradstreet, were data products. I've led teams that have built complex customer-facing websites, reporting systems, software applications, and even APIs. It's this combination of more than a decade of product management experience and 20-plus years' experience in the world of data that gives me the confidence to say that the integration of product management into the world of data management will lead to a massive improvement in the performance of data functions.

Great product managers can go both "deep" and "wide" across a variety of disciplines spanning the production, marketing, and consumption of a product – which requires them to understand nearly every operational aspect involved in running a business. The most important knowledge they can develop, however, is a deep appreciation for the needs and wants of their customers. It's this focus on understanding customers that makes product management a great, and I believe necessary, step in the evolution of any data team – especially one built around more positive, growth-centered mindsets. But developing more of a structured approach to understanding customers on data teams is not the only reason why integrating the discipline of product management into a data team is a great idea.

Thinking back to Chapter 2, when discussing many of the ways that limiting mindsets are manifesting in data teams, the discipline of product management is a powerful antidote for almost *all* of them. This is because product management provides a time-tested framework that allows those who adopt it to quantify the trade-offs involved in producing a good and the benefits a consumer realizes from it. There is very little that is "all or nothing" in product management, as every consideration made by a skilled product manager exists on a spectrum that requires a balance between competing forces, like price and quality, or speed and durability. Accountability is inherent to the product management role – as products will either make money or lose money. Product managers must lead broad and diverse teams of people who do not report to them and must find ways to unite a group under a common cause – often when those group members may have incentives not fully aligned to those of the product function. Ironically, the key traits that make product managers successful are strikingly like what CDOs consistently cite as their primary reasons for failure. But unlike the CDO role, the role of the product manager is well established, well understood, and has been well proven to deliver value over time.

The P&L North Star

An entire book could be written focused only on how to fully integrate the discipline of product management into a data team – and I suspect this will be my next major writing effort. But for now, my goal here is to share some high-level and high-value actions and perspectives that all data heroes can start integrating into their data operations. The first involves a thought experiment. The experiment goes like this:

> "If you had to run your data and analytics team as a profit and loss (P&L), where you put a price tag on every product or service you provide and where sustained consumer demand for those products and services was critical for your success, could you operate profitably?"

Given the depth of my knowledge of the data function at companies today, I can confidently assert that most data organizations are a *long* way from being able to operate as any form of viable P&L. This is not a judgment; it's a very well-formed opinion. And there are likely many among you who would have some strong opinions that say that data teams, because of their place as a "shared service" in an organization, should never be subject to the same level of operational scrutiny as a product organization. You might be right, but arguing the merits of the thought experiment isn't the point.

The point of this thought experiment is that it provides an excellent lens through which to evaluate your overall team strategy, and your evolving product-centric operating model. It provides a "forcing function" that you can use to help better understand if your actions as a data leader are moving your organization closer to being customer and product centric or farther away. Running your data team like a P&L would necessarily require you to deeply understand:

- Your customer needs and problems
- The best solutions to meet those needs
- The cost of building the solutions
- The amount a customer would pay for those solutions
- The time and money needed to support/train your customers
- Your customer retention and satisfaction
- The organization needed to build, market, and support your customers

Solving all these interconnected forces is the very essence of product management. You know what customers need, you build and deliver solutions to meet those needs, and both parties experience a net positive value exchange. This may sound simple enough – and it conceptually is – but successfully executing a product strategy isn't that simple. The long list of very high-profile product failures, at some of the most successful brands on the planet, is a testament to the difficulty.

> "My definition (of a data product) is more of just taking a product management approach to data. And if that's at the table level, the report level, or the Excel spreadsheet level – I don't really care what level it goes to. It's more of an understanding that this product, what we put together, will have a beginning, and middle, and an end."
>
> Eric Zwiefel, former CDAO at Microsoft Americas;
> CDO Matters, *episode #41*

Still, there is valuable guidance in thinking of their organizations as P&Ls for data leaders, and there are steps they can take today to slowly move their organizations in this direction. Keep in mind that I'm not suggesting you need to *immediately* adopt a P&L approach within your data functions. I'm instead recommending that slowly evolving your product strategies and overall operating models toward something that could – in theory – successfully operate as a P&L will help better position your organization to reap the benefits of more growth-centric mindsets.

When you distill all the critical success factors of product management noted earlier into a single theme, it's the idea that value realization is the ultimate driving force of any potential course of action. And these forces have very little tolerance for mindsets that are focused on anything other than building great products. When you apply this into managing a data team, I am confident that over time the results will be transformational.

Hire a Product Manager

If there was only one recommendation I would make to any CDO looking to leverage the benefits of product management within their organizations, it would be to hire a skilled product manager. The connection between hiring a product manager and promoting more positive mindsets rests in their ability to implement the processes and methodologies that will pivot the data team from a technology focus to a customer focus – where accountability for quantifiable customer success is a hallmark of the role. Rather than blame others for the inability of a data team to provide business value, a successful product manager would own the blame – and would seek the feedback needed to make the improvements needed to improve their products.

Thanks to the growth of the popularity of data products, the last two years have seen a significant increase in the number of people with the words *data product* in their titles – most particularly the title of "data product owner." In my experience, most of these people have been repurposed from other legacy data and analytics roles, often out of data governance, business analysis, or project management functions. Unfortunately, just changing the title of somebody to "data product owner" is not the change I'm suggesting.

I recommend hiring a skilled product manager into a data team, with an established background in product management. It's a distinct discipline requiring specific skills that people with data backgrounds typically do not have. While it's certainly possible to train a data person to become a product manager, that person is not likely to get the training they need from within a data team. For this reason, in most situations I would assert that it's far easier, and far more efficient, to hire somebody with a product management pedigree than to upskill an existing employee. Also, training a product manager on data, from within a data team, should not be a major undertaking. The discipline of product management is transferable to any industry or product, and the idea a product manager would need to adapt their skills to a different type of product (or industry) is commonplace.

There are likely many smaller data teams, where it would be difficult for a CDO to justify a dedicated head count to a data product manager. While it would be impossible for me to draw a hard line for what this size of team would be to justify a product manager, I suspect that any data and analytics function at companies with under several hundreds of millions of dollars in revenue would potentially fall into this category. Still, even for these companies, finding ways to implement the perspectives and approaches outlined here, and that are supported by the discipline of product management, would be highly beneficial.

One of the primary benefits of hiring a skilled and experienced product manager is that they could help train the rest of the data organization on the methodologies that product managers utilize to understand their customers, define their needs, and build profitable products. A key part of their responsibilities would be to define and implement a product management framework – adapted to the specific needs of a data and analytics team and embracing all the key tenants discussed here.

> "Monetization is an interesting discussion, as there is value to the data. It is an asset, and we're starting to think of our data as products. . . . (We) are just standing up our product management organization. We have a master data management product manager. We have a catalog or metadata management product manager. We have a visualization product manager, and we're standing up a business operations product manager. And I am sure we will have many other roles in the product space as we evolve."
>
> *Justin Magruder, CDO of SAIC;*
> CDO Matters, *episode #12*

This means any CDO would need to approach the inclusion of a product management function very much from the perspective of that person being a change agent in the data organization. They would need to be empowered to recommend and implement significant changes and would need to have the leadership skills needed to influence those changes across the entire organization.

Embrace User- and Customer-Centric Design Methodologies

One of the many changes a skilled product manager would help to integrate to a data and analytics function is a focus on user-centric design (UCD). In product management, user-centric design is a critical function within the process of understanding customer requirements, where real users are directly engaged to best understand their needs. It will follow a very hands-on, iterative process where product designs are proposed and tested with users, where user feedback and alignment are required before any product can be released into a production environment. This will also include product usability testing, which will ensure the design of any customer-facing interface is easy to navigate and use.

In my experience as a product leader and manager, some of my most enlightening moments have come during UCD sessions and usability tests. Many of these insights were surely the difference between building an average product and a great product. As a natural problem solver, I take great pride in being able to translate user needs into product requirements – but as diligent as I've been during those processes, I've always learned more through UCD sessions than I could ever have learned simply by asking questions of my customers. This is especially the case with heavy dependencies on user interfaces, where you could only learn of how good (or bad) your designs are until you put them in front of actual human beings.

There are two key deliverables of user-centric design: functional requirements and user interface (UI) or user experience (UX) requirements. The first refers to the features and capabilities of your product, and the second refers to its overall usability. As a product manager I've used several different methods to capture functional requirements using UCD principles, but perhaps my favorite has been a process created by the design company IDEO (www.ideo.com). I have fond memories of holding day-long UCD sessions with my customers to develop a deep understanding of their needs. For anyone with a more positive mindset, the collaborative, problem-solving nature of these sessions, which are firmly rooted in having empathy for customers, is an exceptionally rewarding experience.

I also have vivid memories of spending what seemed like countless hours in a UX lab in Dallas, Texas, doing usability testing for the products I managed while at Dun & Bradstreet. The lab was a rectangular room, where the back wall of the room was made entirely of frosted, one-way glass, where on one side, users sitting in front of computers would interact with our proposed designs and be given a specific task. On the other side of the glass, our product team (including me as the product lead) would observe what the users were doing, gauging how easy (or hard) it was for them to accomplish the task. We would rely on basic designs and largely nonfunctional wireframes, but the interactions would very closely mimic what we believed would be the optimal given our captured requirements to date.

I can't recall a single major test conducted in that room that did not result in a significant change to both the UI requirements, and the functional requirements. This is proof that it's impossible to fully understand how anyone will interact with a product until you put that product in their hands. This is just one of the many benefits that a product management function will provide to a data and analytics team.

In addition to building better, easier to use products, this focus on user-centric design methodologies will help data leaders to instill more positive mindsets within their teams because of this focus on user engagement and feedback – especially because feedback is a requirement of the process. The highly collaborative nature of UCD sessions, both for functional UX requirements, will also help to promote more positive mindsets, given collaboration is a hallmark of more growth-centric individuals. Data teams previously not sufficiently engaged, or getting an insufficient level of feedback from their clients, will immediately benefit. This will help data teams to evolve, to build better products, and to increase customer satisfaction.

The criticality of user-centric design in building products that the customer wants to use is often lost in environments where CDOs have consciously chosen more "do it yourself" (DIY) product delivery models, often under the guise of the "democratization" of data. This is not to say that a limited number of customers, especially those in organizations that business functions have their own analytical resources, will not prefer DIY models. Many will. However, even in these situations, there should be a rigorous amount of user-centric design and usability testing on the systems, processes, and data that will be accessed in the process to ensure that every step of the data product lifecycle works. Just turning end users loose on a data catalog and giving them access to a BI tool is not serving anyone's best interests.

Hire a Value Engineer and Measure the Cost and Benefit of Everything

Another key component of a focus on integrating the discipline of product management into a data and analytics function is a requirement to hire a value engineer (or possibly several of them), where the primary responsibility of this person will be twofold:

- Measuring the costs of the data and analytics function, including the costs related to all data products and services
- Measuring the business benefits realized by all data products and services

When you combine these two measures, it becomes clear the role of this person will be the measure the ROI of the data and analytics function within your organization.

As I noted earlier in Chapter 6, I suspect that many of you who are reading this are possibly thinking "It's impossible to measure the business value of data." But I'm here to tell you, *it is not*. You can measure anything – including the "intangibles" of a business, like data. Providing specifics on how to develop measures for the value of data (or a data product) is beyond the scope of this book, but I invite you to check out *How to Measure Anything* by Douglas Hubbard, or *Infonomics* by Douglas Laney. Both will give you a good head start with some practical methods you can deploy to start measuring the business value of data.

> "The first thing a CDO would need to assist their teams with on data quality is coming up with a compelling business case. . . . In the beginning of that, you know you're going to need to spend some money to do that, but you don't actually know (yet) what the benefits are going to be up front because you don't know the

extent of the problem. Coming up with that compelling business case is a key thing a CDO needs to be supporting the team with."

Robert Hawker, author of Practical Data Quality;
CDO Matters, *episode #47*

Many of you may also be wondering why quantifying the value of data is necessary given your CFO, and the Generally Accepted Accounting Principles (GAAP) they follow, does not recognize data as a balance sheet asset. The answer here is simple. Our businesses run on financial measures, and just because your CFO or the accounting profession doesn't (yet) recognize data as a balance sheet asset doesn't mean that you shouldn't measure its value. Your business is scored on profitability, and I strongly believe our business functions should be, too.

Thinking back to Chapter 4, the ongoing refusal of CDOs to measure their value acts as a wellspring for the promotion of highly limiting mindsets in your organizations because it promotes and supports a lack of accountability. The antidote to this source of negativity, and the primary reason why you need a value engineer, is to measure the value of your data products and services.

In quantifying both the costs and benefits of your data products and services (which would necessarily also include all the core data infrastructure and management costs), the value engineer must combine a relatively rare combination of analytical acumen and also interpersonal skills. This is because they will need to work extremely closely with their customers to understand how data is being operationalized, and the downstream impacts it's having on business effectiveness. This also means a value engineer must have a strong grounding in your business operations and understand how all the functional major drivers of a business (like finance, procurement, marketing, etc.) "fit" together to support complex cross-functional processes.

Figure 7.1 shows a tool I've used extensively in my many conversations with CDOs and other data leaders to help them visualize the difference between data metrics and business metrics. These connections must exist at multiple levels, starting at a business and data strategy level and working down all the way to individual fields of data. As there are connections vertically from strategic metrics to transactional data, so too are there connections between business metrics (like customer satisfaction) and data metrics (like the quality of a customer record).

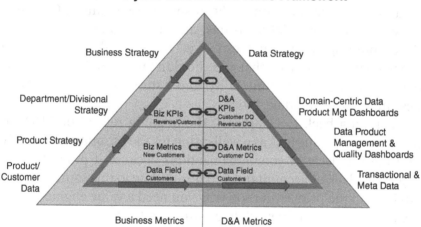

Figure 7.1 The Data and Analytics Metrics and Value Framework

This pyramid graphic is a useful tool to help more senior-level executives to conceptualize how they could start to model the impacts of their work, but a value engineer would need to take this high-level framework one step further – and dive deeper into individual KPIs.

> "What was beautiful about the Salesforce culture was the fact they have this V2MOM process, which is basically this top-to-bottom down publication of all the business strategies across the entire company. So, what is Salesforce at the top level, at the Mark level? What is he focused on? What are the goals, what are the objectives? And even what the measures, the KPIs they are trying

to hit. This goes to his directs, and their directs, and so on. You get this roll up of what every single person in the company is working on.... For somebody like us in the data field, it became really easy for me to start to quantify where we are providing data value.... I could align really easily into those business strategies."

Wendy Turner-Williams, former CDO of Tableau
(acquired by Salesforce, Inc.);
CDO Matters, episode #36

One of the more useful tools I've used in the past when managing value engineers to provide the detail necessary to map all the influences data have on business performance is a business value driver map (see Figure 7.2).

As you can see in Figure 7.2, these maps can tend to get complex, but on the bright side, there will be three key factors that will help to limit the scope related to building value maps for any value engineer:

- The Pareto principle will apply – where 80% of the value of data will come from 20% of the data, which will typically align to "master" data (like customer, supplier, product, etc.). This means you don't need to map every field of data for every business process – only those that are driving the most value for the business.
- There are many industry-standard models value engineers could use as a starting point.
- Business leaders will typically have a limited number of specific KPIs they are measured on, which will provide a natural prioritization for any value engineer trying to understand how data is influencing those KPIs.

Much to my chagrin, the role of a value engineer is not widely adopted today, especially within data and analytics teams. And like the role of a product manager, this is not a role I would recommend that any CDO attempts to develop internally from within their existing team. It's a unique skill set, where the backgrounds and experience of these professionals are typically from a finance or accounting function.

Example Performance Driver Tree

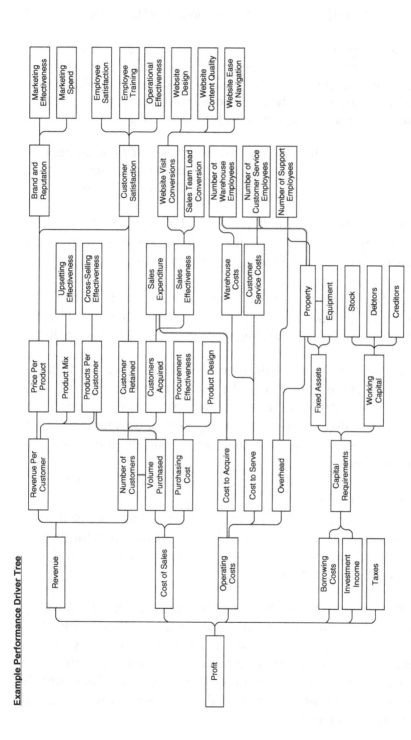

Figure 7.2 Business value driver map. https://www.superchargedfinance.com/blog/how-to-define-value-drivers

This combination of a limited supply of skilled people and a relatively unique skill set means it could be a challenge for CDOs to recruit for this role, but I simply cannot under-emphasize the criticality of it. If data teams are to get beyond the paralyzing grip of limiting mindsets and begin the process of assuming accountability for the value they provide to their customers, then having a specialist who knows how to model the impact of better data on business performance is critical.

On the bright side, there are individuals within organizations today who have very similar roles and who could be easily repurposed to support a data function. The two places where these professionals will most likely be found are within financial planning and analysis (FP&A) functions, or product management roles – and more specifically – product-centric roles focused on pricing. In both roles, you will find highly analytical individuals who have the skills to develop the models necessary to measure the impact of indirect forces on the business, and they'll likely have the skills and behaviors needed to actively collaborate with others in helping to create their outputs. A great starting point for a CDO, especially one in a small or midsize company, could be to approach their CFO to request support from an FP&A function in helping to create a business case for a larger-scale data initiative.

> "My plea to data leaders is really think about the business value that means the most to your leadership, and communicate your changes, challenges, and improvements based on how those value drivers are performing."
>
> *Anjali Bansal, Sr. Director of Analytics, Cervello;*
> CDO Matters, *episode #55*

Like many of the recommendations I'm making for future data heroes in this book, I could write an entire book on the single issue of quantifying the business impacts of better data – and perhaps one day I will. My goal here is not to educate you on how to build detailed business value driver maps or value models but to stress their importance and to illustrate that doing so is both feasible and critical.

Implement a "Go to Market" Function; Repackage Governance and Literacy

Any organization centered around building and selling products will necessarily need to include what is known as a go to market (GTM) function. A typical GTM function will "live" in a product management organization, and one designed for an internally facing data and analytics function would include the following:

- Defining and executing a GTM strategy and plan
- Understanding buyer personas/ideal customer profiles
- Defining and communicating the product core value prop/product marketing
- Customer enablement and support (to replace "data governance")
- Customer training (to replace "data literacy")
- Product pricing
- Channel/product distribution
- Marketing and PR
- Metrics and feedback/analytics

I purposefully highlighted that my recommendations here are for an *internally facing* data and analytics team because the GTM roles are substantially different for companies externally marketing and selling their data products. Additional GTM responsibilities, like performing competitive intelligence, are needed for these companies. However, for companies where data *is* their core product, I would naturally assume that they are already deeply embracing product management.[1]

Once again, we find the focus on customer success and the need to constantly adjust the GTM strategy and plan based on customer

---

[1] If you're interested in taking a deeper dive around the nuances of being a CDO at a company where data is the primary product, I would invite you to check out a conversation I had on my podcast, *CDO Matters*, with Saleem Khan, the CDO of Discovery Data.

feedback as the two primary reasons why implementing a GTM plan will play a meaningful role in the pivot of a data organization toward more positive mindsets. GTM plans are living, breathing practices that must be constantly adjusted based on what the product managers are learning from their customers. The requirement to seek feedback and adapt your product and GTM strategies based on that feedback will require the data team to formalize processes to quantify and manage customer feedback. This requirement will lay a foundation from which to make feedback a necessary and critical aspect of the daily operations of a growth-focused data team.

It's important to note that GTM functions are typically bound to specific product launches or lifecycles, and the requirements of one GTM product may differ completely from another. For example, the training requirements for a highly customized data product, built for a group of highly skilled users, would be completely different than the training requirements of a product built for a broad audience of users with less data knowledge.

The experienced product manager you hire to own responsibility to implement the broader product management discipline within your team should be expected to have experience in managing a GTM function – even if they may not have direct experience in owning any one individual aspect of it. A key to success in adopting a GTM function will be to start very small and grow the capabilities within your product team slowly. I recommend an initial focus on *two key areas* that I believe will have outsized impacts on your ability to promote more positive mindsets in your organization.

Changing Your Data Governance Function to a Customer Enablement Function

Data governance is a critical enabling capability of any data and analytics function, yet most data governance programs struggle to provide any meaningful value beyond the basics needed to ensure a data organization complies with regulatory or audit requirements. A central theme within the definition of the word *governance* is the concept of control, and I firmly believe it's the perspective of data governance as a control mechanism, when implemented and managed by in an organization dominated by mindsets which limit growth, that's severely limiting its value as a program.

The current challenges of data governance run much deeper than just a marketing or PR problem. I touched on the inverted nature of the cost/benefits of data governance earlier in Chapter 4, which helps to reinforce a negative perception of data governance by those subject to its controls. It also helps to ensure organizations will continue to only do the minimum required to conform – and often substantially less. When implemented by data teams rife with mindsets that embrace the status quo, the approach to implementing these controls – some of which are tied to regulatory requirements – tends to align with frameworks that haven't been meaningfully updated in decades. The operating models supporting these governance programs are typically top-down, focused on analytics only, one-size-fits-all, and completely out of step with how those subject to the controls run their businesses. It's a recipe for a disaster that's playing out right now in hundreds and hundreds of companies across the globe, and it's a big reason why so many CDOs are struggling.

The way out of this stalemate is for data leaders to find a way to treat data governance more like a service. Thinking back to the idea of a P&L "north star," apply the same thought exercise to the world of data governance. What would be required for a business unit to want to engage with a data governance program – and even possibly be willing to pay for it?

This may sound entirely too far-fetched to anyone who's been in the world of data and analytics for any length of time, but I don't believe it is. And I believe a great place to start with this transition is to stop calling it "data governance" and instead call it "customer enablement." The key transition here, which will play a growing role in shifting the mindsets of those managing governance programs, is the focus on *enabling* customers – and not controlling them through data use or access policies. It's 100% correct to assert that a simple name change won't be nearly enough to meaningfully alter the trajectory of an industry as large as the field of data governance, and you would be right. Over the years we've fallen prey to making superficial changes to our programs under the guise of remarketing (or renaming) them, and that's most certainly not what I'm advocating here. Far from it.

What I am advocating is a holistic, service-oriented approach that would include all the recommendations I'm making in this book. If you deeply commit to shifting your data organization to embrace positive mindsets, through a focus on customer centricity and product management, I will argue you would necessarily need to change your approach to data governance toward one more focused on customer enablement. A continued focus on governance as primarily a control mechanism will be anachronistic to your goal of customer success.

> "People are already governing their data, through ownership and accountability being devolved to the end user of the data. There is this funny thing that happens, whereas as soon as data is in an IT managed system, like Tableau of PowerBI, suddenly the onus is on IT, the responsibility and accountability for the data. And I've never really understood why."
>
> *Bethany Lyons, principal consultant at Assured;*
> CDO Matters, *episode #25*

The insights needed to completely pivot a governance function from one that is focused on enforcing rules to one focused on customer success is yet another topic that could require the focus of an entire book. Figure 7.3 is a quick summary of some of the positive, growth-centered perspectives that a data team would need to embrace when making this shift.

When taking more of an enablement focus to governance, data product managers will most certainly encounter situations where the need of one customer does not align to the need of the other – and where the data used to fill that need is shared across them. Misaligned needs and incentives are a big problem in governance programs today, especially with legacy programs that try to enforce a "one-size-fits-all" approach to governance.

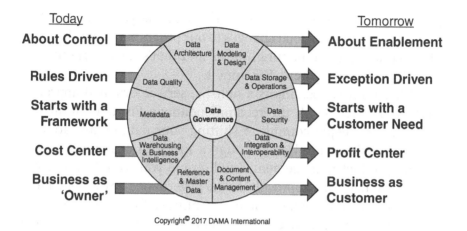

Figure 7.3 Growth-centered perspectives

However, under a product management model, the proposed economic benefits of any customer request are well quantified and well communicated. In the case of conflicting needs, a focus on product management would require the need with the highest ROI to the organization to take precedence. It may also be the case that the ROI of developing distinct data products for each customer need may be economically viable, even if it's operationally less efficient.

In "one-size-fits-all" approaches to governance, where data teams are run only as cost centers, there are heavy incentives for the leaders of governance programs to avoid duplicating efforts and to seek as much reuse of data, tools, and processes as possible. I've seen this play out many times with enterprise MDM programs – where there is a business need for many versions of "truth" for a given domain, but, thanks to a centralized, top-down governance program (which is focused on keeping the costs of managing data as low as possible), the budget will essentially allow for only one version of truth – which often aligns to the CFO version of that truth.

Taking a customer- and product-centric approach to data governance will promote positive mindsets and make your governance program far more flexible and adaptable than they've ever been. A rules-driven approach will necessarily need to give way to an approach that opens the door to having multiple sets of rules based on the benefit they provide to the company.

Your C-suite, your CFO, your regulators, and your auditors will continue to remain your customers, and you'll very obviously need to make them happy through the ongoing enforcement of data policies – which you will. But in a data organization that embraces product management staffed with people who have positive, growth-centric mindsets, keeping your regulators happy will not necessarily need to come at the expense of everyone else.

It will also remain true that you'll continue to have data that is widely shared across functions and processes, where there will need to be some consensus between organizations on the management of that data for your business processes to run as efficiently as possible. Unlike what's been proposed by the data mesh, the sharing of data (and by extension, the policies used to manage that data) across functions will not simply organically evolve. There are practically no incentives in the business for that evolution to take place. This means there will remain a role for a centralized data team, supported by a product manager, to work with both groups to determine the best solutions possible.

Changing a Data Literacy Focus to a Customer Training Function

In a data organization dominated by positive mindsets, where the focus is building extremely well-designed products that customers want to use (and would be willing to pay for), I would fully expect that the need for a training function will be marginal – but likely still necessary. All good GTM functions have a training or customer enablement component, both for internal and for external users. However, unlike the perspective embraced by most data literacy programs, an experienced product manager will not assume that a lack of customer skills is the biggest problem faced by data customers from day one. Instead, the skill levels of customers would be well known and well in advance of the creation of any new product. Those customer skill levels would play into the overall design and usability of the product, where the product manager would balance the development and design costs needed to build a highly intuitive product that didn't require any training versus any costs needed to train users on products that may somewhat be less intuitive.

In a data team where a legacy "data literacy" function is subsumed into a GTM function, there is a holistic focus on building products that are easy to use and at a cost that justifies the expected benefits. However, even in situations where a product manager is fully aware of the user skills, has done the best job possible to ensure their product has gone through rigorous UI/UX testing, and likely even significant prototyping, there are likely going to be some situations where customer training is required. This training function will become the evolution of any company focused today on data literacy, where investments in training customers on data "methods and processes" will be eliminated, where those efforts will instead shift toward investing in building better products that provide quantifiable value.

> "You need to understand how the organization is making money and saving money, and you need to be able to connect your data work as directly as possible to how the organization is making or saving money. And if you are not able to express that, you're not being successful. Period. And I think that's the shift we need to have. And to do that, you need to understand how the business works. We always say data literacy, but how about business literacy?"
>
> Dr. Juan Sequeda, principal scientist at data.world;
> CDO Matters, *episode #8*

The need for customer training or enablement function is typically going to be greatest at the time a new product is launched, but a commitment to training must happen at a programmatic level and extend beyond the initial product launch. New customers are constantly joining the organization, and their skills and capabilities are also evolving over time. A product management function necessarily needs to support the training needs of all customers across all phases of the product lifecycle. In some limited situations, where regulatory concerns demand it, there will likely be some requirements for mandatory customer training on data products or services, with regular recurring certifications. Again, these requirements would generally be well known in advance of the implementation of any new product or governance policy and would be integrated into their supporting GTM plan.

Separate Data Management from Data Product Management (and GTM)

One of the bigger challenges faced by any data and analytics team that may consider the implementation of product management into their organization is the reality that today, data teams are responsible for both procuring and processing their raw materials *and* building their products. In a globalized world where organizations are incentivized to hyper-specialize, there remain very few large companies with this span of control over both their supply chains and manufacturing processes. These companies are known as "vertically integrated," and the best example of these would be large energy companies, particularly oil and gas – like Chevron or Exon Mobile.

Conversely, almost all data teams are vertically integrated and control both the extraction and processing of raw materials and the creation of finished products. However, drawing a hard line between the creation of raw materials and finished goods is largely not how most data teams function today. Instead, the operating models of most teams take the approach of managing data through a continuous pipeline, where data is moved, manipulated, and published in a continuous process. Raw unrefined data goes in one end, and some form of consumable data, often in the form of analytics, comes out of the other.

There is some growing focus in the analytics world on what many would call a "medallion" architecture (which classifies data as either "bronze, silver, or gold" depending on where it is in a data management process), and it's a useful tool to understand the "state" of data within a data pipeline. However, the idea that data could be both a finished good that a customer might be willing to pay for, and a raw material used within another product, is perplexing to many – especially within data teams long beguiled by "all-or-nothing" patterns of thinking. The fact data can be both a raw material and a "finished good" is at the heart of much of the ongoing debate and confusion around the definition of data products.[2]

I recommend CDOs looking to leverage product management to promote more positive mindsets in their organizations are well served to organizationally separate classic data management functions from data product management. In the context of building great products customers want to buy, for all intents and purposes, most data management functions align to a data supply chain – not product management. Separating the supply chain from the product development process will ensure there is clarity on who "owns" the satisfaction of the customer within a data team, creating greater accountability, and promoting more positive mindsets.

Making this separation will add one more level of accountability in a data organization that does not exist today. Resources that today work on the creation or refinement of data raw materials will need to become accountable to product managers, who will need to collaborate with data stewards, data modelers, or data engineers to ensure the methods used within the supply chain are creating the raw materials needed to create great products. This separation partially exists today in terms of the separation of data management from analytics functions; however, CDOs looking to promote more positive mindsets by having more clearly defined lines of accountability in their organizations should make this separation more overt, and well communicated.

---

[2] In episode #62 of the *CDO Matters* podcast, I go into detail around the issue of the definition of a data product. Check out https://profisee.com/podcast/cdo-matters-ep-62-data-products-demystified.

Evolve Your Organization Toward Customer and Product Centricity

The last major consideration for any data leader looking to utilize the discipline of product management to promote more positive mindsets is the organizational structure and supporting responsibilities that will best enable this transition. Mindsets are manifested in people but also in groups, so the way a group is aligned to task – which in our case is building great data products – will have a significant influence on the ability to shift the mindset of a large group.

In this chapter I've already touched on some of these more critical roles, including the product manager and the value engineer. I've also recommended the separation of product management from classic data management. If there were only three changes you, as a senior data leader, could make to your data organization after reading this book, those are the top three I recommend.

However, when looking at the broader data and analytics function and typical organization, there are many other changes that I am confident will best position CDOs and other leaders of data functions to support a transition toward a more customer and product-centric organization rooted in more positive mindsets.

Let's start at the top, with a high-level review of a potential organizational chart that I believe is well suited to support a product and customer-centric focus (see Figure 7.4). Please keep in mind that unless you are F2000 company, it's highly unlikely any one of these noted responsibilities will justify a dedicated full-time employee. What's being shared is inclusive of all responsibilities and not necessarily the individual roles of the individuals who will own those responsibilities.

Also keep in mind that what is recommended here is best suited for a more centralized data and analytics function managed, typically managed today within an IT function. It's conceivable that many of the teams and roles identified here could also exist within data teams of individual business functions or domains. This would lead to greater domain flexibility, but it would also lead to significant inefficiencies at a cross function or enterprise level, which could ultimately lead to more centralization over time.

It's important to remember that a core premise of this book is that *the* biggest roadblock to data and analytics success is the embrace of overly limiting mindsets – and not inefficient organizational designs or operating models. This means that the constant see-saw back and forth between data operating models of centralization and decentralization (including federation) that we've experienced over the last two decades is very much a symptom of these negative mindsets, and not a cure for them. I firmly believe that if the recommendations made here are widely adopted, that what we consider today as more "centralized" approaches to data and analytics will become wildly successful and that companies will no longer see a need to dismantle these centralized groups in favor of giving individual domains more autonomy – since the needs of the domains will be satisfied unlike any time in the past. In other words, the belief that domain autonomy is a hard dependency for getting value from data will quickly become a myth – all thanks to a more widespread embrace of mindsets that focus on product and customer success.

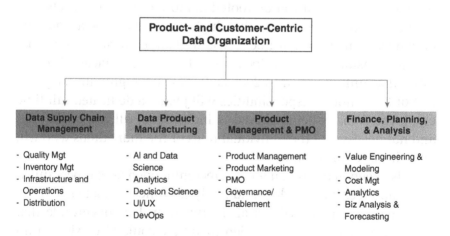

Figure 7.4   Organizational chart

Data Supply Chain Management

The data supply chain management team is responsible for gathering, processing, and storing the data raw materials that are used by downstream processes to create consumer-ready data products. This includes data consumed by business software applications. The data supply chain team takes requirements from the data product management team, and the costs of this team are allocated back to specific data products.

This team would include data quality, MDM, observability, and any stewardship owned within a more centralized data team (this model could also be applied to a functional data team, where its more common for stewardship resources to align). This team would also manage any data discovery or profiling and the creation and management of an internally facing data catalog and glossary. This catalog *may* also be used by the product team to distribute data products, but managing the underlying infrastructure of the data catalog would be primarily a supply chain function.

This team would manage any of the infrastructure and operations for both data management and analytics, including any data lakes and warehouses and any supporting architecture for those systems. They would also be responsible for the movement of data through the data supply chain, including any legacy ETL or data pipelines, data integration, visualization, and semantic layers. This team must support the data engineering and "wrangling" needed for both traditional analytics and also any data science functions.

Data Product Manufacturing (or Development)

The data supply chain management team is responsible for gathering, processing, and storing the data raw materials that are used by downstream processes to create consumer-ready data products. This includes data consumed by operational business software applications. The data supply chain team takes requirements from the data product management team, and the costs of this team are allocated back to specific data products.

The data product manufacturing team includes an AI and data science team, an analytics team, a decision science team, a UI/UX team, and a DevOps team. The AI and analytics teams would likely not be any different from how those teams look today in most functions, but the addition of a team focused only on decision science, and on UI/UX, would be new to most. DevOps would be focused on the processes of getting products into production environments and managing those environments.

Decision science is an evolving discipline that seeks to empower the customers of data teams to make better decisions and to solve extremely complex, cross-functional business problems. It is a new approach to the combination of data, classic analytics, advanced analytics and AI/ML, and business process optimization that aims to help provide guidance on how to make better decisions. It also requires the outcomes of those decisions to be quantified and attributed. An effective decision science function would know which decisions led to positive business outcomes and which did not. I would not expect most data teams to have the skills needed to embark on a decision science path today, or even in the very near future, but I am confident it's ultimately where all data teams need to eventually evolve to.

Data Product Management and PMO

The data product management function interfaces with customers from across the organization and defines the requirements needed to deliver value from data products and related services. They define the data product strategy (in close collaboration with the CDO), and they manage the product roadmaps and provide inputs on the raw materials needed to build their products to the manufacturing and supply chain teams. All data products and services have a cost, where those costs are allocated to business units consuming those products or insights. The key role of this team is to define exactly *what* the data and analytics function will build, deploy, manage, and govern each year – which would necessarily require that this team is intimately involved in defining the scope of all major initiatives.

The project management office (PMO) is a shared service, cross-functional group that manages the roadmaps and deliverables for every group in the data function. They are responsible for ensuring all major initiatives are delivered on time and on budget, which means they work closely with others across the team to ensure all efforts are well estimated and adequately resourced.

The data governance function will also live in this team, and their primary responsibility is to ensure both the successful definition and management of governance policies and their implementation across the wider organization. Referring to the three-ring Venn diagram in Chapter 4 that outlines the three "levels" of data governance in all organizations, the data governance team in a CDO organization will have responsibility for the successful governance of all "global" and "regional" data. This means data governors will collaborate with product managers to ensure that governance policies align with product requirements and strategies, and they will closely interact with functional data governance and stewardship resources to ensure successful implementation of all governance policies.

An important distinction in this organizational alignment, and one touched on earlier, is the idea that the data governance function must pivot away from control and toward customer enablement. A great way to help in this transition is to hire product managers to oversee the data governance function, particularly those in manager- or director-level positions who are responsible for data governance today. The focus here is on *positioning the governance function as a service*, supported by a service (or product) manager. Again, any reasonably experienced product manager would be skilled in the process of managing a service (and not a product), given the two are very closely aligned (services are tasked based, products are tangibles). While it's unlikely a CDO would be able to recruit a product manager with deep experience in data governance, training a product manager in the requirements to support a data governance function is entirely feasible. Training any existing governance experts in the discipline of product management would be more costly and time-consuming and, for many, likely unavoidable.

A final, and extremely important function in this team, is product marketing, which is a critical aspect of any GTM program. The primary roles of this function are to support user enablement and training, internal marketing and communications, customer support, and customer satisfaction. The focus on internal marketing and communication is an extremely important one, since it's this group that will need to ensure the rest of the organization is aware of the value the data team is delivering to the organization. This team will tell the "data stories" needed for the wider organization to understand the role that data is playing in optimizing their business and enabling more effective decision-making. This team will also play a critical role in gathering user input via a support function, which will help to facilitate the accountability and feedback loops necessary to promote more growth-centric mindsets across the data team.

Finance, Planning, and Analysis

The fourth pillar of a product- and customer-centric data team focused on building more positive, growth-centric mindsets is finance, planning, and analysis (FP&A). A recurring theme in the discussions of highly limiting mindsets is a lack of accurate insights within most data organizations on both the cost of their services and the benefit they provide to their companies. Therefore, to facilitate the transition toward a data team grounded in positive mindsets, producing this cost/benefit data is of critical importance. This is the function of the FP&A team.

Professionals in the analytics FP&A team will be responsible for providing accurate financial plans and budgets for the data and analytics function and will work closely with customers in both the functional business units and the corporate finance function to gain alignment on budgets and forecasts. They will ensure that the necessary costs for data products and services are accurately passed back to their customers via the cost allocation methods embraced at a corporate level.

The value engineers who are building the cost/benefit estimates for all data products and services will align to this team, so too will business and systems analysts whose job will be to ensure the costs of running a data function, and procuring any new systems or infrastructure, will be supported by expected value as modeled by the value engineers.

Another important function in this team is the analytics group, which like everyone else on this team, is a cross-functional, shared service. The scope of this team is to produce the analytical insights needed to optimize the efficiency (and ultimately, profitability) of the wider data and analytics team. The scope of this analytics group is internal to the data function and separate from the product development team, providing analytical solutions for customers outside the D&A team.

As we discussed in earlier chapters, mindsets can affect individual actions, but in the cumulative, they also affect the perspectives and actions of a group. This means it's imperative for CDOs and other data leaders who are intent on developing more positive mindsets within their organizations to take the steps necessary to create an organization that will be conducive to promoting more accountability, more customer centricity, and more growth. The successful integration of product management as a discipline within the data and analytics function will go a long way to this end.

Chapter 8
Embrace Agility and a Relentless Focus on Value Delivery

One of the more interesting research conclusions reviewed earlier in Chapter 2 shattered the widely held belief that a widespread embrace of a "data culture" is a necessary dependency for a CDO to deliver value. What research shows is that the opposite is true: the delivery of value influences a corporate culture. This necessarily means that a highly effective tool for a data leader to drive the organization toward a widespread embrace of more positive mindsets is to deliver value from data. As intuitive and logical as they may seem, a widespread embrace of limiting mindsets – particularly an embrace of an external locus of control – continues to enable many CDOs to assume that cultural forces outside their organization are a much bigger hindrance than the culture of their own team.

The importance of using small successes, delivered consistently and repeatedly over time, as a lever to positively influence the mindsets of the members of the data and analytics function is the focus of this chapter. Here we will discuss the role that taking an agile, iterative approach to defining and delivering on a data strategy will have in promoting more positive mindsets on a data team.

> "There is another word I use often, which is agility. Have agility. Have flexibility in the way you operate. Test things. Learn, and then be able to move in a nimble fashion. Don't be wedded to a particular process for several years and then realize it doesn't work, because then you've just wasted a lot of money."
>
> *Samir Sharma, CEO of Datazuum;*
> CDO Matters *podcast, episode #11*

A key consideration throughout the chapter is the focus on taking a minimum viable product (MVP) approach to product development efforts – both for first iterations of a data product and for subsequent enhancements or improvements. The idea of delivering the simplest version of a product needed to solve a valuable customer problem will also be applied to the process of building a data strategy – a key to success for any data and analytics leader.

The Data Strategy MVP

In the push to develop a team more focused on positive mindsets, data leaders must not forget the importance of a data strategy – which will establish a shared vision for the future and the high-level plan that will be used to reach that future state. In my time as an industry analyst, I had hundreds of conversations with CDOs about their data strategies – where it was commonplace for a new CDO to believe it would take upward of a year to complete a "fully baked" data strategy. At a time when CDO tenures are hovering around 18 months, taking a year to define a data strategy (let alone make any real progress on implementing it) is a foolhardy approach.

A better approach, and one razor focused on the delivery of short-term business value, is what I call the Data Strategy MVP (see Figure 8.1).

DATA STRATEGY MVP – KEY ATTRIBUTES

Figure 8.1   Data Strategy MVP

The Data Strategy MVP consists of two layers. The outer ring includes key organizational constraints that CDOs will not be able to significantly change in the short term (less than 6 months). It is at this level where the MVP data strategy will be defined. The inner ring is the operating model of the data and analytics function, which defines all the critical capabilities needed from a data function to deliver on the strategy.

The strategy starts on the outer ring with the creation of a draft strategy document, which will be the first iteration of a document that will be constantly updated and enhanced over time. Rather than position the existing culture and organizational maturity of the organization as dependencies for a successful implementation of the strategy, taking an MVP approach requires a CDO to assume these are constraints to the strategy, and not something that will be changed in the short term. An MVP approach here would also refute the need for any large-scale maturity assessments or "as is" evaluations from large consulting firms – where I would instead recommend having data product managers directly engage customers to quickly assess the readiness of the organization for any data-related efforts.

The goal for all CDOs or equivalents is to use a team approach, focused on developing a quick understanding of customer needs, the overall business vision and strategy, and existing organizational realities to develop a draft data strategy in under a month. From here, data leaders can move to the next ring down and focus on quickly understanding what is needed to deliver the first of many outcome-driven MVPs.

The inner ring is the operating model of the data and analytics function. For current in-scope, top-priority initiatives supporting the data strategy, it includes the following:

i. Success Metrics and Business Cases
ii. Scope, Approach, and Roadmap
iii. Data Governance Model
iv. The Data and Analytics Organizational Model
v. The Data and Analytics Product Management Discipline
vi. Enabling Technology and Infrastructure

Ultimately the delivery of the strategy and operating model is the responsibility of the CDO (or equivalent), but that person will need to work in close collaboration with several members of their teams through the entire process described in this chapter – most notably their product and project managers, and value engineers.

When it comes to data strategy, two key foundations of the Data Hero Mindset are that culture is best influenced by the delivery of value, and that a data strategy *must* be a living document that is entirely grounded by the ability of the data organization to deliver value. What this means is that I strongly recommend most efforts of a CDO who seeks to leverage the power of more positive, growth-centric mindsets should be on their operating model, and ensuring they are able to deliver on whatever promises they make to the organization. It is through the successful delivery of value that the company culture will tilt in the favor of a CDO and the paralyzing impacts of limiting mindsets will be negated – so the focus must necessarily be on the inner ring of this framework.

This is not to suggest CDOs don't need to understand the overall, company-wide vision, strategy, and goals. They absolutely do. And they must also ensure that their efforts are reasonably aligned to these higher-level strategies. However, keep in mind that culture and maturity – two critical influences on your strategy – are outcomes, and not dependencies of your strategy. The MVP model states that as you increase your operational excellence and your ability to deliver value, your culture and maturity will necessarily improve, as will the mindsets of everyone in your organization. With this in mind, let's dive more deeply into the critical aspects of any data and analytics operating model.

Success Metrics/Business Cases

Taking an MVP approach means that CDOs will not define *every* potential outcome from every potential data initiative for their organization but, instead, a limited number (I suggest no more than three) of material business outcomes that could be enabled through the products and services enabled by their team within the next 9-12 months. These outcomes, which necessarily would be measured by existing business KPIs, would optimally be defined in close collaboration with functional business leaders who are willing and able to partner with a CDO. This partnership would also include a willingness to fund the work, through whatever cost allocation or chargeback methods are embraced by the company.

The importance for CDOs to work with customers who want to partner with them is critical, especially for newer CDOs who have yet to establish a track record or in situations where limiting mindsets may be running rampant (and the organization has a lot of "learned helplessness" around getting value from larger data initiatives). In these more jaded organizations where there's been a longer history of a failure of data teams to provide meaningful value, data leaders must do everything in their power to stack the deck in their favor, and that includes picking the right customers. In some situations, this may require a CDO to focus on an early-stage initiative supporting a business function that may not clearly align to the top priorities as defined in the corporate strategy. In this situation, getting the support of the C-suite on this potential divergence is critical, as working with a partner customer who is heavily invested in your success, and supportive of your efforts, is way more valuable than towing the company line.

I've seen far too many situations where a CDO does the right thing by the corporate strategy (or by a CEO or CIO edict) but ends up having to partner with a reluctant and disbelieving customer who subsequently ends up sabotaging or subverting the efforts of the data team. This happens far too often, and for a CDO working to ingrain more positive mindsets, trying to force or manipulate a customer who doesn't want your help will end up doing more harm than good.

Picking the right customer doesn't mean there won't be positive ROI for the company – there necessarily *must* be meaningful business benefits from every initiative considered in an early phase data strategy, especially if the goal is to leverage business outcomes to influence a more positive, growth-centric culture. It does mean, however, that choosing the data initiatives to work on is not purely a function of those initiatives with the highest ROI to the organization. Other considerations, like the openness of the customer and the feasibility of the initiative, are also critically important.

At this stage, listening to customers and developing a working knowledge of their key challenges and opportunities is of paramount importance. This is why having your product managers deeply involved in this phase, and all phases of the definition of your data strategy, is critical.

Your goal in this phase of understanding how you will operationalize your strategy with your operating model is fourfold:

1) To understand the willingness and eagerness of a customer to want to partner with you on a solution.
2) To understand and quantify the expected business benefits that will come from delivering a solution for your customers.

3) To get to a level of comfort that the solutions needed by customers could be delivered within a reasonably short time frame, optimally within 3 months.
4) To reach a level of clarity around expected benefits, whereby you could prioritize each initiative based on a combination of a willingness to work with you, and expected benefits.

Given you'll have very few specifics to work with from the perspective of the customer requirements – which are most certainly bound to change once you get further into the development process – the willingness of the customer to adapt and work with you in the absence of crystal clear specifics is also something you also need to pay close attention to.

Once the right customers and potential early-phase initiatives supporting the data strategy are identified by your product manager(s), the CDO would have their value engineers estimate the cost and benefit of each of these deliverables and work with their PMOs (who are taking their inputs from product managers) to develop a high-level understanding of the people, time, and infrastructure needed to deliver on them. This work from project managers, in close collaboration with product managers and value engineers, is the genesis of an early-phase roadmap for the data and analytics function, and it's a critical aspect of taking an MVP approach to a data strategy.

Scope, Approach, and Roadmap

There are many who would argue that including a roadmap as a deliverable within any business strategy is not appropriate and that a data strategy shouldn't be "encumbered" by the constraints of a roadmap – but I strongly disagree. A strategy without a roadmap is an academic exercise and recommending a strategy that hasn't at least been "sized" by a product team increases the chances that it's unfeasible (or impractical) for an organization to readily implement what's being recommended.

Recommending a data strategy that can't be implemented is a boon for any consultants hired to address the "gaps" between the strategy and the operational capabilities of a data function, but the current reality of most CDOs requires a different approach. Most CDOs will have a maximum of two years to both define a strategy and show value from it, so taking the precious time to enrich consultants on any prolonged capability or maturity assessments (which generally follow boilerplate methodologies) seems ill-advised.

The scope, approach, and roadmap for each of the top-defined deliverables in an MVP data strategy will heavily influence other "downstream" aspects of the operating model, including the product requirements and GTM, any necessary governance requirements, and the supporting technical infrastructure. From this point forward in the implementation of the deliverables associated with the data strategy MVP, it's important to remember that an MVP approach is required at every stage and should be applied to every dependency of a data initiative. In other words, when I talk about a product or governance framework, I'm not talking about implementing *all* aspects of that framework. I am only talking about *the minimum amount of that framework needed to successfully deliver on the expected business outcomes defined in the MVP*. Such a focus aligns to an outcome or value-driven approach to defining a product or governance requirements and will best position data leaders seeking to leverage success as a tool for building a more growth-centered organization.

> "Many of the AI achievers have achieved value on the way. So, although they had something they were striving towards, some aspiration, they seem to have incremental value creation on many steps on that way. So that keeps them going, and that keeps them motivated. We compare it to a marathon. So, we have the final finish line in mind, but...we keep running because we have little wins on the way. I think that's a good way of looking at it, and a good learning from many of the AI pioneers and achievers."
>
> Dr. Michael Proksch, *chief scientist at AccelerEd and co-author of* The Secrets of AI Value Creation; CDO Matters *podcast, episode #60*

The main task within of this phase of your data strategy definition is one of analysis – where your product manager(s) are working closely with members of your Data Product Manufacturing team to come up with extremely high-level estimates of the scope of each potential initiative. Once those estimates are in place, they will work closely with project managers and value engineers to make a recommendation on the top three initiatives that will be tackled first based on a combination of the scope, technical feasibility, level of effort, and expected business benefits. These three initiatives will form a "phase one" roadmap in support of your data strategy.

Given that enterprise data teams will be working closely across all major lines of business, the analysis during this phase will likely include far more than just three potential projects. This number will likely be closer to over a dozen (if not more), where those initiatives all fulfill the criteria of a having an eager customer, a well-defined problem that will generate tangible benefits, and can be executed in a reasonably short period of time. Given the goal is to have a high-level data strategy in under a month, it will be impossible to have any sort of detailed specifications on project requirements – but that's not the goal. The goal here is to have a high-level understanding of a limited number of possible initiatives that should be focused on, first – where additional rigor will be applied once development on those initiatives begins to ensure full clarity on requirements.

Any potential initiative not included in the short-term roadmap will need to be added to a backlog of potential projects, which will form the roadmap that accompanies your data strategy. It is reasonable to assume that the total level of effort for all these initiatives will likely begin to exceed two (or more) years, which starts to provide more visibility on the longer-term roadmap for the data function.

The Data Governance Model

In previous chapters I've discussed the problems with taking a more bottom-up, framework-driven approach to data governance. This approach will help to reinforce the status quo and will do little to help ingrain more positive mindsets in the data organization. Instead, data leaders seeking to instill more positive mindsets through the iterative and repetitive delivery of business value must instead focus on enabling the minimum amount of data governance needed to deliver on the expected customer outcomes.

Here's a specific example. Let's assume that as a part of a broader corporate strategy to focus on world-class customer support, a CDO aligns on the creation of a customer "360°" view as a key deliverable within their strategy MVP, where the key business metric being supported is customer satisfaction. The MVP approach here would dictate that the scope of that "360°" view would be the minimum needed to drive meaningful customer value. This means that not every nugget of information about the customer would need to be gathered – only enough data to provide the insights needed to improve customer satisfaction. This means that it's more likely the MVP would be closer to a "customer 180" than a true 360° view.

Taking customer data from across the organization to create a single view of the full relationship with that customer is a classic master data management problem, and it's one I am extremely familiar with. From a data governance perspective, what must be decided is the minimum amount of data governance needed to solve the immediate problem. In practical terms, the minimum to solve a single customer view problem would likely include data governance policies that define the following:

- A cross-functional customer definition
- The data quality standards of the data used in the analysis, both the raw data from the source systems and for the new consolidated customer
- The business rules used for matching disparate customer records together
- The access rights to view the data

This is the minimum data governance work that would be needed for an initiative this size and could be delivered in a fraction of the time as compared to an effort focused on an entire governance framework. This is not to suggest that reaching consensus on a cross-functional customer definition will be easy. Often, this can be a contentious process, given lines of business will be adamant that their definition of the customer is the right definition. Ultimately, the right definition, and the "winning" viewpoint, will depend entirely on who the customer is for these business insights and the business problem trying to be solved. Given that this new 360° view is being built to increase customer satisfaction, the lines of business (LOBs) with the most influence over customer satisfaction (likely product and sales/marketing) should have a disproportionate influence on the final decision.

The responsibility to determine the minimum level of governance requirements for any initiative included in your MVP data strategy will fall to the data governance product manager, and their inputs will be critical to understand the overall feasibility and scope of any initiative. Including initiatives within your strategy MVP that have extremely complex data governance requirements should be scrutinized heavily and avoided wherever possible. One such example is a focus on building an "operational" style of MDM – one where gold master records are pushed into source systems – given the governance requirements for this initiative are extremely complex. This is not to suggest that a project of this governance complexity will never be initiated – but rather – that data organizations that are looking to leverage the power of value delivery to break free from the status quo through the promotion of a growth mindset are best suited to focus on efforts with lower overall failure risks.

The Data and Analytics Organizational Model

I touched on the optimal data and analytics organization and roles needed to support a more product- and customer-centric focus in Chapter 7. However, it's worth noting that the MVP approach also requires data leaders to take an MVP approach to their organization. What I outlined earlier is an optimal "end state" for a data and analytics function, and for any CDO in the early stages of a push to re-architect their team toward more positive mindsets, it may be that they only need to focus on a few key roles or that a very select few people are many different hats at the same time. To me, the *bare minimum* required changes that a CDO should make to a more traditional data organization would be the addition of the data product management and value engineering roles. The other organizational changes outlined in the previous chapter could be phased in incrementally, over time. CDOs building a data function from scratch would obviously have more flexibility, and this scenario does happen with greater frequency at midsize companies.[1]

D&A Product Management

Over the past two years, data products have been close to the top of the hype cycle, and the concept of building products in a data function has quickly gone from relative obscurity to the top discussion point at data conferences. I believe much of this hype is a byproduct of the waning popularity of the Data Mesh, which has "data products" as one of its four core operating pillars.

For better or worse, there is no single definition for *data products* within the data industry. Here is my definition: *A data product is a finished good (or service) created by a data team, built to solve a specific customer problem, that the customer would otherwise be willing to pay for.* However, within the broader data and analytics industry, the concept of data products exists on a spectrum, representing two very different perspectives of the definition of a data product on either end (see Figure 8.2).

On one end (the left side of Figure 8.2), data products exist to help drive scalability and efficiencies within a data function and are created to benefit those customers who would ultimately build analytical insights with them. This view of data products sees them as essentially raw materials that would be used by downstream processes to build more "finished" products, like analytics insights or data science models. I believe this view of data products is held by

---

[1] I had an amazing conversation with Joyce Myers, the CDO of MTSI, on episode #52 of the *CDO Matters* podcast on this very topic. Joyce is building a data function from scratch and has plans to significantly scale out her team slowly over time.

DATA PRODUCT SPECTRUM

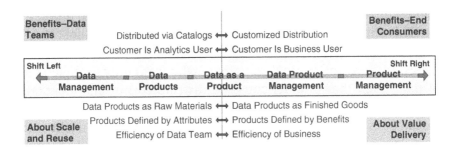

Figure 8.2 Definition of a data product

many data practitioners and was very elegantly detailed in the book *Data Management at Scale* by my friend and *CDO Matters* podcast guest Piethein Strengholt.[2]

At the other end of the spectrum (on the right side of Figure 8.2), data products are end-consumer-ready, finished products that are designed specifically to solve a customer problem. Created through a product management process, these data products are goods that end consumers would otherwise be willing to pay for and have a value that can be quantified and tracked. This perspective on data products is less common but is certainly the view most embraced by anyone with a product management background.

I am a huge believer in a "shift right" approach to data products and see it as having the best potential to drive transformational benefits for companies serious about implementing data products. However, as I noted in a previous chapter, I am also a believer in the benefits that come from the fact that the data function is "vertically integrated," with control over its own supply chain. This means that the optimal focus for a data team integrating a product management function would be to embrace *both* ends of this spectrum. CDOs must

---

[2] Strengholt, Piethein. *Data Management at Scale: Best Practices for Enterprise Architecture*. O'Reilly, April 2023. In addition to his book, Piethein was gracious enough to be a guest on my podcast, *CDO Matters*, where we discuss data products in more detail. Check out https://profisee.com/podcast/cdo-matters-ep-44-data-management-at-scale.

focus on building excellent products, but they must also focus on having a highly efficient data supply chain capable of producing the highest quality raw inputs to any data product or analytical process.

This approach also supports the idea that a data product "SKU" could be created anywhere on the spectrum based on the customer needs. If there are internal customers who want only a single field of data, then that product could be distributed through a catalog and consumed by an end customer. For customers who want more finished, "shrink-wrapped" analytical solutions (like a dashboard or a data visualization), then those could be distributed through customized channels with higher levels of support and training. The same data element sold individually could also be included as a raw material used in a more customized solution.

When considering how to apply an "MVP" approach to data product management, here is yet another area where an experienced product manager will play a critical role in helping evolve your data organization. Any reasonably skilled product manager will have experience in applying more agile methodologies to product management and development and will be extremely familiar with the process of working with customers to determine the bare minimum needed from a product for it to deliver value.

The same is true with building out your product management and GTM functions, where the MVP approach dictates that you apply the minimum amount of these disciplines needed to successfully deliver a product. The GTM model defined earlier is optimally an end state, but taking an MVP approach means you'll focus only on the minimum needed from your GTM program to successfully launch this individual deliverable.

Technology and Infrastructure

One way that data professionals promote the status quo is through an excessive focus on technology. This would suggest that to break the grip of limiting mindsets and the status quo – less of a focus on technology is needed. I believe this is a fundamentally true statement, since data professionals need to shift their top priorities away from technology and toward customer success. But it also doesn't mean that technology won't play an important role in helping to promote a data organization focused on positive mindsets. It most certainly will.

When data professionals put customers first, implement product management, and take a highly iterative approach focused on value, the focus on technology will necessarily need to shift away from one focused on "why" to one more focused on "how." Technology is just one tool that data professionals with positive, growth-centered mindsets will use to support the iterative deployment of great products that deliver exceptional value. Technology will also be levered to drive added levels of scale and efficiencies in the data supply chain, which will help to drive down the costs of their services and deliver more innovative products.

Taking an MVP approach to deploying technology certainly has its merits, but data leaders must also proceed with a certain degree of caution. They must seek input from experienced systems and data architects to ensure that any short-term choices on technology, which lean more toward a focus on an MVP, do not unnecessarily hinder any longer-term efforts to scale the data function in the future. Based on the data and business strategies, data leaders may find themselves in situations where some short-term investments in capabilities that deliver more functionality than is needed in any given MVP is warranted.

Looking back at our previous example of building customer 360, there will be decisions that must be made in terms of what technologies are used to solve this problem. MDM is first and foremost a discipline, and MDM problems can most certainly be solved with or without buying MDM software. You can create a "master customer file" by hand in an Excel spreadsheet and address the core requirements of a "360" using entirely an entirely manual approach, but doing so will be a highly inefficient and time-consuming undertaking. This means there will very likely be a valid business case for a data leader to invest in infrastructure that provides capabilities well beyond what is needed for any one MVP.

Having high up-front infrastructure costs, with the expectation those costs will be fully recouped over time, is nothing new in the world of product management and development – or for that matter – more "traditional" approaches to data and analytics. However, in my experience, once a company hits a certain size and scale and when there is a robust business case built for an investment in data and analytics technology, those business cases for technology investments are relatively easy to justify. There is no single "magic number" to describe the size of company where investing in things like data quality, MDM, or advanced analytical technologies will always be cost-justified, but herein lies the importance of working with your value engineer to quantify the cost/benefit of any investments you make. Either the investment will be justified or it won't.

Wash, Rinse, and Repeat

The MVP approach to defining and implementing a data strategy intent on promoting more positive mindsets in a company requires a repeating, iterative approach as represented in Figure 8.3.

Every iterative release of a data product, service, or infrastructure supporting your data strategy will necessarily drive incremental customer value, which will positively impact the culture of the organization and the mindsets of everyone in it. Optimally, the wheels here turn in cycles of *weeks*, and not months or years. Each turn will be immediately followed by another release, and another chance to deliver value. With each release, your GTM function will be promoting your successes internally across the wider company both inside and outside the data function – as people in and out of your data team will need to be aware of the value you're bringing to the company.

Another important aspect of these iterations is the opportunity to seek feedback and adjust both your data strategy and supporting operating model based on what you've learned in prior releases. A "retrospective" should be part of every MVP, where the organization takes time to adjust their plans based on what's working and what needs additional focus.

Over time, with a continued focus on iterative MVP releases, the data and analytics function will slowly begin to "fill in" any of the

MVP ITERATIVE APPROACH

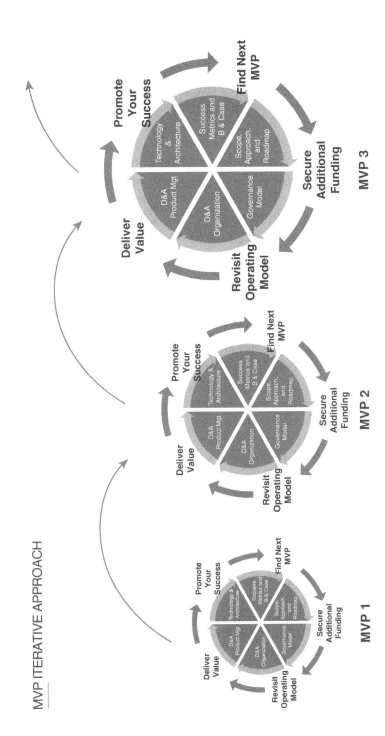

Figure 8.3 Iterative MVP approach

gaps within their governance or product management frameworks – including any gaps around data governance policies, or enabling capabilities of a data product management, or a data supply chain management function. The idea of building and enhancing your skills and capabilities is the fundamental difference between a value-driven approach to implementing a data strategy (which is exactly what I am advocating here) and a framework-driven approach. The value-driven approach requires you to focus only on policies and capabilities needed to deliver value for any one individual MVP, where the totality of any given framework will be defined and implemented slowly over time, based on customer needs. Your skills and capabilities will be built from the bottom up, where the capabilities or governance policies implemented are only those needed to support the delivery of short-term value. On the other hand, a framework driven approach will require you to implement *all* of capabilities required by the framework, a process that (in theory) will never fully end. This means making the implementation of any framework – like the data governance framework defined in the Data Management Book of Knowledge (DMBoK) – a dependency for the short-term success of a data function is a recipe for failure that will only serve to reinforce limiting mindsets.

> "If organizations do not focus on the cultural and foundational aspects of governing, securing, managing, and democratizing data, they will continue to face the same challenges they have encountered over the past decades. While these foundations are crucial, they are often deprioritized because it is difficult for organizations to demonstrate ROI related to these. Based on my experience with hundreds of engagements, I have found that integrating these foundations with business solutions and use cases creates tangible ROI. Also, organizations do not need to wait for a full transformation to realize value. Instead, they should adopt a LEAN Transformation approach, breaking the cycle into 3–6 month increments."
>
> *Emerson Gatchalian, CDO at Microsoft Global Blackbelt, Americas;*
> CDO Matters *podcast, episode #58*

Data professionals taking this MVP approach should expect the scope of each MVP to slowly increase, as they gradually improve their capabilities, teams, and team skills over time. Each MVP release will build on the last, which will subsequently scale the overall "maturity" of the data and analytics function. With each additional release, and each additional delivery of value, the culture and mindsets of the organization will also improve. The organization will gradually shift slowly from one focused on the status quo to one focused on growth and development. Success will breed more success, and mindsets will shift to the positive.

Chapter 9
Look Inward Before Looking Outward

In the previous three chapters I've shared many highly tactical, operational steps that data leaders can take related to the priorities, roles, responsibilities, and organizational structures that I believe will create the most fertile ground possible for more positive mindsets to emerge. Yes, mindsets are very much a psychological phenomenon, but as I've outlined in the previous chapters, there are some very concrete steps CDOs can take to create the organizational "scaffolding" needed to drastically increase the likelihood that a focus on the status quo will give way to a focus on growth and development for everyone in the data and analytics function – including the CDO. These include focusing on customer success, implementing product management into the data function, and embracing a more agile, MVP-driven approach to the delivery of a data strategy and supporting operating model.

In this chapter we'll discuss some of the individual behaviors that all CDOs who want to pivot their organizations toward more positive, growth-centric mindsets should model. These behaviors, and the steps taken to promote them, should be openly communicated and promoted as a part of an ongoing focus on organizational health in the data function – where a departmental priority on building more positive, growth-centric mindsets is openly communicated. Most importantly, these behaviors should be embraced by the CDO and all the data leadership and should be modeled in both words and deeds.

In Chapter 2 I outlined the primary characteristics of people (and organizations) with more positive mindsets. While it would be easy for me to simply say "be more resilient" or "collaborate more" (as we covered in Chapter 2, both resilience and an openness to collaborate are two attributes of people with a more growth-centered mindset), I believe there are other, more foundational behaviors that also need to be embraced. When we model the behaviors covered in this chapter and couple them with the actions outlined in Chapters 6–8, I'm confident that you, and your organization, will be in the best position possible to promote a culture of growth.

The primary theme of this chapter is best summarized by the idea of data leaders, and everyone on the data team must look inward before looking outward. Put another way, CDOs must model the behaviors they want others to embrace and align their actions with their words. In doing so, they will promote a culture of high integrity and accountability that shuns blame and constantly seeks to improve. Others in the data function will see their leaders leading by example, acting in alignment with their stated goal of becoming focused on positive, growth-centric mindsets, and will be more likely to embrace the same.

Be Humble

Very early in my career I managed to somehow convince myself that not knowing something was a sign of weakness and that taking an approach of "faking it until I make it" was the right one. It didn't take me long before I figured out this was the exact wrong approach and that the only way I could be fully open to growing and developing was to admit I lacked knowledge.

In many ways, I was forced into this learning when I took a position leading a large team of highly skilled software engineers for several years during my tenure at AOL. Being a nontechnical person with zero skills at writing code or building databases, I was so deficient in technical acumen that it would have been completely impossible for me to even fake having *any* sort of technical acumen. My team would have seen right through me, and my integrity would have been shot.

> "The mentality of engineers is that they are very skeptical... they almost have a heat seeking missile for spotting people that aren't one of them. You have to understand the persona of an engineer. They are very, very nerdy. (They) are typically very smart, very sharp, and it's kind of like its own competitive game in some ways. It's nerds trying to out-nerd each other. That's just kind of how it is. So, (as a new data leader) you just have to know that upfront, they are sizing you up whether you like it or not."
>
> *Joe Reis, co-author of* Fundamentals of Data Engineering; CDO Matters, *episode #33*

Instead, all my early days as a team leader of a group of skilled software engineers were filled with heaping doses of humility – a behavior that I managed to eventually leverage to my advantage. Since I couldn't even fathom being prescriptive to my team in terms of how we would apply technology to solve a given problem, I was forced to take a different approach. Rather than tell my team how to solve a problem, I became a blackbelt at describing a given customer problem and all our various limitations (time, money, resources) – a skill my team came to value as much, or even more, than if I had the same technical skills they had. The ability to describe a business challenge and customer requirements in extreme detail, in a way that an engineer could act on, was the genesis for my career in product management. It was also an incredibly valuable lesson in the importance of humility, and how being vulnerable to your team and to your customers doesn't make you weak; it can strengthen you.

Embracing humility, accompanied by an openness to being vulnerable in situations where you lack skills or experience, are two behaviors that all data leaders who want to promote more growth mindsets should welcome. This may be discomforting to many, but the rewards that come from your authenticity will drastically outweigh any perceived benefits that come from avoiding that discomfort by trying to be somebody you're not. A majority of CDOs are their company's first CDO, so it makes complete sense that both the company and the CDO are learning together how to get the most from the role. A CDO focused on building more positive mindsets in their organization will acknowledge (and embrace) the newness of the role and its lack of detailed definition but will seek to leverage humility and a willingness to learn as powerful counterbalance to some of the chaos and lack of clarity that inevitably comes with a new role.

I consider humility as a necessary dependency in the quest to develop more of a positive mindset, because, without it, there's always the possibility that you don't believe you need to learn or that you don't need to grow. When you're humble, you admit that it's impossible you could know everything and that it's entirely likely you're wrong – even when you're fully convinced that you're right. This doesn't mean you need to become any less decisive or assertive in your leadership style – it just means you're willing to acknowledge that there are always others who will know more than you, that there is a benefit to assembling a group of people with diverse set of opinions and backgrounds, and that sometimes you'll fail.

> "This shows up all the time when people look at the limitations of statistical modeling. If your data is drawn from a limited set of experiments, you really don't know what would happen in a world in which you can introduce an innovation that's never been done before. So that's a real challenge, and it's an example of the kind of thing we should have some humility about on what we can do with statistical modeling. We can do a great job in predicting other data that are similar to the data on which we've trained

the model, but often, we cannot make any predictions for what would happen in a world where we break how different observables are related to each other."

Chris Wiggins, chief data scientist at the New York Times; CDO Matters, *episode #24*

Embrace Critical Thinking

Critical thinking is the process of actively and skillfully synthesizing information to make rational and informed judgments or to solve complex problems. Critical thinking requires you to question all assumptions and to apply heaping doses of skepticism in your evaluation – which will necessarily require you to assess the credibility of any or all sources of information.

For example, if you hear a consultant make a certain claim, critical thinking will force you to question all the facts used to make that claim. It would also force you to question the motivations of the person making the claim and to acknowledge that other dynamics may be at play that skew the perspective of the person making the claim. Here is an example. If a consultant says "The data quality of companies in the manufacturing sector is poor," then critical thought would necessarily require you to ask these questions:

- How many manufacturing companies has this person worked with, and would that represent a statistically significant sample size of manufacturing companies?
- What methodologies were used in assessing the data quality, and could those methods stand up to any scientific or academic rigor?
- Was the data quality of every business process of every company in the sample measured?

- What would motivate a consultant to make such a statement, and how do they benefit from creating the narrative that the statement is true?
- And on, and on...

Taking this approach would quickly allow you to determine, with relative confidence, that the assertion is a statement of opinion and not a statement of fact – and as stated – is little more than hyperbole.

Earlier in Chapter 3 I touched on how many in the data and analytics industry rely excessively on platitudes, like "garbage in, garbage out," and how doing so promotes mindsets that hinder growth. Hyperbolic statements are closely related to platitudes, and any data leader seeking to engrain more positive mindsets in their organizations should be wary of their use in their organizations – particularly when it comes to people using them to describe the state of data, or data consumers, in the company. The widespread embrace of more positive mindsets in any data organization will necessarily require it to value facts over clichés or overly dramatic assertions. A highly effective tool that everyone can use to sway the organization toward more fact-based decisions and perspectives is critical thinking.

However, since it requires you to question your assumptions, critical thinking requires diligence, energy, and a certain degree of bravery. Rather than assuming something is true, for whatever reason, critical thought requires you to question those assumptions and to apply the effort needed to develop the facts needed for a rational analysis. Critical thinking also requires that any assertion of fact that isn't backed by facts – regardless of who is making the assertion – be challenged. This is where the data hero in everyone will need to emerge, given that assertions of C-level executives, thought leaders, analysts, and consultants would all necessarily be subjected to the same rigor of critical thought.

Given the heroism needed to question authoritative voices, it's easy to see how the status quo can take such a firm grip on an organization – which is exactly what's happened in many data teams today. If the organization doesn't embrace growth mindsets and there are no incentives or opportunities to question authority, then the relative safety of the status quo is logically the best option. Job security becomes a function of not "rocking the boat," and innovation and risk taking become a thing of the past.

Data leaders seeking more positive mindsets would be well served to promote more critical thought in their organizations. This can happen through formalized training and development around the process of critical thought and through rewarding those who embrace those behaviors. More important, people must feel like they have the freedom to question authority and that – if they do – they will not face any sort of negative consequences or retribution for doing so. The most important factor in developing a team of data heroes willing to embrace critical thinking is having a leader who is willing to be questioned and to see those situations as opportunities to grow and develop – and not an attack on their knowledge or authority.

Lead by Example

The most important catalysts in driving the changes needed for any data team to break free from the paralyzing impacts of limiting mindsets are the behaviors of the data leader. The words and actions of the leader set the tone for the entire organization, which means any meaningful attempt to change the culture of the team toward one of growth will require the CDO to lead by example. If the team sees the leader saying one thing but doing another, that leader's credibility will be lost, and the organization may continue to succumb to the gravitational pull of the status quo.

There are several key behaviors and practices that heroic data leaders must embrace in their efforts to lead by example. The first is to actively *seek constructive feedback*. This can happen informally across a myriad of interactions with team members on any given day, including email communications, team meetings, or simply by wandering around the office and asking team members for feedback.

More formal processes can also be put into place, including things like having team members provide feedback to a leader on an annual performance review. I am a huge believer in having team feedback play a role in the evaluation of any leader (and having some proportion of leader compensation tied to those ratings), and the same is also true with getting feedback from customers. If a data team embraces more of a product management approach as I advocated earlier in Chapter 7, implementing the methods to receive feedback on customer satisfaction will need to be put in place, as they are a necessary ingredient in building great products. This customer feedback data could be easily leveraged into an annual review process for a data team lead.

Another important behavior during this transition to more positive ways of thinking is for data leaders to *act with integrity*. In a nutshell, acting with integrity means your words and your deeds are aligned. You say what you will do, and you do what you say. In many ways, acting with integrity means that you'll be modeling the behaviors you want others, both in and out of the data team, to embrace.

There is perhaps no better example of this than the idea of being more "data driven." Putting aside the platitudinous nature of the phrase itself, if you want others across the organization to use data to make decisions, then *you* must also use data to make decisions. The failure of a data leader to use hard data to make decisions will provide evidence to the entire company that the data organization isn't actually that serious about data – and the reputation and integration of the team would be irreparably harmed. This is exactly what I believe is happening at many companies today, largely without the data leaders even realizing it.

The following are the biggest opportunities for data leaders to "walk the walk" when it comes to being more data driven within their organization:

- Creating data to measure the business value of the products and services they provide
- Using these measures of value to help guide and prioritize the efforts of the team

- Using these measures within the incentive plans of the data leader and key members of the management team
- Using these measures to determine and fund the annual budgets for the data function

These are some significant changes that will take time for any data leader to implement, but they will go a long way to aligning the actions of many data leaders with their words. They will also make the job of running a data team infinitely easier – since many of the biggest challenges related to funding, staffing, and customer engagement are significantly assuaged when a data leader can prove the value of the products and services they bring to an organization.

When leading by example, heroic data leaders must also *have empathy* for their customers and their team members – particularly while in a transitional phase toward more positive mindsets. Having empathy and compassion allows data leaders to frame mistakes as opportunities to learn and grow. Having empathy for your team members will also help create a more psychologically safe work environment, where people will feel more empowered to take risks, question authority, share ideas, and admit mistakes. As a result, empathetic data leaders will also create an environment of greater trust, team cohesion, and collaboration.

> "To get people working with you, you need to spend more time listening than anything else, so you can really understand what a day in their life looks like for them. Then probe them with questions to figure out where their data blockers are, what's preventing them from doing their job right the first time, and their frustration points. Then you connect the dots with how governance and good data practices can actually help them get to where they want to be. That's really where I would start."
>
> John Moran, senior director of governance and AI,
> Thermo Fisher Scientific;
> CDO Matters *podcast, episode #6*

The same is true for customers. Heroic data leaders who are serious about healing and growing their relationships with their customers most approach them from a position of empathy and understanding. Recognizing the stress of people's jobs and the many difficult trade-offs everyone must make every day (like the trade-off between speed and quality, for example) is the key to breaking free from the mindsets that embrace the misguided beliefs that their customers lack skill or don't care about data.

A powerful, but simple, tool data leaders can use to develop more empathy and create more trust within their teams is to embrace more active listening skills. Active listening requires that all attention be focused on the person speaking, where the listener avoids any temptation to develop (or verbalize) a response to what is being said until the speaker has fully finished articulating their position. Rather than immediately respond, active listening requires the listener to slow down and invite the speaker to provide more clarity and details through the use of probing, open-ended questions – even after a speaker has articulated their position. These questions are designed to reinforce the belief that the listener is 100% engaged in the conversation and is investing the time needed to fully and completely understand the perspective of the other person. Creating an environment where an employee can be fully "heard" in an interaction with a data leader will help that person to believe that the listener cares and has empathy for the speaker. Listening before speaking and taking the time to fully understand the perspective of another are things we can all benefit from.

A final behavior that any data leader seeking to lead by example can embrace is to become what Satya Nadella, CEO of Microsoft, calls becoming the "learner in chief." Heroic data leaders will set an example for their teams by putting a premium on all opportunities to grow and develop. Again, these actions can be formal and informal. Less formal opportunities will come in every potential interaction with staff and with customers. Embracing simple behaviors, like being highly inquisitive and curious with team members, can go a long way to promoting the perspective that a team leader is sincerely focused on learning. Asking questions, being an active listener, or embracing critical thinking will all show a team that the leader is seeking to assemble as many facts and insights on a given issue as possible.

"We know thing aren't perfect in data and analytics, so there's an iterative mindset. I love the phrase 'learn fast'. Nelson Mandela is one of my heroes. I don't know how many books I have behind me from him, but he had a phrase that went something like this . . . 'I never lose. I win, or I learn. I either win, or I learn.'"

Jordan Morrow, author and SVP of data and AI transformation at AgileOne;
CDO Matters *podcast, episode #51*

A great example of a slightly less formal focus on learning and development, successfully utilized by one of my brilliant peers at Profisee, is a weekly "book club" focused on helping our business development representatives to become better sellers. A book is assigned by the team lead, and every week a given number of chapters are reviewed by the entire team (including the leader) in a group setting, where everyone shares their key takeaways from that week's reading assignments. Not only does this foster collaboration and a better team dynamic, but it's also a great way for a leader to give tangible proof of the team's commitment to learning.

Examples of more formal opportunities, implemented through more structured programs or policies, to express a team leader's commitment to growth, are plentiful. Allocating a proportion of a team's annual budget to individual training is critical (typically as some form of reimbursement for training-related costs), as is supporting the ongoing training of members of the data team. This could include incentives, or even bonuses, for employees who attain new professional certifications. Two such certifications that could help any organization seeking to implement all the recommendations noted in this book would include DAMA's Certified Data Management Professional (CDMP), or the Product Management Certification from the Pragmatic Institute.[1] These certifications would be helpful for both team members and data leaders, especially those with little experience in product management.

---

[1] DAMA CDMP Certification: https://cdmp.info. The Pragmatic Institute Product Management Certification: https://www.pragmaticinstitute.com/product

There is also no shortage of opportunities to learn while attending data and analytics industry events. Two of the events that are particularly good in their focus on learning and development for data professionals are the events hosted by DATAVERSITY, including the Data Governance and Information Quality (DGIQ) conferences, typically held in the summer in California and in the winter in Washington DC.[2] I have attended many of these events over the years (and was given the honor of presenting a keynote speech at the DGIQ Conference in December 2024) and I fully recommend them. For more senior data leaders, the CDOIQ Symposium, held every year in Cambridge, Massachusetts, is an excellent option for both learning and professional networking.[3]

Data leaders could also invest in their own training and development programs for their employees, either in partnership with their HR departments or on their own. These programs could include learning modules for all the key behaviors and practices highlighted throughout the book (above and beyond the skills already expected of a data and analytics team), including product management, critical thinking, and active listening. As a part of a more formalized focus on employee development, heroic data leaders would be well served to support the idea of a specific portion of all employees' time being spent on learning. Even a single hour a week allocated on team members' calendars for training could go a long way to demonstrating the leader's commitment to the development of his team members.

For those smaller companies unable to build their own training programs, there are several commercial options available for data professionals – many of them entirely free. These include the training programs offered by DATAVERSITY, the Data Management University (DMU), and the Institute for Certification of Computing Professionals (ICCP).[4] Beyond these formal training programs,

---
[2] https://www.dataversity.net
[3] https://cdoiq2024.org
[4] DATAVERSITY: https://www.dataversity.net ICCP: https://onlinecourses.iccp.org Data Management University: https://datamanagementu.talentlms.com

opportunities to learn from other data professionals and thought leaders (like yours truly) abound across a variety of online channels, including LinkedIn, Substack, and even YouTube. If you're looking to find free training on just about any data-related topic online, you will find an abundance of it.

As a part of any recurring team meetings, especially those focused on reviewing quarterly or annual performance, data leaders could further exemplify a commitment to learning by allocating a portion of those meetings to a review of the "key learnings" for each employee. Just as employees will typically review any key accomplishments toward company, department, or customer goals, they could also include any new learning as one of those key accomplishments. Those learnings could even be included as required deliverables for every employee within their annual goals.

A data leader who embodies the "learner in chief" mentality openly publicizes their own growth and development goals and their progress to that goal. They are also humble and admit situations where they may lack knowledge in a certain area. "Faking it until you make it" simply isn't an option for any 'learner in chief' who is acting with integrity. Like challenging authority, being vulnerable about your own shortcomings requires bravery, which is yet another reason why I'm calling anyone who embraces these behaviors as data heroes. The mindfulness and fortitude required to lead by example won't necessarily be easy, but the rewards will be transformational for both the leader and the team.

A final opportunity for CDOs to lead by example is to be highly *mindful of the words and language they choose*. Wherever possible, data leaders should seek to frame issues in the positive, and not the negative. For example, it's quite common for data professionals to talk about customer "pain points" or challenges. Those same issues could just as easily be framed using more positive words, focused instead on benefits that would come from resolving those issues. Another example is something I touched on previously, which is consistently referring to data as "garbage." Simply using the word "*opportunity*" instead of *challenge* may sound subtle but in the aggregate, and over time, can go a long way to helping promote more of a positive focus within the business.

> "If we call them issues, if we call them pain points, if we call them friction points, all of these kind of have a negative connotation to them, right? And then the businesspeople who have been successful are (saying) 'wait a minute – are you calling my baby ugly?' In reality, what we're doing is pointing out opportunities for improvement. Sometimes it's just finding that right switch of language, from pain to opportunity. You have to find the language that resonates."
>
> Joyce Myers, CDO MTSI;
CDO Matters podcast, episode #52

Those taking the steps needed to become a heroic data leader must tread a fine line between highlighting improvement opportunities and being perceived by their team as somebody who is being overly critical or negative. A critical aspect of any journey to embrace more of a growth mindset requires people to question the status quo and challenge approaches that no longer serve both individuals and their companies. When leaders challenge their teams to do things differently, they need to be intimately aware of the degree to which many people are deeply invested in the status quo and that all change is inherently discomforting. This will require leaders to be constantly mindful of the words they choose, their overall tone, and the framing of the narratives or stories they use to support their case. This will require energy and diligence, and it will require leaders to seek constant feedback on their effectiveness.

Make Room for Failure

It may seem slightly counterintuitive to assert that promoting a mindset focused on growth would require one embrace failure. But as we discussed earlier in Chapter 2, research has shown that people with positive, growth-centric mindsets are able to leverage failures as a critical ingredient in the learning process. This means any data leader seeking to promote more positive mindsets must develop a culture where failures are seen as learning opportunities. This is not to suggest that failures should be promoted, but rather, used as a tool for learning and development.

As with all these behaviors, it's critical for the CDO to lead by example and be willing to share their own experiences with failure. This will reinforce humility and authenticity and help to create a work environment where others feel like they can share (and grow from) their individual failures.

A story I tell often to my clients is that the first three times I was leading projects to implement MDM at one of my previous companies were dismal failures. I don't sugarcoat the fact that many poor decisions were made, and far too many corners were cut. I failed to fully understand how customer master data was being used in multiple downstream systems and processes, including the processes used to incentivize our salespeople. By changing aspects of the customer data that I wrongly assumed were entirely benign, there was a ripple effect that materially changed the compensation of our sales executives. This situation caused the entire MDM initiative to be shelved for nearly two years while we addressed some of the bigger process issues related to sales territory assignments and incentives.

In another situation, I failed to secure funding for an MDM initiative by building a business case that was entirely focused on improving data quality, and not business results. The benefits that were pitched to the CFO had zero visible connection to his priority KPIs, so our funding request was denied. This forced us to essentially bootstrap an MDM without the funding needed for data stewardship or enterprise-class MDM software, two constraints that forced us to be highly creative – but also significantly hampered our efforts.

In both situations I was able to learn some incredibly important lessons about how to approach a large-scale MDM initiative and, more importantly, how *not* to approach such an effort. I have carried those lessons with me throughout my career, and they have helped to inform my choices, as well as the choices of hundreds of data leaders I've consulted.

I have not been shy about sharing details on my failures. In fact, I even shared them during my interview process to become an MDM analyst for Gartner. Taking this approach allowed me to show that I'm capable of learning and that I embrace a growth mindset. It also showed that I have the credentials that can only be gained from hands-on experience doing the work of a data professional. Rather than position me as a failure, sharing my stories of failure during my Gartner interview process significantly worked to my advantage. This is why I can confidently recommend a similar approach for any data leader seeking to build their credibility and promote more positive mindsets in their team.

> "I've learned more from the mistakes I've made than the successes I've had... (failure) opens the door to that growth, but I think the reason is because, when you have a failure, as long as you have a growth mindset, you recognize and acknowledge that failure, and then you know, ok, there is something – at least one thing – but probably multiple options of things I can do better. When you have a success, you often don't go back and say, 'oh here is all thing things that went well.'"
>
> Meagan Boson, VP of business performance at Oldcastle; CDO Matters *podcast, episode #63*

Beyond sharing stories of failures, data leaders can also put more formalized processes into their workflows to enable their teams to learn from failures – and successes. A fantastic tool for this is to create what many, particularly those from a software development background, would typically call a *postmortem* after every major initiative. However, I'm not a huge fan of the word *postmortem* since the same word is used by medical examiners for entirely different, and for more macabre, purposes. I much prefer the phrase "lessons learned" to describe the process of taking time to review what worked and what didn't work. "Lessons learned" has much more of a positive, growth-centric tone and better aligns to the intent of this process.

In these "lessons learned" sessions, a tone must be set by the data leader where these meetings are seen as opportunities to learn, and not blame. Failures must be normalized as a necessary step in the learning process, where any overt focus on blame could have the exact opposite impact – where a culture of fear is promoted over one of growth. Finding the right balance between accountability and blame is delicate but not impossible. When discussing and reviewing failures in the past, I've found success in referring to the broader team, or our processes, when discussing what went wrong (e.g., "what did *we* get wrong?" or "where did *our* QA process break?"), but then referring to individual people when discussing what needs to change in the future (e.g., what can *you* do differently next time?).

It's also important in these "lessons learned" sessions to focus on matters of fact and not opinion. This means the team leaders driving these sessions should spend time in advance of the session to gather the necessary facts, with full alignment from the team members responsible for any area or process that is going to be reviewed. A focus on issues of fact will remove any subjectivity or assumptions and limit the opportunity for emotions to play an excessive role.

The goal of these sessions is twofold: (1) to celebrate successes, and (2) to highlight opportunities to improve in the future. In the case of the latter, it's not necessarily the goal of these sessions to put detailed remediation plans in place – that can happen in subsequent meetings. Rather, the goal will be to reach some consensus on the root causes, and the steps the team believes should be taken to avoid similar situations in the future. In the case of celebrating successes, time should be taken to highlight individuals who were heroic in their efforts to ensure a successful delivery, especially in situations where there may have been a previous failure that was successfully overcome.

Data leaders committed to promoting more positive, growth-centered mindsets must create a team culture where failure is viewed, by everyone, as a necessary ingredient in the learning process.

This will create an environment more conducive to risk taking an innovation. It will ultimately lead to far greater levels of accountability, since the lack of reprisals and blame will help to remove the fear and vulnerability associated with taking full agency over one's actions.

As we discussed earlier, when initiatives with positive intent are implemented into organizations rife with limiting mindsets, it's common for the outcomes of those efforts to have the exact opposite effect. An example would be using a data literacy program with a goal of making it easier to understand reports, but where the net result is the creation of more frustrated users because the data in the reports is not fit for purpose. However, when initiatives with positive intent are implemented into organizations that embrace a positive mindset, the impacts are exponentially positive. This is exactly how a failure can ultimately become a lever of success. If the right mindset is in place, simple things can drive heroic impacts.

Be Practical

Perhaps the greatest antidote for any data leader seeking to jettison "all-or-nothing" thinking patterns is to more widely embrace practicality. More specifically, value-driven practicality. A common theme in my many discussions with more successful CDOs over the years has been they tend to have a bias to action, where often those actions will often buck established best practices. It could be argued that taking more of an agile, MVP-driven approach to building and managing data products will necessarily require more practicality – and that may be true. However, being overt about a focus on practical approaches that work to deliver business value is still an approach worth embracing.

I previously touched on the issue of data ownership and how trying to force data customers to "own" data that is widely shared is a recipe for failure – even when many well-established governance frameworks, including DAMA, recommend it. Taking a more practical approach to ensuring that shared data is well governed and well managed requires a heroic data leader to shun the best practice and apply management practices that can actually work. Many of the recommendations in this book come from having tried, and failed, in applying these best practices.

If something works (and helps to drive value for customers), even if it's not aligned to what most would consider a best practice, you should embrace it. Another example here is around the issue of data cleanups being a necessary dependency for excellence in data management. Data cleanups are costly, time-consuming, and never-ending. If you can still deliver meaningful value without an excessive focus on data cleanups, fantastic. Don't assume that just because your consultant or your vendor are both telling you that data cleanups are required, that they are. A more practical approach demands that you focus first on what will drive meaningful value in the shortest amount of time.

Being more practical will also free you to embrace your intuition and avoid analysis paralysis in situations where you need to make quick decisions. The preference is always to have the right data at the right time, but often, urgency will demand a more practical approach. When this happens, embracing more of a growth mindset rooted in practicality will require you to seek the feedback needed to understand if that decision drove the right outcomes. If it didn't, that failure is a learning opportunity that you can carry forward so that the next time you're faced with a similar situation, the outcome will improve.

> "I'm a big proponent of heuristics. I don't think, even from a data science perspective, I don't think we would be where we are today if we didn't have heuristics, and we did go out and test those theories . . . . The more you embrace that, and work with the data and heuristics together, the gut feelings, or instincts and lived experiences together, the better your holistic understanding is going to be."
>
> *Dr. Santona Tuli, head of data at Upsolver;*
> CDO Matters *podcast, episode #43*

A key takeaway here is that practicality requires a focus on outcomes, and not methods. There may indeed be times when taking a methodical approach to solving a problem also happens to be the most practical, but that will often not be the case. Practicality also demands a heroic data leader to be more adaptable and to abandon any rigid, over-excessively structured approaches to solving any given problem when simpler, more pragmatic options are available.

Chapter 10
Looking Forward

Over the last two years since the commercial explosion of generative AI and the widespread awareness of the potential that data has within our companies, I've been extremely bullish on the future of the data profession and of chief data officers. As I said in Chapter 1, we are living in a golden age of data and analytics, and the opportunities before us to drive truly transformational value from data are unparalleled in the history of our industry. This means the future could indeed be very bright, but the many barriers supported by mindsets that oppose growth are substantial – but not insurmountable.

For the remainder of the book, we'll explore a future state where mindsets of growth and positivity have become the norm, and where heroic acts of data leadership are commonplace. What would this future state "look" like, and what will it mean for the future of our professions and our companies?

Natively Digital

In 2001 the American educator and writer Marc Prenksy coined the term "*digital natives*" within a series of two articles he wrote to describe a generation of your people who have grown up surrounded by digital technology, such as computers and the Internet.[1] These people are inherently more fluent and savvy on the use of digital technologies than the "digital immigrants" (like me), who were born before them and were not raised from childhood using them. Since Prensky coined the term, it's been adapted to also describe companies with deep digital roots. Three examples often labeled as "digital natives" are Amazon, Netflix, and Uber, but there are many, many more.

While there's no consensus on what differentiates a digital native besides a widespread embrace of "digital technologies" (a largely meaningless distinction), it's obvious that timing and technology alone are insufficient to distinguish a true digital native. However, three attributes consistently highlighted in articles and research focused on digitally native companies are customer centricity, agility and innovation, and a heavy reliance on data for making decisions at every level of the organization.

When you take a deeper look into the culture of the companies described as digital natives, many common attributes appear – most of which have something else in common – which is a close resemblance to the attributes that describe positive mindsets. Even if a company may not publicly espouse the importance of positive, growth-centric mindsets, it's quite clear they are at the root of how many of these digital natives aspire to operate.

Take Amazon, for example, which widely promotes its 16 leadership principles as critical to its business success. These include a "customer obsession," "learn and be curious," "ownership," and "invent and simplify," among others.[2] Netflix embraces values like "candor" (you willingly receive and give feedback), "courage" (you are vulnerable in search for the truth; you are willing to risk failure, or challenge the status quo), and "curiosity" (you learn rapidly and eagerly; you are as interested in other people's ideas as your own;

---

[1] https://www.marcprensky.com/writing/Prensky%20-%20Digital%20Natives,%20Digital%20Immigrants%20-%20Part1.pdf.
[2] https://www.amazon.jobs/content/en/our-workplace/leadership-principles

you're humble about what you don't yet know). The words used to describe each of these core values are those of Netflix and are published on a publicly facing website.[3]

When considering how the data function is typically supported in these companies, more commonalities appear. This includes a tendency to have federated operating models where data and analytics capabilities are deeply interwoven into the operating models of individual business functions. The lines between the "data team" and the "business team" are often completely nonexistent, as the use of data becomes intrinsic to the operations of the business function. Netflix is a perfect example of this, as is the work underway at Nestle's Purina division discussed in Chapter 2. Corporate data functions continue to exist to support cross-functional and enterprise-wide use cases, but individual business functions are given the flexibility to create what is necessary to best support their customer needs.

Another distinguishing feature of digital natives is that data is deeply engrained into their product delivery, development, and innovation efforts. A great example of this is Uber, where the use of real-time data is critical to the daily operations of their business – and if you removed it (or made it difficult to access) – the entire business would literally collapse. The same is true for many other digital natives, where the idea that daily operations could function, at scale, without access to highly accurate and relevant data, is laughable. At these companies you cannot separate the operations of the business, and the value it delivers to clients, from the availability of data. While many companies may make aspirational claims about data becoming their "lifeblood," for digital natives, data is at the very core of how they operate.

> "And what I noticed in the, I'll say AI-native companies, so the ones that have just started up in the last two or three years, is their data science function is ingrained from the beginning. And

---

[3]https://jobs.netflix.com/culture

so even if I don't have a data scientist on the call with me, the data science nomenclature, the concerns, the goals are just kind of baked into their process."

Shubh Sinha, CEO and co-founder, Integral;
CDO Matters podcast, episode 64

There most certainly are some downsides to the extremely federated, if not completely decentralized, approaches that many digital natives take with their data and analytics operating models. The primary critique of these approaches is twofold: (1) the silos that will naturally tend to evolve when you give more autonomy to individual lines of business to manage their data, and (2) these silos will lead to inefficiencies that must be overcome when it comes to enabling more cross-functional or global uses of data. These are valid concerns and will often drive many organizations toward more top-down, centralized patterns of managing data.

A great example of a highly federated approach to data management is at Microsoft – a company (and a CEO) that is committed to embracing more of a growth mindset. The evolution of data management at Microsoft from a centralized, to a more federated approach, is thoroughly documented in the book *Data Management Strategy at Microsoft: Best practices from a tech giant's decade-long data transformation journey*, by my friend Aleksejs Plotnikovs.[4] In this book Aleksejs outlines how Microsoft has slowly pivoted away from a more "command and control" approach to data to one where individual business units/domains have relative autonomy. This autonomy is not without a cost, however, in that even a company as wildly successful as Microsoft, they still struggle with providing customer insights at a global level. As painful as it was to read, Aleksejs provides the stark details of the *four* failed attempts Microsoft has made at a global MDM solution.

---

[4] Plotnikovs, A. (2024) *Data Management Strategy at Microsoft: Best Practices from a Tech Giant's Decade-long Data Transformation Journey.* Packt Publishing.

When acknowledging the costs associated of the federated approaches to data management that are favored by digital natives, the benefits must also be considered. When heroic data leaders deeply embrace the recommendations I've made in this book, particularly around developing robust metrics to understand the value of their data products and services, they will know both the costs and benefits of their actions. In data organizations not embracing these approaches, decisions are being made by CDOs to embrace (or shun) a given operating model with zero visibility on their financial impact. A perfect example of this highlighted in Chapter 4 is the data mesh – where many CDOs have raced to embrace an unproven operating model without any idea of what it costs. In a future-state data function that deeply embraces the tenants of product management and customer centricity, and where positive mindsets flourish, the decision to federate (or centralize) is made using hard data to back the decision, not intuition.

A last very significant thing that differentiates many digital natives is their success in business, and the speed at which they've grown. The "magnificent seven" companies, all of which share many attributes of a digital native, have seen their market capitalization grow more than 5x the average company on the S&P 500 over the last decade. The combined sales of the three most digitally native companies of the magnificent seven, Amazon, Meta, and Google, is over $1T USD – making the combined incomes of these three companies greater than the GDPs of all but 20 sovereign nations on the planet. And at the time of writing this book, not one of these companies has existed for more than 30 years. Given this stunning performance, it's quite clear these digital natives are doing something right.

I see digital natives as shining examples of what can happen when data leaders harness positive mindsets to bridge the gap between the current value of data to companies, and its potential value. When we embrace the behaviors of people with positive mindsets and when we take the brave steps within our data organizations to allow those mindsets to flourish, we become more like these digital natives.

"Making better decisions is going to be essential to be competitive. So people running batch processes, whether you're reloading once a day or once a month or once a quarter. It's like trying to cross a street when you can only see how it looked five minutes ago. It's not competitive. In the future you are going to see real time accounting of who is who, and who is related to who, fast enough to make decisions as it's happening, not after the fact. I think the most competitive organizations are going to be able to make sense of what they know while they're observing it so they can do something about it."

Jeff Jonas, CEO of Senzing;
CDO Matters *podcast, episode #16*

Data and AI Haves and Have-Nots

As companies, and their data leaders, make the changes necessary for positive mindsets to flourish, we will slowly start to see a growing divide between the data "haves" and the data "have-nots." Those heroic data leaders who deeply ingrain data into the operations of their businesses will overcome the many roadblocks to widespread data and AI adoption discussed in earlier chapters, and the benefits of their actions will quickly enable nonlinear returns – particularly by comparison to those companies stuck in the mire of the data status quo. The use of AI will play an outsized role and will create a virtuous cycle where the more a given company differentiates, the more difficult it will be for others to catch up. We are already seeing this to a limited degree with digital natives within the "magnificent seven," but this is only just the beginning of an AI-fueled transformation that will disproportionately benefit those organizations who are able to effectively harness its power. This is particularly the case for the intersection of AI and quantum computing, but that's a topic for a future book.

"We are standing on the brink of an enormous technical revolution, and it's going to change the way we live, work, and relate to each other. . . . So, the question becomes, as leaders of this digital technology, are we really thinking about how we create human value, and not just financial value? Are we really thinking about how we are benefiting people and not simply exploiting them? In other words, are we doing well, and doing good?

Dr. Cheryl Flink, PhD, SVP at Truist Leadership Institute;
CDO Matters *podcast, episode #7*

As a self-professed capitalist, I am not overly concerned that there is a reasonable chance that riches enabled by AI will disproportionately flow into a select few companies, especially since I believe so strongly that there is a way for every business to unlock the potential of data in their organizations. That said, I suspect that in time there will be some serious conversations at a societal level that will likely unfold should this digital disparity between companies become so acute that competition with them becomes effectively impossible. This is not a new phenomenon, as two companies within the magnificent seven, Google and Microsoft, are intimately aware of what can happen when you raise the ire of anti-trust regulators. Should Tesla and Nvidia continue to dominate their respective markets for the foreseeable future, I suspect that they too may also come under similar scrutiny.

In the interim, I'm confident that many data leaders, and many companies, will make the changes needed to finally realize the transformative power of data – and these changes will be a good thing, especially for the careers of data leaders behind them.

DataOps and the Convergence of Data and Product Functions

As more and more data leaders follow this heroic path, I believe that organizations will slowly begin to see the natural fit that exists between a data function and a product function and that extracting the most value from data "looks" much like the processes of extracting value from any product or service. When organizations see that treating data like a product requires both product and supply chain management – two functions they are likely already supporting, and often doing very well – there will be an increasing number of them that start to adapt their product organizations to integrate data management. Data management and governance will pivot from being a cost center to one that is viewed as critical business enablement function – and potentially even one that become a revenue generator for the company, which leads me to the ideas of data monetization and sharing.

One potential way to look at this merging of product and data is through an adaptation of the existing term *DataOps*. Gartner defines DataOps as follows:

> "DataOps is a collaborative data management practice focused on improving the communication, integration and automation of data flows between data managers and data consumers across an organization. The goal of DataOps is to deliver value faster by creating predictable delivery and change management of data, data models and related artifacts. DataOps uses technology to automate the design, deployment and management of data delivery with appropriate levels of governance, and it uses metadata to improve the usability and value of data in a dynamic environment."[5]

The shortcoming of this definition, insofar as we're talking about how the data function better integrates to the product function, is that the value is delivered through improved data management functions (notably, predictable delivery of data) – and not necessarily improved business performance. Yes, we most certainly want to run the data function more effectively, and we also want to build great data and analytics products and services. However, in a future where the data function is dominated by positive mindsets, the data of an organization also becomes intrinsic to how the broader company operates. Like today's digital natives, the product development and innovation cycles are deeply influenced and interconnected to data, which means that any "DataOps" focus of

---

[5] https://www.gartner.com/en/information-technology/glossary/dataops

the future would necessarily also need to extend beyond data products, and into all the products and services offered by the company.

> "I believe that establishing flexible, autonomous horizontal teams tasked with managing their applications and taking ownership of their data and data-related processes is essential. In my view, these should be multi-disciplinary teams that adopt DevOps and DataOps practices. Such an approach promotes scalability. Relying on a single team for all tasks is not a scalable model; spreading responsibilities across various teams enhances efficiency and supports scalability."
>
> *Piethein Strengholt, author of* Data Management at Scale *and CDO of Microsoft Netherlands;*
> CDO Matters *podcast, episode #44*

Data Monetization and Widespread Data Sharing

A natural by-product of many of the changes I'm advocating in this book will be that organizations will start to better understand how data could potentially be monetized to consumers outside their organizations – since that's essentially what I'm advocating from the perspective of building (and valuing) great data products for internal customers. If an organization knows what the costs and benefits are of its data-related products and services, regardless of who is consuming them, and if the data function is more closely aligned to the product function, then it's only logical that some would start to externally monetize those data assets.

In my experiences, having seen the failure of many data marketplace efforts, the biggest challenges historically for organizations that have expressed an interest in monetizing their data for external consumers are the following:

- They lack product management skills within the data function.
- They don't know the value of their products.
- Lawyers see data as critical intellectual property that should not be widely distributed.
- Concerns about privacy, or lack of sufficient governance on data.

When data leaders ingrain more positive mindsets in their organizations and they implement changes to their organizations and processes needed to promote those mindsets, all but one of these challenges to data monetization will be marginalized. The only one not necessarily addressed in the recommendations of this book is the one dealing with lawyers and their comfort levels around externally distributing data.

What I have learned over my many years in business is that there are two approaches you can take with lawyers. You can seek their approval, or you can challenge them to provide the legal framework needed for you to pursue a given course of action. The latter is my preferred approach, in that you're far more likely to receive actionable guidance and encounter less resistance. The former is an invitation for a lawyer to say "no," and given the inherent conservatism we want and expect from lawyers, a negative response is far more likely for any request that has the slightest potential to increase business risk.

Even if a lawyer is happy with a data monetization plan, there is still a valid question to be asked about if CDOs should monetize their data, given competing priorities and scarce resources. As AI increasingly automates data governance and management functions, there will likely come a time when a CDO will have the choice to downsize their organization or seek to deploy those resources to other tasks that ultimately drive more value for their companies. Rather than reduce their team size, I suspect many will choose to re-deploy data management resources to other efforts, including data monetization.

> "To your point about sharing data, some companies are productizing it. A veterinary recently did this, one of our clients, where they standardized their definitions of vets, medication, health care terms, naming conventions, and they offer that as a product to the veterinarians that are starting their practice and buying all these data management and processing solutions. It was a standard data model, as standardized metadata ontologies for relationships, taxonomies for hierarchical relationships and descriptions,

and they are generating revenue from that by providing it to the industry. So, there is value out there"

Lulit Tesfaye, partner and VP at Enterprise Knowledge;
CDO Matters *podcast, episode #46*

Another evolution of a data function that more widely embraces positive mindsets is data sharing. A broader focus on understanding exactly how data is used in an organization, and the value it drives, will provide data leaders complete clarity on exactly what data drives competitive differentiation, and what does not. Growth-centric data leaders who know how their data is used, and who are more open to risk taking and innovation, will naturally seek novel approaches to driving even more value. One of those approaches is data sharing.

Master data management exists because there are economies of scale that are created when an organization can use data to break functional silos within an organization. If you consider that each individual business is itself a silo, it stands to reason that there may be incredible value for companies, particularly those who already partnered across a complex value or supply chain, to leverage data sharing to increase efficiencies on a broader scale, across a wide network of companies. Data organizations that embrace more innovation in their operations will naturally seek to share data with other companies that they depend on, in more strategic (and less transactional) ways. This is particularly the case when it comes to supporting ESG and sustainability use cases, where there will be plenty of opportunities for companies to share data across complex supply chains. In the short term, regulation will drive the adoption of data sharing in some parts of the world (particularly Europe), and ESG reporting requirements and related regulations will drive the adoption of data sharing. But for everywhere else, data sharing will be adopted more slowly and will be an indicator of a more innovative and adaptable data organization.

Beyond the opportunities to leverage data sharing to drive cross-organizational process efficiencies, the growing use of data to drive competitive differentiation across GenAI-based language models, or via more traditional machine learning or causal AI use cases, will also stimulate more data sharing and monetization. As the market for GenAI solutions evolves, the companies building these models will naturally seek to find ways to differentiate their products in support of more specific, domain-specific solutions. Instead of building generalist models (and chatbots or agents), many will seek to adapt or fine tune their core models to become far more specialized. This will happen only with access to hyper-specialized bodies of data that today are not publicly available. Small and midsize companies without the resources or skills to build or adapt their own language models will have increasing opportunities to monetize or share this data. Many will look to partner with other smaller companies to "pool" their data resources to be able to compete with much larger, deep-pocketed competitors that do have the resources to build their own AI-based solutions. Regardless of the use case motivating the desire to share or monetize data, more adaptable and innovative data functions of the future will inevitably find themselves more in cooperation with other businesses than ever before.

Data Consortiums and Governance Networks

The more that data functions with more positive, growth-centric mindsets seek to leverage data monetization and sharing to drive incremental value for their customers, the more the need will arise for companies to formalize partnerships to support the governance of data being shared across them. These partnerships will often take the form of a data consortium, or similar, where the mandate of that organization is to create and implement a framework for managing the data that is shared between its members. A critical aspect of this framework will be the establishment of a body of data governance policies, including things like quality measures and data verification methods.

Data consortiums are not new and have long been used to create standards for data that is widely shared across companies or complex business processes. The success of these consortiums has been extremely mixed, with many high-profile initiatives failing to gain traction. Two examples of failed attempts to facilitate data sharing across companies have been the Open Data Alliance (ended in 2018) and TradeLens (ended in 2022).[6] However, not all attempts at data consortiums have been failures.

One of the more successful consortiums is the Global Standards One (GS1) consortium, which for the last 50 years has been the entity responsible for maintaining the data standards for the bar codes that appear on consumer-packaged goods.[7] Consortiums are typically nonprofits that are created and funded by the individual companies that benefit from using the standards, but not always. One of the biggest and more successful data consortiums on the planet is my old employer Dun & Bradstreet (D&B), which is a $2.3B USD for-profit publicly traded company. The core of D&B's operation is a consortium of companies that share their accounts receivable data with D&B, which then uses this information to create credit ratings for corporate entities. Companies that participate in the consortium receive free access to a limited set of data from D&B, but those that do not participate can still buy access to the D&B data via annual subscriptions.

Another consortium that's evolved in the last decade that I find quite interesting is CDQ, which evolved out of the University of St. Gallen in Switzerland in 2011.[8] It's a group of 31 primarily European manufacturing companies that have grouped together to share data related to their customers and suppliers. CDQ handles the implementation and management of the governance policies and tasks supporting this shared data set, including data stewardship. An update to any one individual supplier record at one of the

---

[6]The Open Data Alliance was a group of 320 companies working to share data specific to the operation of data centers, and included Microsoft, BMW, and Lockheed Martin in its membership. TradeLens was an effort pushed by IBM and Maersk to adopt blockchain-based technologies across the global shipping industry to track the movement around shipping containers and their cargo.
[7]See www.gs1.org.
[8]See www.cdq.com.

member companies benefits all 31 members of the consortium. This is a perfect example of MDM being applied across a group of companies, instead of within a single company.

I find the CDQ model interesting because I believe that in time, as more heroic data leaders start to emerge, models like CDQ will increasingly become the norm. Innovative CDOs will seek to offload low-value, resource-intensive tasks that do not help to drive a competitive advantage for a company, such as data stewardship or data verification for corporate master data. This will happen because my experience shows me that the processes companies use to verify and manage this data are remarkably similar. I'll give you a specific example.

Sometime in 2016 I was in the office of the SVP of procurement for an F100 high tech company, and we were discussing how to use data to accelerate their process for onboarding new suppliers. This SVP said something that made a lasting impression on me, which was "If I know for a fact that one of our biggest competitors is already using a given supplier, can't I use that insight to help accelerate a decision to onboard that supplier within our company?" In essence, what this SVP of procurement was saying was that she would be comfortable using the data quality and validation processes of her competitor. In other words, she would be comfortable in taking more of a shared approach to governing her supplier data. This is exactly what CDQ is doing, and I firmly believe that, in time, more of these governance networks will evolve – with a twist.

Today, data consortiums largely operate as "hub-and-spoke" models, where a single entity is responsible for managing and governing a shared data set. The cost to maintain the network is supported through membership fees or are paid as subscription fees to for-profit entities like D&B. In the future, opportunities exist for companies to take more of a peer-to-peer approach to creating and managing these governance networks, where the "hub" intermediary is cut out of the equation and companies work directly with other companies to create these governance and data sharing networks. Blockchain technologies are a particularly interesting option here, as they support both a shared (and completely trustless) governance framework and the ability for anyone who contributes to the network to receive "compensation" every time a new record is updated or added to the chain. I shared some of my thoughts on how blockchain technologies could be leveraged to create a network of shared data in an article published in Forbes in 2022.[9] However, as the failure of blockchain-dependent TradeLens highlights, creating the network effects needed to disrupt legacy approaches to managing these data consortiums and cut out any "middleman" will not be an easy task.

Still, I am confident the benefits that many companies, particularly smaller and midsize enterprises, will reap in the future through more collaborative management of data that is shared across complex value or supply chains will be material. The successes of some data consortiums are proof positive they can work and consumer demands are strong.[10] Heroic data leaders are those who are willing to take the bold steps to realize the economies of scale that will exist through more widespread sharing of both data and its management.

Data Sustainability

Another important by-product of the growth of data heroism at companies across the globe will be an increasing focus on the criticality of sustainable practices in data and analytics. I firmly believe that it's only a matter of time before CDOs are required to support a sustainability mandate, like "net zero" data management policies. To a certain degree, some of these forces are already underway, particularly in the European Union.

---

[9] See https://www.forbes.com/councils/forbestechcouncil/2022/09/15/how-blockchain-can-save-data-governance.

[10] Take, for example, a situation in the United States of having to manually complete "new patient" forms every time you change or add a healthcare provider. Capturing this data once and sharing it in a trusted and privacy-compliant way via a governance or sharing network, would be significantly more efficient and patient-friendly.

"I foresee very shortly, in the world of companies with boards, that risk subcommittee of an audit committee of a board, is one day going to say 'so, tell me about this algorithm that you used to release this product to market. What unintended consequences have you planned for, Mr. or Ms. CDO?. How can we have missed this thing that has environmental, or social, or human rights impacts that we didn't know about?'"

Renee B. Lahti, former CIO of Symantec, Hitachi Vantara, and SC Johnson; CDO Matters *podcast, episode #27*

For example, the Digital Product Passport (DPP) was created through the EU's passage of the Ecodesign for Sustainable Products Regulation (ESPR) in July 2024.[11] The DPP is a digital record containing detailed data about a products lifecycle, including its country of origin, the materials used to create it, and its environmental impact. DPPs are designed to promote sustainability by providing consumers, businesses, and regulators with transparent and accessible product information data and will be slowly implemented for certain product categories over the next five years, starting with batteries in 2026. The DPP is a great example of a regulatory agency enforcing data standards (and sharing) with the express purpose of driving more sustainable business practices, but I also happen to believe that many data functions – especially those heavily influenced by more positive mindsets – will *voluntarily* start to adopt more sustainable data practices. Why?

The answer here is simple. Our current data management practices are potentially harmful to our environment, and they don't have to be. They are harmful because in part we have a massive problem with data hoarding in the world of data and analytics, where recent data suggests that anywhere from 40% to 90% of

---

[11] See https://data.europa.eu/en/news-events/news/eus-digital-product-passport-advancing-transparency-and-sustainability?utm_source=chatgpt.com.

all data is "dark" – meaning that it's just collecting digital dust and will never be used for an analytical or operational purpose.[12] However, this dark data is still sitting in hard drives on computers that are consuming scarce energy. One recent estimate has data centers emitting more greenhouse gasses than the global airline industry, where the average data center consumes enough electricity to power 50,000 homes.[13] Quite obviously not all computers in data centers are being used to store dark data (and plenty of data is being used regularly), but the simple fact that a nontrivial amount of data will never be used highlights a massive opportunity to improve our data management practices.

Given my many conversations with data leaders over the years and my own experience in data leadership, I can say with certainty that our data hoarding problem is a result of a fear-based approach to data management – which runs completely counter to a more positive, growth-centric approach. The fear driving data hoarding is based on a concern that one day in the future, a data consumer will want a report, and as data professionals, we won't be able to produce it. You can run a report on anything happening in your core business applications, but only so long as your analytical systems are proactively capturing the data effluent from those applications.

I can recall many situations when as a data leader I've sat across the table from software engineers, or business customers, who are working on creating a new business application or making significant alterations to existing applications. My data analysts would naturally ask "What reports do you need?" and far too often, the answer is "We're not entirely sure." When this happens, the data team will have a choice of two extreme opposites: either capture all the data generated by that application in the anticipation it *might* be used in the future or not capture any data at all. Most of the time, data professionals will err on the side of caution, where the

---

[12]https://www.datacenterdynamics.com/en/opinions/the-elephant-in-the-data-center-shedding-light-on-dark-data/?utm_source=chatgpt.com
[13]https://greenly.earth/en-us/blog/ecology-news/what-is-the-carbon-footprint-of-data-storage

fear of being unable to support a potential future request is enough to trigger an investment in the data center costs needed to store all that data. Individually these investments may be small (I've been told often that "storage is cheap"), but in the aggregate, there are creating significant externalities that are not widely discussed in the data and analytics industry. I wrote an article for *Forbes* in the summer of 2023 to help raise awareness on this issue, but as an industry, we still have a long way to go.[14]

> "If we're not helping to activate the data, then honestly, we shouldn't even have it. There is no need for the data to be in BlueConic if you don't have an intended purpose for it. This is why our model centers on the use cases you plan to support with the data, rather than that 'data ingestion and figure it out later' kind of approach."
>
> Cory Munchbach, CEO of BlueConic;
> CDO Matters *podcast, episode #3*

Organizations under the influence of more positive mindsets, however, will take a drastically different approach. Instead of just blindly storing all data in the digital equivalent of a rainy-day fund that never gets spent, data teams under the influence of more growth-centric mindsets, while also embracing a product management approach, will require a detailed cost–benefit report be created for any new data product or service. The status quo of data hoarding will be questioned through the diligence required to build great, cost-effective products. The costs will optimally include not only recurring operating expenses for data storage but also any higher-level societal costs that are associated with making choices, which involve consuming scarce energy resources.

When it comes to data teams making decisions that involve significant energy consumption within data centers, data hoarding is just the tip of the iceberg. The increasing hype associated with AI is

---

[14]https://www.forbes.com/councils/forbestechcouncil/2023/07/20/a-cdo-call-to-action-stop-hoarding-data-save-the-planet

Looking Forward

also causing new levels of scrutiny around the issue of the energy being used to create or utilize GenAI-based solutions, including large language models. Data from 2024 suggests that GenAI-based queries consumed 10 times more energy than a Google search. Goldman Sachs estimates that data center power demand will grow 160% by 2023, which will increase the total power consumed by data centers from 1% to 2% of overall global power, to 3–4% by the end of the decade.[15] The critical dependency that the growth of AI has on access to abundant energy explains why many tech companies are making significant investments in nuclear energy. This includes Microsoft's plan to revitalize the Three Mile Island nuclear plant in Pennsylvania, as well as Amazon's plan to develop four small modular reactors (SMRs) over the next several years.[16]

Both Amazon and Microsoft have aggressive net-zero goals, and these investments in carbon-free nuclear energy will allow them to support those goals while securing the energy needed to significantly expand their AI footprints. I firmly believe that as more companies adopt more positive mindsets toward the management of their data, they will also follow the examples set by the likes of Amazon and Microsoft to seek to apply more sustainable data management practices – regardless of if those practices are mandated by regulators (like what's happening in Europe) or if they're being voluntarily adopted.

A key dependency on this focus toward sustainability in data management will necessarily require companies to break from the paralyzing grip of the status quo. Mindsets that hinder growth promote a lack of accountability in data organizations, thereby enabling behaviors like data hoarding and an inability to understand the cost/benefit of any data product or service. When positive mindsets flourish, a culture of accountability will also flourish, and data leaders (and their corporate leadership) will be well-positioned to

---

[15]https://www.goldmansachs.com/insights/articles/AI-poised-to-drive-160-increase-in-power-demand
[16]https://www.aboutamazon.com/news/sustainability/amazon-nuclear-small-modular-reactor-net-carbon-zero

make informed decisions about what's best for both the company, and the environment.

The actions needed to embrace more sustainability in data have some rather simple origins – and they start with data leaders taking a complete inventory of their data estates, where it's determined exactly what data is being used, how it's being used, and the estimated costs and benefits of that usage. Developing this visibility would naturally complement the evolution of a product management (and product lifecycle) focus within a data function and (ironically) allow the data function to become more data driven. Decisions about what data to retain and what data to archive can be made using a rational framework that's been developed through the lens of both the customer needs and the cost to support those needs. The same is true with any data products or services, like dashboards or visualizations, which may be repeatedly published but never (or infrequently) used. Rather than relying on fear to justify the retention of data in perpetuity, heroic data leaders will embrace the behaviors needed to be more accountable to the sustainability goals of their organizations.

> "Just because you have data and you don't know what it is, it doesn't mean it goes to the cloud. You can go 100% to the cloud, but you are wasting space in the cloud. So, know what your data does, know what it is, know what its classifications are, its use purposes. And then use appropriate cloud services, and every hyperscaler has a tiered capability in this data space, to give you the best bang for your buck. So, if you don't know what's going on, on prem, it's not going to help you in the cloud."
>
> *Ayman Husain, customer engineering leader, Google;*
> CDO Matters *podcast, episode #61*

Data as an Asset

Forward leaning and innovative data teams that embrace more positive mindsets will allow for data to become viewed as a business-critical asset within their organizations. While I remain skeptical that the governing body of the accounting profession in the United States, which is the Financial Accounting Standards Board (FASB), will ever warm to the idea of treating data as a balance sheet asset, this doesn't mean companies won't operate as if data is an asset. It's true that there's been a longstanding debate on the merits of considering data as an asset (for example, assets are typically "tangible," and data is not), but when it comes to allowing for a company to realize the full potential of data, I don't believe any of these debates necessarily need to be resolved.

What's most important is that organizations evolve to a point where data is viewed by everyone in the company as critical to the successful operation of their business. This is not the case today, because if it were, I wouldn't have written this book. When data leaders take the bold steps needed to promote more positive mindsets within the data function, the groundwork will be laid for the entire organization to eventually change how it perceives data. Data will no longer be seen by many as simply a byproduct of the business and will instead be seen as a critical business input.

This shift away from the perception of data as a business exhaust is fundamental – and perhaps one of the most critical outcomes of a more widespread embrace of positive mindsets in the data function. When this happens, the general perceptions surrounding all aspects of data, including the data function itself, will also shift. Data will not be one of the last things considered when business functions seek to streamline or optimize their operations, it will be one of the first things they consider.

If you recall from previous chapters, I noted several times that initiatives with otherwise positive intentions, when implemented by data organizations rife with highly limiting mindsets, will often have the exact opposite impacts. CDOs will see that their efforts to promote more adoption of data through programs like data literacy or data governance will ultimately end up creating less adoption of data – or even animosity with their customers. However, when positive mindsets are the norm in a data function (and are promoted by all the tactics recommended in this book), data leaders won't need to aggressively push the organization to adopt data. Instead, the demand for data will come from customers who appreciate its value.

As much as data leaders today may want their organizations to see the value of data, limiting mindsets hinder them from operating in a way that promotes the ability for data to be viewed as an asset. A widespread embrace of more positive mindsets, promoted by the actions of a heroic data leader, enables a paradigm shift where data customers will create the demand needed for CDOs (and their teams) to feel valued. Instead of pushing a data agenda, the data agenda will be pulled forward by data customers who couldn't imagine operating without the products and services provided by their data and analytics function.

In Closing

It's an amazing time to be in the data business, as there's never been a great opportunity for data professionals to advance their careers and to advance the use of data as a transformational force in their companies. We've been struggling to realize the potential of data for far too long, and the time is right for a change – and I am optimistic that we will change. I trust that after reading this book, you now share this optimism far more than you did before reading it.

I chose to use a hero metaphor in this book, because the story of a hero who embarks on an epic journey is as old as humankind. A hero goes on an adventure and faces many trials and obstacles and gains the knowledge and insights needed to overcome them. In the end, the hero emerges transformed and serves as a powerful inspiration for others to take a similar path. The trait I admire the most about the hero is bravery – and that's exactly what I think it will take for all data leaders to transform their careers, their teams, and their companies. Nobody ever said the journey was easy – and the journey of a data hero is no different.

It will take bravery to question the status quo. It will take bravery to question your consultants. It will take bravery to question the pundits and thought leaders who are motivated to keep things the way they are. It will take bravery to embrace more risk and to shun practices and perspectives that are widely embraced. In taking these brave steps, you will be challenged, and you will be questioned. The journey will undoubtedly feel rather lonely, and you'll likely question why you're going so far out on a limb, when the safety and security of the status quo is so easily attained.

Take peace in knowing you won't be fully alone and that there's a small – but growing – community of data professionals, including myself, who have preceded you on this path, and who are working tirelessly to break the paralyzing grip of the status quo. You can find us on LinkedIn (and several other public channels), where we use the power of social media to amplify and advance many of the perspectives of data heroism outlined in this book. I welcome you to engage with me and others in my growing LinkedIn community, but you can also find me presenting at data conferences and sharing my perspectives on my podcast, *CDO Matters*. I am fully committed to the success of CDOs – and anyone who wants to become a CDO – and will happily assist you, in whatever way I can, on your journey.

Lastly, I welcome any feedback you may have on the content of this book. I am committed to my own growth and development and would welcome any suggestions or criticisms you have on how I can better serve my career and my customers. You can find me on LinkedIn @malhawker.

Good luck with your journey!

Index

A
Accenture, 122–123
accountability, 45–49, 52
active listening, 224
adaptability, as a trait of positive mindset and data heroism, 25–27
aggregation, of data, 86
agility
    about, 195–196
    data and analytics organizational model, 205–213
    data governance model, 203–205
    Data Strategy MVP, 196–199
    scope, approach, and roadmap, 201–203
    success metrics/business cases, 199–201
AI Readiness, 102, 107
Alibaba, 39
aligning incentives, 155–156
All Feedback Is a Gift (Lundin and Goldsmith), 34–35
Allen, Paul (executive), 37
all-or-nothing thinking, 42–45, 68, 96–102, 137–138, 165, 186, 232
Amazon, 236, 239, 253
America Online (AOL), 45–49, 52–55, 164
analyst relations (AR) role, 129
anti-hero
    about, 63–64
    blaming customers for product failures, 69–76
    data culture as a dependency to deliver value, 80–83
    data first, 76–80
    data literacy, 69–76
    data-driven culture, 76–80
    deterministic all-or-nothing thinking, 96–102
    garbage in, garbage out (GIGO), 83–88
    seeing negative intentions in others, 88–96
    unwillingness to quantify value of data, 64–69

App Exchange, 59
approach, scope, roadmap, and, 201–203
artificial intelligence (AI), 5, 190, 240–241
"as-is" assessment, 124
asset, data as an, 254–256

B
Ballmer, Steve (CEO), 37
Bansak, Anjali (Sr. Director of Analytics), 177
barter, 48
Be Data Literate (Morrow), 51, 70, 111
behaviors
  about, 215–216
  being humble, 216–219
  being practical, 232–234
  of CDOs, 215–234
  embracing critical thinking, 219–221
  leading by example, 221–228
  making room for failure, 228–232
  values and, 21–22
benefits, measuring, 172–178
"best-practices" approach, 124
BlackBerry, 27
blaming, 49–52, 69–76, 138
Blockbuster, 27
blockchain technologies, 248–249
Boson, Meagan (VP), 230
brand integrity, 127
Buffett, Warren (businessman), 90
business cases, 199–201
business metrics, 173–174
business processes, focusing on, 152–153
business requirements document (BRD), 153
business stakeholders, 81

C
candor, 236
CDO Club, 71
CDO Matters (podcast), 11, 122, 206, 207, 257
CDQ model, 247–248
centralization, 159
Certified Data Management Professional (CDMP), 225
challenges, avoiding, 52–56
change/changing
  data governance function to customer enablement function, 179–183
  data literacy focus to customer training function, 183–185
  resisting, 56–59
  willingness to, as a trait of positive mindset and data heroism, 25–27
ChatGPT, 96, 98, 100, 141, 143
Chevron, 185
"Chief Data Officer Year End Review," 71
Chief Data Officers (CDOs), 6–7, 8, 24
Claude, 141, 143
client inquiries, 112
client relationships, strength of, 127
Cognizant, 110
collaboration, 36–40, 77
constructive candor, 35
constructive feedback, 221
consultant influences, 120–128
Consumer Direct Offense, 25–26
content creators, 135–136
Coors, 79
corporate culture, mindset and, 21–24
Corporate Culture and Performance (Kotter and Heskett), 23–24
costs, measuring, 172–178
courage, 236

Index

Covey, Stephen (author), 61
critical thinking, embracing, 219–221
criticism, openness to, as a trait of positive mindset and data heroism, 34–36
CRM software, 154
cross-functional data management, 28
cross-functional processes, 94–95
curiosity, 236
curmudgeons, 58–59
customer enablement function, changing data governance function to, 179–183
customer feedback, 158
customer obsession, 236
customer-centric approach
   about, 147–149
   aligning incentives, 155–156
   assuming positive intentions, 153–155
   to data governance, 182–183
   data-driven compared with customer-driven, 149–152
   design methodologies for, 169–172
   feedback loops, 157–158
   focusing on customers instead of technology, 152–153
   having empathy, 153–155
   moving organizations towards, 187–193
   organizational structures, roles and responsibilities, 158–161
   proactive engagement, 157–158
   success metrics, 155–156
customer-driven, data-driven compared with, 149–152
customers
   blaming for product failures, 69–76
   changing data literacy focus to training function, 183–185

D

data analyst, influences for, 112–120
data and analytics
   about, 63–64
   aggregation of data, 86
   blaming customers for product failures, 69–76
   convergence with product functions, 241–243
   cross-functional nature of data, 28
   data as an asset, 254–256
   data as garbage, 227–228
   data culture as a dependency to deliver value, 80–83
   data first, 76–80
   data literacy, 69–76
   data-driven culture, 76–80
   democratization of data, 171
   deterministic all-or-nothing thinking, 96–102
   garbage in, garbage out (GIGO), 83–88
   growth of data, 3–4
   haves and have nots, 240–241
   need for data, 4–5
   objective quality of data, 90
   organizational model, 205–213
   product management, 206–208
   roadblocks to, 114
   seeing negative intentions in others, 88–96
   selling data, 150
   subjective quality of data, 90
   unwillingness to quantify value of data, 64–69
Data and Analytics Metrics and Value Framework, 174
data cleanups, 233
data consortiums, 246–249
data culture, 23–24, 80–83, 151, 195
data driven

INDEX

data driven (*continued*)
  about, 75
  being more, 15
  customer-driven compared with, 149–152
  extreme forms of, 76–80
data driven companies, 7
data first, extreme forms of, 76–80
data governance
  about, 81, 91–92, 94–95, 101, 161
  changing to customer enablement function, 179–183
  complexity of, 96
  customer-centric approach to, 182–183
  data literacy and, 178–186
  levels of, 191
  model, 203–205
  networks, 246–249
  "one-size-fits-all" approach to, 180–182
  positioning as a service, 191–192
  product-centric approach to, 182–183
  in project management office (PMO), 191
Data Governance and Information Quality (DGIQ) conference, 226
Data Hero Mindset, 14, 24–40, 198
data hoarding, 252, 253–254
data leaders, 65–66, 160
data literacy
  about, 69–76, 110, 111
  changing to customer training function, 183–185
  data governance and, 178–186
Data Literacy Project, 110–111
data management, separating from data product management and GTM, 185–186
Data Management Association (DAMA), 91, 225

Data Management at Scale (Strengholt), 207
Data Management Book of Knowledge (DMBOK), 91, 212
Data Management Strategy at Microsoft: Best practices from a tech giant's decade-long data transformation journey (Plotnikovs), 238
Data Management University (DMU), 226
data mesh, 31, 121, 159, 206
Data Mesh (Dehghani), 121
data metrics, 173–174
data monetization, 243–246
data owner, 91, 93, 96
data ownership, 232–233
data product management
  project management office (PMO) and, 190–192
  separating from data management and GTM, 185–186
data products
  about, 168
  concept of, 33–34
  defined, 206, 207
  manufacturing (or development), 189–190
  owners of, 168
data professionals, as content creators, 136
data quality
  complexity of, 96
  definition of, 85
  metrics for, 67
  tools for, 101
data sharing, 243–246
data skills, 70, 75
data stories, 192
Data Strategy MVP, 196–199
data supply chain management, 189
data sustainability, 249–254
data warehouses, 101

Index

DataLounge, 26
DataOps, 241–243
The Data Whisperer (Taylor), 108
DATAVERSITY, 226
decentralization, 159, 160
decision science, 190
defeatist attitude, 57
Dehghani, Zhamak (author), 121
Deloitte, 122–123
democratization of data, 171
design methodologies, 169–172
deterministic thinking, in a probabilistic world, 96–102
developing empathy, 223–224
DevOps, 190
digital immigrants, 236
digital natives, 235–240
Digital Product Passport (DPP), 250
digital technologies, 236
digital transformation, 156
direct market research, at software companies, 131
direct-to-consumer (DTC) sales, 25–26
do it yourself (DIY) product delivery models, 171
Drucker, Peter, 21
Dun & Bradstreet (D&B), 164, 170–171, 247, 248
Durgin, Veronika (data leader), 29, 159–160
Dweck, Carol (psychologist), 18–19, 22, 36, 37–38, 49

E

Eastman Kodak, 27
Ecodesign for Sustainable Products Regulation (ESPR), 250
Einstein, Albert (scientist), 12
emotional contagion, 22–23
empathy, 153–155, 223–224
engagement, proactive, 157–158
Enron Corporation, 47
ESG, 245
Everett, Dan (business owner), 57

Experian, 110
external locus of control, 50–52, 53, 74, 79, 84, 89
Exxon Mobile, 185

F

failure, 30–34, 228–232
federated approach, 160
feedback, openness to, as a trait of positive mindset and data heroism, 34–36
feedback loops, 157–158
finance, planning, and analytics (FP&A), 177, 192–193
Financial Accounting Standards Board (FASB), 255
Finkle, Len (CEO), 18
fixed mindset, 18–19
Flink, Cheryl (SVP), 240–241
focusing on foundations, 97
forcing function, 166
Foster, Jason (CEO), 163–164
future state
 about, 235, 256–257
 artificial intelligence haves and have nots, 240–241
 convergence of data and product functions, 241–243
 data as an asset, 254–256
 data consortiums, 246–249
 data haves and have nots, 240–241
 data monetization, 243–246
 data sustainability, 249–254
 DataOps, 241–243
 digital natives, 235–240
 governance networks, 246–249
 widespread data sharing, 243–246

G

garbage in, garbage out (GIGO), 83–88, 97, 137
Gartner, 8, 107, 110, 111, 112–120, 123–124, 130, 230, 242

Gatchalian, Emerson (CDO), 212
Gates, Bill (CEO), 37
Gemini, 141, 143
Generally Accepted Accounting Principle (GAAP), 173
Generative AI (GenAI), 4–5, 31, 39, 97–98, 99, 100–101, 102, 140–141, 245–246
global pandemic, 25–26
Global Standards One (GS1) consortium, 247
go to market (GTM) function
  about, 210
  implementing, 178–186
  MVP and, 208
  separating from data management and data product management, 185–186
gold rush, 4–5
gold standard, 124
Goldman Sachs, 253
Goldsmith, Marshall (author), 34–35
Google, 38, 239, 241
Google Trends, 111
growth mindset, 18, 157
growth-centered perspectives, 182
Gusmus, Reed (CMO), 134–135

H

Harvard Business Review (HBR), 97
Hawker, Malcolm (author), 1–16
Hawker, Robert (author), 172–173
Heskett, James L. (author), 23–24
hiring
  product managers, 167–169
  value engineers, 172–178
Hit Refresh (Nadella), 37–38, 147–148
The Hive concept, 32–33
Hoover, 59, 164
How to Measure Anything (Hubbard), 172
Hubbard, Douglas (author), 172
humble, being, 216–219
humility, embracing, 217–218
Husain, Ayman (customer engineering leader), 254
hype cycle, 118, 123–124

I

IBM, 7, 39
IDEO, 170
implementing go to market (GTM) function, 178–186
incentives, aligning, 155–156
influencers, as content creators, 136
Infonomics (Laney), 172
Information Technology Ecosystem Feedback Loop, 105–112
infrastructure, technology and, 208–210
inner ring, in Data Strategy MVP, 197–199
innovation, as a trait of positive mindset and data heroism, 30–34
Institute for Certification of Computing Professionals (ICCP), 226
integrity, acting with, 222
intent, failure to see positive, 59–61
intentions, assuming positive, 153–155
internal locus of control, 50–51
internally facing data and analytics team, 178
invent and simplify, 236
iterative approach, 210–212
ITSM standards, 157

J

job exchange programs, 154
job shadowing, 153
job sharing, 153
Jonas, Jeff (CEO), 240

K

key performance indicators (KPIs), 174–175, 199
Khan, Saleem (CDPO), 150
Kimball, Doug (CMO), 158
Kotter, John P. (author), 23–24

L

Lahti, Renee B. (CIO), 250
Laney, Douglas (author), 64–65, 172
large language models (LLMs), 98–99, 140–144, 252–253
leading by example, 221–228
learn and be curious, 236
learned helplessness, 57–58, 199
learner in chief, 224, 227
lessons learned, 230–232
limiting mindsets
    about, 13–14, 18–20, 41
    all-or-nothing thinking, 42–45
    avoiding challenges, 52–56
    blaming others, 49–52
    embracing status quo, 56–59
    failure to see positive intent, 59–61
    lack of accountability, 45–49
    reluctance to take risks, 52–56
    resisting change, 56–59
lines of business (LOBs), 205
LinkedIn, 11–12, 107, 133–140, 227
literacy programs, 74
LlaMa, 99
locus of control, 50–52, 53, 74, 79, 84, 89
loss aversion, 55
Lundin, Stephen C. (author), 34–35
Lyons, Bethany (consultant), 181

M

machine learning (ML), 190
Madsen, Laura (author), 13
Magic Quadrant, 31, 124, 129
Magruder, Justin (CDO), 169
market realities, 105
master data, 91–92
master data management (MDM), 92, 205, 209–210, 229–230, 245
MDM Hubs, 101
measuring costs and benefits, 172–178
medallion architecture, 185–186
Merck, 28
Meta, 99, 239
methods, literacy programs with an emphasis on, 74
Microsoft, 24, 37–39, 97, 224, 238, 241, 253
Mindset: The New Psychology of Success (Dweck), 18–19, 36, 49
mindsets
    about, 17–21
    of CDOs, 24
    corporate culture and, 21–24
    limiting, 13–14
    shifting, 19
    values compared with, 22
minimum viable product (MVP), 196, 204, 205, 208, 209, 210–213
modeled metrics, 67–68
Mohan, Sanjeev (founder), 80
monetization, 169
Moran, John (senior director of governance), 223
Morrow, Jordan (author), 51, 70–71, 111, 225
MS Copilot, 143
Munchbach, Cory (CEO), 252
Munger, Charlie (businessman), 90
Myers, Joyce (CDO), 206, 228

N

Nadella, Sataya (CEO), 37–40, 147–148, 224
naysayers, 58–59

negative emotional contagion, 23
negative feedback loop, 13
negative intentions, 88–96, 138
negative mindsets, 188
Nelson, Hala (data leader), 29
Nestlé, 32–33
net zero, 249, 253
Netflix, 236, 237
networks, data governance, 246–249
Nike, 25–26, 55
norms, 21
Nvidia, 241

O
"one-size-fits-all" approach, to data governance, 180–182
Open Data Alliance, 247
operating models, 159
operational style, of MDM, 205
operations-centric roles, 154
organizations
  accountability as a cornerstone of health of, 52
  data driven, 7
  federation and size of, 160–161
  moving toward customer and product centricity, 187–193
  organizational culture, 21
  organizational structures, 158–161
outer ring, in Data Strategy MVP, 197–199
ownership, 236

P
pain points, 227
Pareto principle, 175
Perez, Joe (CTO), 157
perfectionism, psychology of, 52
Plotnikovs, Aleksejs (author), 238
positive emotional contagion, 22–23
positive intentions, 59–61, 153–155
positive mindset, 17, 24–40

postmortem, 230
Power BI, 110
power dynamics, within collaborations, 77
practical, being, 232–234
practice guilds, 33
Pragmatic Institute, 225
Prensky, Marc (educator), 235–236
proactive engagement, 157–158
"The Problems with Data Literacy" article, 71–72
Proctor and Gamble, 156
product management
  about, 163–165
  in data and analytics, 206–208
  embracing user- and customer-centric design methodologies, 169–172
  governance and literacy, 178–186
  hiring product managers, 167–169
  hiring value engineers, 172–178
  implementing "go to market" functions, 178–186
  measuring costs and benefits, 172–178
  moving organization toward customer and product centricity, 187–193
  profit and loss (P&L), 165–167
  roles in, 177
Product Management Certification, 225
product managers, 164–165, 167–169
product-centric approach, 182–183, 187–193
productivity, impacts on, 74
products
  blaming customers for failure of, 69–76
  convergence of data with functions of, 241–243
  marketing, 192

Profisee, 18, 35–36, 40, 97, 122, 134, 225
profit and loss (P&L), 165–167
profit margins, in consulting, 123
project management office (PMO), 190–192, 201
Proksch, Michael (scientist), 202
psychology, of perfectionism, 52
Purina, 32–34, 40, 237
PwC, 122–123

Q
Qlik, 110–111

R
Radio Shack, 27
Rashidi, Sol (CDO), 28–29, 40, 58–59
Redman, Tom (author), 10
reinforcement analytics
    about, 103–104
    analyst influences, 112–120
    consultant influences, 120–128
    Information Technology Ecosystem Feedback Loop, 105–112
    market realities, 105
    social media influences, 133–140
    technology influences, 140–145
    vendor influences, 128–133
Reis, Joe (data leader), 29, 217
resiliency, as a trait of positive mindset and data heroism, 27–30
resisting change, 56–59
retrieval-augmented generation (RAG), 99
retrospective, 210
return on investment (ROI), 7
risk-taking, 30–34, 52–56
roadmap, scope, approach, and, 201–203
roles and responsibilities, 158–161
Rotter, Julian (psychologist), 50
Royal Caribbean, 28
rules-driven approach, 182–183

S
Sagraves, Allison, 7
Salesforce.com (SFDC), 59
Sarbanes-Oxley Act, 47
Schmarzo, Bill (author), 156
scope, approach, roadmap and, 201–203
Sears, 27
Securities and Exchange Commission (SEC), 47–48
self-fulfilling prophecy, 115
selling data, 150
Semantic Pedanticism Feedback Loop, 105
Sequeda, Juan (scientist), 184
service desk approach, 157
shadow data teams, 159–160
shadow IT groups, 82
Sharma, Samir (CEO), 196
shift right approach, 207
Short, Eddie (consultant), 125–126
silver bullets, 79–80
Sinha, Shubh (CEO), 237–238
SKU, 208
Smale, John (CEO), 156
small modular reactors (SMRs), 253
social media influences, 133–140
software companies, 130, 137
Sony Music, 28
The Speed of Trust (Covey), 61
statement of work (SOW), 127
status quo, embracing, 56–59
status quo bias, 55
Stouse, Mark (CEO), 43
Strengholt, Piethein (author), 207, 243
subscriptions, to analyst firms, 122
Substack, 227
success
    data culture and, 23–24
    metrics for, 155–156, 199–201
sunk cost fallacy, 58
supply chain, 186
surveys, 131–132

T

Tabb, Chris (data leader), 29
Tableau, 110
Taylor, Scott (author), 108
techniques, literacy programs with an emphasis on, 74
technology
    focusing on, 152–153
    influences for, 140–145
    infrastructure and, 208–210
Tesfaye, Lulit (VP), 244–245
Tesla, 241
ThoughtWorks, 121
Three Mile Island nuclear plant, 253
Toys "R" Us, 27
TradeLens, 247, 249
Tuli, Santona (head of data), 233
Turner-Williams, Wendy (CDO), 174–175
"2024 AI Business Predictions" report, 98
Tyco, 47

U

Uber, 236, 237
University of St. Gallen, 247
user experience (UX), 170, 184, 190
user interface (UI), 170, 190
user-centric design (UCD) methodologies, 169–172

V

value delivery
    about, 195–196
    data and analytics organizational model, 205–213
    data governance model, 203–205
    Data Strategy MVP, 196–199
    scope, approach, and roadmap, 201–203
    success metrics/business cases, 199–201
value engineering, 156
value engineers, 172–178, 193
values
    behaviors and, 21–22
    concept of, 67
    of data, 64–69
    data culture as a dependency to deliver, 80–83
    mindsets compared with, 22
    realizing, 74–75
vendor influences, 128–133

W

Wiggins, Chris (data scientist), 219
willingness to change, as a trait of positive mindset and data heroism, 25–27
Winterbottom, Kyle (CEO), 66
WorldCom, 47

Y

Young, Lawrence (Value Consultant), 69
Your AI Survival Guide (Rashidi), 28, 58–59
YouTube, 227

Z

Zenk, Brian (VP), 32–33
Zwiefel, Eric (CDAO), 167